D. JAMES KENNEDY

THE
MAN
AND
HIS
MINISTRY

D. JAMES

KENNEDY

THE
MAN
AND HIS
MINISTRY

Herbert Lee Williams, Ph.D.

CORAL RIDGE MINISTRIES
Fort Lauderdale

Williams, Herbert Lee.
    D. James Kennedy: the man and his ministry / Herbert Lee Williams.
        p.   cm.
    Includes bibliographical references.
    ISBN 0-8407-7475-3
    1. Kennedy, D. James (Dennis James), 1930- . 2. Evangelists-United States—
Biography. 3. Presbyterian Church—United States Clergy—Biography. 4. Coral
Ridge Presbyterian Church (Fort Lauderdale, Fla.)—History. 5. Evangelism
Explosion, Inc.—History. 6. Fort Lauderdale (Fla.)—Church history. I. Title.
BX9225.K44W54   1990
269J.2'092—dc20
    [B]   90 33560
                                                               CIP

To
Mary
Elizabeth

Willing helper,
honest critic,
truest of all friends,
beloved wife

CONTENTS

PART THREE: THE MAN OF VISION

PART FOUR: THE MAN OF LETTERS

PART FIVE: THE MAN AND HIS COUNTRY

PART SIX: THE MAN AND HIS LEGACY

D. JAMES KENNEDY

A.B., M.Div., M.Th., D.D., D.Sac.Lit.,
Ph.D., Litt.D., D.Sac.Theol., D.Humane Let.

PREFACE

Let's imagine, just for a moment that you're a tourist in South Florida. You've been motoring up the Gold Coast, all the way from Miami's plush banking houses and teeming inner cities to Fort Lauderdale's crowded beaches. You've been duly charmed by endless miles of pastel high-rises, by long strips of glitzy entertainment palaces, and by ever-changing vistas of an ocean swarming with pleasure craft ranging from shallow-water catamarans to globe-girdling yachts to island-bound cruise ships loaded with vacationers.

You get the impression that you're in a two-valued world—fun and commerce. The feeling is constantly reinforced by the unbroken flow of merchandising messages along the way. If it's not pleasure, it's business; if it's not business, it's pleasure. And sometimes you're not sure that either one is entirely aboveboard. Legitimate or not, this is sun-fun-mon country.

Let's say you swing over onto Federal Highway right through Fort Lauderdale's bustling downtown and on northward across rightly named Commercial Boulevard. You're in for something of a culture shock.

Suddenly appearing in your windshield, just beyond the last liquor store on the left, is a gleaming white image from another world. With a stately spire that lifts its delicate faceted glass heavenward to a height of three hundred feet above the secular scene below—gracefully framed by identical but smaller spires on either side—it may be the most beautiful church building in America.

It is the Coral Ridge Presbyterian Church.

What you're seeing is more than a landmark. It is a testimony to the living faith, the total commitment, and the inspired genius of one man—D. James Kennedy.

Like the magnificent structure that symbolizes his Christ-honored ministry, the life story of Dr. Kennedy also confronts the casual observer with something of a culture shock. Imagine once more, if you will, an ordinary Arthur Murray dance instructor being plucked out of his Tampa studio by the hand of God to become the guiding force of one of the fastest-growing churches in any denomination. Imagine such a prospect being used by the Holy Spirit to re-energize in our time the Great Commission; he has called it Evangelism Explosion International and has carried Christ's original strategy for "discipling all nations" into every nation and every territory on earth. The strategy works in the Church today just as dynamically as it did in the three centuries after it was imparted to the apostles and before it was bottled up by ecclesiastical bureaucracy.

The same miracle-working God who called a lowly Amos from his fig-gathering in the wasteland of Tekoa (a man who was not a prophet, neither a prophet's son) to thunder forth His word to Israel—the same God is at work among us today. The prayerful intent of this book is to make known, to disseminate as widely as possible, the inspiring story behind the miracle that transformed D. James Kennedy into a pastor, scholar, evangelist, trainer of soul-winners, best-selling author, crusader for righteousness in American life and government, and patriot preacher of our time.

This is not the first biographical work about D. James Kennedy. In 1972, David C. Cook Publishing Company of Colorado Springs, Colorado, published *The Kennedy Explosion*, a 125-page record of the early years written by E. Russell Chandler, former religion writer at the *Los Angeles Times*. His informative summary emphasized the phenomenal development of Evangelism Explosion.

Sincere thanks are due to Anne Kennedy for supplying pictures and letters; to Ruth Rohm for her help on the beginning history of the church; to Ruth Cotts for her encouragement and assistance in the library; and especially to Mary Anne Bunker, executive secretary, for the invaluable aid she willingly and cheerfully provided for many months. I am deeply grateful to members of the church staff and to all others who helped to make the research more a pleasure than a task.

Inscribed in large letters on the outer wall of the Coral Ridge Presbyterian Church is a simple proclamation that perhaps comes closest to expressing the uniqueness of the mind and the ministry of Dr. Kennedy: "Excellence In All Things And All Things To God's Glory." A small bronze plaque inside the sanctuary echoes the sentiment: "To God Be The Glory; Great Things He Hath Done." I share in the desire that all honor be ascribed to the One to whom it is due as we consider together this most unusual record of excellence for His glory.

HERBERT LEE WILLIAMS
JANUARY 1990

PREFACE TO THE REVISED EDITION

"Dear friend, if you have never dreamed a godly dream, I hope you will. God has given you a mind to dream such dreams. What can you dream? What can you think of that could be done that would glorify God? If you had a written guarantee that you could not possibly fail, what would you attempt? I urge you to think about that, because you have just such a written guarantee from the Lord God Almighty: 'I can do all things through Christ which strengthens me.' I hope some of you are going to think about that, and dream a dream."

At the 40th anniversary celebration of Coral Ridge Presbyterian Church, Dr. D. James Kennedy was doing what he does best—dreaming, and inspiring others to dream as well.

"Forty years ago I dreamed a dream. This land was sand spurs and thistles and weeds. But I dreamed a dream of a church where multiplied thousands of people would come to glorify God; where the music would lift His name up gloriously; where people would be converted by the power of the Gospel. I dreamed that dream, and I opened my eyes, and there was a field of sand spurs and weeds."

And so the story goes. Turning thistles and weeds into wonders for God's glory. Over the years, Jim and Anne Kennedy—and those whom God has brought alongside to help—have kept that dream alive. More than that, they have seen that dream grow and take on new dimensions beyond anything they could have thought or imagined. This revised edition of *D. James Kennedy: The Man and His Ministry* provides the details of the outworking of that initial dream right up to today. The past decade has seen the dream greatly expand to reach more people in more ways than ever before.

But most importantly, the dream has just begun! At that 40th anniversary celebration, Jim Kennedy was not content to reflect on the past. "Looking ahead to the future, I have a dream. As we pierce the mist of time and look forward to another 40 years, I believe—like Moses' 40 years in the wilderness—the play is just beginning."

Do you have a dream? Do you have a dream inspired by the heart of God? We hope so. It is our hope that this book will inspire you to take hold of that dream with all your might and trust in the One who can turn divine dreams into reality. That is the legacy of D. James Kennedy—a legacy that will continue for generations to come.

D. James Kennedy

THE
MAN
AND
HIS
MINISTRY

THE
MAN
OF
THE
WORLD

BORN THE FIRST TIME

Before thou camest forth
out of the womb I sanctified
thee, and I ordained thee a
prophet unto the nations.
—JEREMIAH 1:5

It would be pleasant to begin the life story of one of America's most beloved ministers without shocking the reader. But the life must dictate the telling. No matter how earnest the desire to begin painting in warm colors and harmonious shapes, somber hues of tragic reality are essential to a faithful picture.

For this is the story of a miracle—the transformed and transforming life of D. James Kennedy.

Many preachers and presidents have attributed a major part of whatever success they have known, or hoped to achieve, to the indelible influence of a sainted mother. One famous evangelist repeatedly attests that he never entered a pulpit without an awareness that his mother's prayers preceded him. And humankind has testified over centuries to the loving maternal imprint that had the most to do with the shaping of their lives.

By painful contrast, here is a man of God whose memories take him back to a home devastated by the curse of alcoholism. For a child needing tenderness, there was often terror; in the place of empathy, frequent embarrassment. Nevertheless, under the guiding hand of God's providence, the experience of growing up in a family unregenerated by the Holy Spirit would serve to accentuate the miracle that no one anticipated. As a forgotten poet expressed it:

> The greatest miracle of all,
> The sages taught of yore,
> Is life itself. But search again:
> The transformed life is more.

The real beginning of the Kennedy story was 1930—in itself a year worth remembering:

- President Herbert Hoover was literally run out of office by a fire in the White House. While temporary space was being prepared for him in General Pershing's office, the president vacationed on Florida's Long Key.

- A banking group headed by J. P. Morgan and Company, in a brave effort to resurrect the stock market, announced the liquidation of the last of its share holdings.

- Admiral Richard Byrd returned from his exciting discoveries in Antarctica, which he had gallantly renamed "Marie Byrd Land" in honor of his spouse.

- The U.S. prohibition commissioner ordered a crackdown on home brew paraphernalia, which he said was "filling the basements of America."

- In accord with the Treaty of Versailles, France dutifully withdrew all its troops from the Rhineland, and Adolf Hitler tensed for the kill as his new Nazi party won 107 seats in the *Reichstag*.

- An alert astronomer named Clyde Tombaugh found a ninth planet in the solar system and, aware of what seemed to be on people's minds in 1930, he dubbed it "Pluto" after Plutus, the Roman god of money.

- In far-off Ethiopia, a likable Haile Selassie was being crowned emperor, lion of Judah, king of kings. In farther-off China, President Chiang Kai-shek became a Christian.

- Col. Charles A. Lindbergh set another sizzling travel record, flying from California to New York in just 14.5 hours.

- On November 3, in the slowly growing city of Augusta, on the Georgia-South Carolina state line, Dennis James Kennedy was born.

The Kennedy news grabbed no headlines in 1930. It rated no more than a couple of lines in condensed agate type tucked away in The Augusta Chronicle's vital statistics columns.

After all, in the beginning the story was about as simple as could be imagined. An industrious Yankee salesman ("Kennedy's the name, glassware's the game") comes south in search of new markets and finds a bride on the banks of the Savannah River. Not too long thereafter, the proud young parents—George Raymond and Ermine Roberson Kennedy—

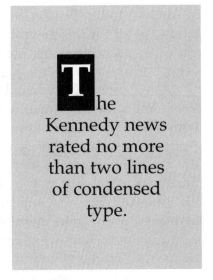

The Kennedy news rated no more than two lines of condensed type.

show off their first born son, whose privilege it is to perpetuate the family name. The following year, the two weeks premature but healthy younger brother, Dennis James, puts in his appearance.

According to the family records, the Kennedy surname is from Old Gaelic and could be spelled either as *Cinneide* or as *Ceannaideach*, both deriving from a term connoting plainness. If applied to appearance, the ancestor word was not overly flattering; but if descriptive of character, as early names tended to be, then "Kennedy" implies a person of plain, open, honest disposition. This ancient clan was later found in both Scotland and Ireland, with the Scots claiming that the Irish branch of the family was sired mostly by "lawless persons" forced to flee from the highlanders, who were proud of their ties to King Robert III in the twelfth century.

The Irish Kennedys, on the other hand, insist that they descended from one "Kennedy, Nephew of Brian Boru, High King of Ireland," dating back to the eleventh century. The surname is reported to be the sixteenth most common in Ireland today, with approximately twenty thousand families listed. No one hazards a guess as to the number of Kennedys in America today. Besides, such genealogical trivia held no interest at all for this newest Kennedy, nor would it attract more than a fraction of his attention in later years. The source of his inspiration is not the past, but the future.

More interested in where he is going than in where he is from, Jim Kennedy draws an almost scriptural inference from the family coat of arms. The "dolphin natant" on the crest reminds him that the symbol of the first-century Church was the fish (because its letters in the Greek stood for "Jesus Christ, Son of God, Savior"). The motto, *Avise la fin*—French for "Consider the end," appears to him almost to restate the first question he asks every prospect: "If you should die today, do you know for certain that you would go to Heaven?" And the powerful belt that surrounds the crest is to him the girdle of truth right out of Ephesians 6:14.

His parents called the thoughtful, shy little boy Jimmy, but to most people for most of his life he has been plain "Jim." Actually, he was the namesake of a rather distinguished Chicago businessman, who was a member of the Board of Trade. Today, on the South Side, there is a Dennis James Kennedy Park, which honors his grandfather. But the bearer who has made the name known internationally in the present generation has never used the "Dennis," partly because his mother did not like the name.

It was many years later that his maternal grandmother made an unexpected request. Approaching her death, the old woman had already laid her burial gown out carefully on her bed. When she learned that her grandson was going to become a preacher, she sent for him just two months before her long life ended. She allowed him to lead her in a prayer of profession of faith in Christ, and then she extracted from him the promise that he would choose "D. James Kennedy" as his official name. Thus it has been ever since. (Certainly a host of other first-initial churchmen—G. Campbell Morgan, J. Sidlow Baxter, J. Hudson Taylor, and J. Vernon McGee— would applaud his grandmother's choice.)

The father of the Kennedy clan is remembered as a "dear, dear man, extremely loving and patient and long suffering." Like most traveling salesmen during the difficult times, he spent much of his time on the road in order to support his family. By 1936, after moving his family to Jacksonville, then being transferred back and forth between there and the home office in Chicago, the elder Kennedy was settled in the big Illinois city, where the family would stay for almost a decade. Six-year-old Jimmy was to carry just two memories of Jacksonville with him. The grown man today cannot recall anything about the school where he took his first timorous step into the educational process, but he clearly remembers the walk to and from the school grounds. His other dim impression from that long-ago period is a vague, undefined consciousness, not only that God had made him, but that God had something He wanted him to do. "It was just a feeling," he says, "that I could not explain."

Jim would live out a good part of his boyhood in an

apartment in a pleasant neighborhood south of Howard Avenue near Evanston. Best of all, the home was only fifty yards from the windy shores of Lake Michigan. Here began a lifelong love affair with water and water sports. Also, the beaches were a handy refuge from an increasingly "unbearable battleground" at home, where his mother's recurring bouts with inebriation were wreaking havoc on the chances of normal family relationships. For a sensitive, affectionate boy to grow to maturity in a home ravaged by the frightful encroachment of alcohol addiction and to escape disabling psychological scars, surely required the intervening hand of God.

That same providential watch care spared Jim's life on a bitter cold winter's day when the surf of Lake Michigan had been transformed by a hard freeze into a fairyland of ice sculpture—and a natural playground for children.

The wind-whipped waves had congealed into volcanic mounds of solid ice at the water's edge. It was great fun to dash up the sides of these ten- or twelve-foot cones and jump over inside where a platform of ice sealed the structure a few feet down from the top. As Jim ran up the slope, leaped into the crater and down onto the diaphragm of ice, his feet went through; only his outspread arms prevented his plunging into the freezing waters feet below. He was stuck, with no way to extricate himself, and if his brother George had not happened to be within hearing distance to come and give him a hand, Jim would have died that day.

If his brother had not happened by, Jim would have died that day.

Nine years of schooling in what was considered, in the 1940s, to be one of the better systems in the country gave no hint of the mental capacity or keenness of insight that would become hallmarks of the matured Kennedy intellect. But during this exposure to the patterns of Midwest speech, his tongue undoubtedly received valuable training in the direction of precise, crisp articulation (as demonstrated by the large number of television news anchor persons recruited from this area of the United States). Jim would find this childhood discipline of considerable use to him later, in the pulpit.

Lacking any special motivational impetus, the young Kennedy ascended the rungs of the educational ladder somewhat lethargically, avoiding distinction along the way. He involved himself in the usual litany of activities shared by American schoolboys: sports competition, flitting grade-school romances, a few heated playground altercations, and intermittent dreams of becoming a scientist, preferably an astronomer.

But as the formative years passed, the church was being given little, if any, chance to influence emerging character traits and attitudes. The family had a nominal affiliation with a local Methodist church, but if the Gospel had anything to say about his situation, Jim never got the message. The prospect of sitting in a Sunday school class to learn something about the Bible held out minimal appeal. Consequently, religion remained totally uncharted territory. It couldn't begin to compete with ice skating.

Membership in the Boy Scouts of America challenged Jim as an energetic teenager, especially during the exciting years of World War II. Jim dearly treasured the opportunity to escape to summer camps like West and Dan Beard in the Michigan wilderness. "Those Boy Scout camps," Jim recalls, "gave me my only true relief from a really difficult life at home. They were my absolute haven of peace, and the greatest joy of my boyhood that I can remember was when it was time to go to summer camp." Jim worked his way up to the rank of Star Scout.

Eventually it was time for something else. The comparative aimlessness of a boy's life was about to undergo a major course correction. The senior Kennedy had begun to suffer from the same asthmatic condition that had led to his father's death a few years before, and he was taking no chances. In 1945 he uprooted the family from what had become familiar home turf and transplanted it to sandy soil and a subtropical climate far below the Mason-Dixon line.

For Jim, living near the warm Gulf of Mexico would mean opportunity for even more water sports. It would also mean more waiting, tougher testing, and even a touch of profligacy before the prodigal son would look toward the Father's home, before he would hear the voice that spun Saul of Tarsus around on the Damascus Road.

HISTORY IN THE MAKING

Wherewithal shall a young man cleanse
his way? by taking heed thereto
according to thy word.
—PSALM 119:9

The relocation was from Northern Illinois, where icicles had measured three or four feet on the eaves of the Kennedy apartment, to South Florida, where Spanish moss decorated tree branches by the same dimension. But to Jim Kennedy, the initial impression was not so much fascination with his new environment as a vague disorientation; the one place where he had developed a comfortable sense of belonging had been left almost fifteen hundred winding miles behind. Only a shy fifteen-year-old can know the anguish of trying to make new friends and to reestablish normal routines in a totally strange setting.

The unexciting confines of Palma Ceia, a suburb on the southern fringe of Tampa, provided scant indication that the new home state really boasted some of the most romantic names in world history—incomparable names that had swirled around Florida like a Gulf hurricane before they came to rest in the earliest encyclopedias.

For example, there was Ponce de Leon, who gave the state its aromatic name and who followed Columbus by only twenty years, in search of the fountain of youth. There was the fearsome Hernando de Soto, who landed with seven hundred men at the Indian village named Tampa in 1539 and began his long northwestward march to discover the Mississippi River and its bluffs at the site of Memphis. There was Sir Francis Drake, who impolitely burned to the ground the continent's very first white city, St. Augustine. And somewhere in there was the almost mythical Jose Gasparilla, the swashbuckling king of the pirates from the Spanish Main, who commandeered the port of Tampa and thus inspired the city's most festive annual celebration.

And in later times there was Andrew Jackson, whose cunning military and political maneuvers finally wrestled Florida away from foreign control. There was the colorful freedom fighter, Osceola, who contemptuously plunged his dagger into the pages of a treaty proposing an end to the Seminole wars. And none other than Teddy Roosevelt himself trained his Rough Riders beside Tampa Bay, which became the point of embarkation for troops headed to Cuba in the Spanish-American War.

A glamorous past, indeed! But, somewhat like the artless Bedouin resting in his goatskin tent in the shadow of the great pyramids with no awareness of their weighty impact on the history of civilizations, young Jim pretty well took his new environment for granted. This high school sophomore's grasp of, and appreciation for, the ponderous lessons of history lay yet in the future.

Neither was he aware that the history of American evangelism was about to undergo a transformation just across town from where he lived. A youth named Billy Graham had come down from his native North Carolina to North Tampa to pursue his theological studies at the Florida Bible Institute, later known as Trinity College. Jim never saw the gaunt young preacher holding forth at the Tampa Municipal Trailer Park before he graduated with the class of 1940. After the Sulphur Springs Baptist Church declined to hire Billy Graham as its pastor, he launched his own career with an evangelistic tour of Florida in his 1927 Chevrolet. Twelve years older than Kennedy, he was soon making history across the United States. It would be a while before Jim followed such an auspicious lead, but their paths eventually would cross many times.

Jim discovered, as time moved along, that his new home-town was a pretty nice place after all—especially during the 1940s. Despite the doubling of population that followed the land rush a couple of decades earlier, only thirty-five people per square mile lived in Florida, according to the demographic charts. This compared very comfortably with the United States average of forty-four per square mile. There was plenty of activity down toward the bay front, where ships laden with phosphate rock, cement, canned citrus, and the famous hand-rolled cigars from one hundred factories in quaint Ibor City (remember Hav-A-Tampa?) steamed out into the Gulf, bound for eastern seaboard cities and for the Panama Canal. For pleasure, the outlying beach resorts of St. Petersburg and Clearwater held out constant invitations.

Jim signaled his transition to early manhood in 1948 by graduation from Henry B. Plant High School with two notable achievements: a substantially improved grade record for the upper-class years and an outstanding musical background. Not only had he become proficient on the clarinet and saxophone, but he was also drum major of the high school band. From there, it was but a step from the institution named for Mr. Plant to one constructed by Mr. Plant, a gentleman who had made himself the patron saint of Tampa some years before. Plant (for whom nearby Plant City is named, along with dozens of public places in Tampa) had opened up the whole territory before the turn of the century with his railroad system, as H. M. Flagler was doing on the

East Coast.

It was the industrious Plant who built the elegant Tampa Bay Hotel. The mammoth structure was one of Florida's true spectacles—its Moorish architecture adorned with enough onion-shaped domes and convoluted trim to stop any tourist in his tracks. In Jim's eighteenth year, this once-famous resort inn housed the University of Tampa, where he launched into a college career that was to be temporarily abandoned after two-and-one-half years.

Those years contained some rough spots, like the hazing for a coveted membership in one of the campus fraternities. In the decades following World War II this ritual was taken seriously by the "Greek brothers." Jim and the other pledges were treated to a molasses-and-feathering in which hands, feet, and hair were transformed into balls of stiff, sticky goo. Then each initiate was covered with a gunnysack and nothing more, put out into the remote countryside around Tampa at two in the morning, and left to make his own unlikely way back to civilization. Other stages of the induction, Jim recalls, included an anointing with genuine skunk secretion which required a week of washing and deodorizing to outwear, plus other diabolical tortures. He was duly admitted to the fraternity, but bowed out in disgust after the first meeting, which was highlighted by vulgar entertainment.

More to his liking was the new sport of water-skiing, at which he soon became proficient enough to open, with a friend, a water-skiing school. While towing skiers, he often gave boat rides to fun-seekers on the beach. On one particular day, his passengers were a young mother who sat in the front of the boat beside him and her small boy of five or six who sat on the seat in the stern. After releasing his skier to coast back into the beach, Jim steered, as usual, into a very tight circle to return the boat to the pier. Suddenly he noticed that the young woman, who had left her seat and was sitting on the forward deck facing the back of the boat, was sliding irretrievably off the deck and out of the boat because of the centrifugal force. He instantly turned loose of everything and made a desperate grab for the woman. That was the wrong thing to do.

Out of control, the boat twisted violently and Jim thought it had taken on a heavy wave. Actually, he discovered that he and his female passenger were out of the boat and in the water. The boat, with the throttle wide open, was now headed at full speed toward the crowd on the beach with the small boy in the stern shouting, "Mommy! Mommy!" An experienced lifeguard and swimmer, Jim started toward the trailing line, hoping to grab it and slow the boat's progress. However, when the young woman began thrashing about and shouting that she couldn't swim, he changed course to go and hold her head above water.

In utter shock, Jim watched the boat, with its bow up at a thirty-degree angle, pick up speed and approach the shore. Fortunately, it was now headed toward the other side of the pier, where uninhabited sand banks about eight feet high were covered with dense undergrowth. As it ran aground, the flat bottom of the speeding boat slid right up the embankment and arched over a tree that stood about twenty feet high. Then the boat, boy, and all disappeared on the other side. By the time Jim and the horrified mother got to shore, all they could see was a thin wisp of smoke from the overheated motor.

Expecting to find the child's mangled body, the two raced through the underbrush and up the bank. But, miraculously, the tree had gently halted the boat's flight and had let it down to the ground with nothing more than a few scratches on the bottom. Even the engine was unharmed. And the little boy? He came running out of the bushes to meet them, shouting, "Mommy! Can we do that again?" Once again, Jim's luck—or something like it—had spared him from impending tragedy.

Meanwhile, on the more positive side, Jim was finding college to be pleasant enough. Deep within his makeup he discovered an affinity for learning and a great interest in the liberal arts. His growing love for literature seemed to be intensified by a Shakespeare course. And soul satisfaction flowed from his association with music.

His music, after all, had put him in college. Although he was not able to provide financial assistance, Jim's father had conscientiously encouraged him to seek a higher education. And Jim's proficiency on the clarinet in high school made him the top performer at the annual band concert during his senior year. The featured work was Gershwin's "Rhapsody in Blue," a difficult composition that opens with a solitary clarinet glissando and contains several other demanding solo clarinet parts.

Without knowing that the University of Tampa's music director would be in the audience, Jim had prepared himself well for the performance. His flawless execution won him a full music scholarship at the university. On the college level, the student quickly became the master of the instrument, and Jim Kennedy was soon playing first-chair clarinet with the band, which meant he was given all the solo parts. And it would not be long before his tall, athletic figure and his sense of rhythm would again single him out as ideal for the role of drum major. He also went out for crew, rowing with the team in the placid mouth of the Hillsboro River. There were some golden days, to be sure, but Jim was not going to come by a college degree easily. Unfortunately, his priorities at that age ranked such extracurricular activities as judo lessons, weight lifting, ping pong, boxing, and

> **T**he sheepskin was abruptly postponed by five years of academic apostasy.

womanizing pretty much on a par with the pursuit of a diploma. The sheepskin was abruptly postponed by five years of academic apostasy.

What in the world could be the lure to draw such a promising youth away from the hallowed halls of ivy? It was a hall of another kind, one where big-band music seldom stopped, pretty girls were in abundance, and Terpsichore was the reigning deity. And it paid good money!

Everybody in America seemed to know about Arthur Murray and his easy-to-learn dancing lessons, which by 1940 had allegedly converted three million wallflowers into ballroom socialites. A popular song, "Arthur Murray Taught Me Dancing in a Hurry," made the Hit Parade. Murray himself, who had planned to be an architect until he happened to win a waltz contest, made (1) the best-seller list twice with his how-to-do-it books, (2) *Who's Who in America* every year for fifty years, and (3) a fortune. His studios across the country eventually numbered 450. So respected was this master teacher of dancing-for-fun that he was invited to write on the subject for *Encyclopaedia Britannica*.

No small wonder, then, that a University of Tampa

At twenty years of age, Jim Kennedy was a bona fide swinger

student, who was already infatuated with music and dancing, should somewhat impulsively respond to a newspaper advertisement placed by the Arthur Murray Studio—or that he should be hired on the spot as an instructor. He was happier on the dance floor than he had been on the campus. At twenty years of age, Jim Kennedy was a bona fide swinger. The steps were no problem for him to pick up and pass on to the endless line of young women seeking self-expression and popularity. From the fox-trot through a dizzying array of Latin rhythms that captivated a generation during the 1950s, he was an expert. As a matter of fact, he was expert enough to take first place in Arthur Murray's All-American competition, a sort of Olympiad of dancers that pitted thousands of instructors against each other. Barely twenty-two, he was chosen to serve as a member of the National Dance Board, a group of mentors responsible for creating and formulating steps for the instructional program. Almost predictably, Kennedy moved up the various levels on the salary scale until he became studio manager of the Tampa franchise.

Had he found his permanent niche? After all, the masculine good looks, the lithe body, and the impeccable dress and manners required by the program (which liked to characterize itself as "the Golden Rule applied to ballroom dancing") made him a natural. How could he do anything but prosper? Even in this admittedly secular setting, Jim demonstrated to himself and to others an attribute that would uniquely identify his true character throughout his life: a commitment to excellence. No matter what kind of activity he would involve himself in, this apparently innate thirst for quality would lead him to seek the goal nearest to perfection.

At this stage, Jim's problem had to do with goal definition. His success was beginning to exact its toll. While the flesh was being fed amply enough, the spirit was suffering from acute malnutrition. There was no room on his busy agenda for church, no interest in quiet Bible-reading, no exposure to godly influence—just the chance association with purely nominal Christians. The moral erosion that so easily besets the young of the species in every generation was becoming chronic and progressive like an unwanted malady. With the genial encouragement of wrongly selected companions, a footloose *bon vivant* could find it easy to slide into some of society's loose habits: corrupt language, occasional drinking, a little carousing, a bit of philandering.

And it was all in the name of a good time, of "getting the most out of this world." The trouble was, Jim hadn't yet caught on to the fact that he really didn't belong to this world. He just didn't know that he belonged to God. He was about to learn.

But first there was Anne.

CHAPTER 3

IT TAKES TWO TO TANGO

*Whoso findeth a wife findeth
a good thing, and obtaineth
favour of the Lord.*
—PROVERBS 18:22

When Anne Lewis showed up at the Tampa Arthur Murray dance studio one breezy night, her arrival signaled a permanent course alteration in Jim Kennedy's life. In fact, Jim got the signal within thirty seconds after she walked into the building. "No doubt about it," he told a fellow instructor. "That's the girl I'm going to marry." Up to that moment, he had hardly given a thought to marriage. After all, he was only twenty-two.

Born in Statesville, North Carolina, Anne shared her mother's maiden name of Craig and her veterinarian father's love for animals of all sizes and descriptions. With Jean and Carolyn, her older and younger sisters, she spent most of her growing-up years in the picturesque town of Lakeland, just thirty-four shopping miles from Tampa.

A frantically busy Presbyterian, whose father, Dr.

Kenneth R. Lewis, was an elder at the church where her mother was president of the women's group and pastor's aide, Anne matured into a diminutive dynamo of enterprise and activity. She sang solos with the choir, she was an avid horsewoman, she worked with children's classes, she played bridge, she modeled for fashion shows, she sewed, she performed on the piano and clarinet, she operated a ham radio at all hours, she was seriously contemplating a dancing career, she was off to Florida State College for Women at seventeen, she was back home the following year to hold down a secretarial job, and she was busy performing as a water ballerina in water-ski shows.

By age nineteen Anne had zeroed in on a degree program at Birmingham-Southern College, where the exuberance of sorority life, participation in all sports, and endless music rehearsals helped to drain off some of her excess energy. Although she majored in Spanish, she was asked to stay on after graduation as an assistant director in the Department of Music at Birmingham-Southern, a position she held for the next four years. After a summer of graduate study at UCLA to get a taste of life in the American West, as well as to prepare for a possible career in elementary or secondary education, she decided to "do Europe" with several sorority sisters—a splendid junket that added to her store of knowledge and depleted her dwindling savings account.

During this time, Anne had successfully supported herself and, as a typical, ambitious working girl, evidenced little interest in forming lasting relationships with boyfriends. One thing she was certain of and never passed up an opportunity to express publicly and emphatically: she would never be married to a preacher! She came by that conviction after her sister, Jean, became the bride of a pastor. "Life in a goldfish bowl is not for me" was her oft-heard declaration. Besides, destiny had put her feet on the road to becoming the executive secretary for a corporation in the giant phosphate industry in Bartow, thirty minutes' drive from home.

Thus she appeared, right on schedule, at that fateful Friday night dance party at Arthur Murray's. Students were encouraged to bring guests to the weekly event at the studio, and Anne was escorted by a young admirer who was just learning to dance. It was his time to go into a smaller room for private instruction, so he deposited Anne in one of the chairs lining the main ballroom where she could wait comfortably. And who do you suppose was circling the floor at the time, teaching a middle-aged woman the basic steps?

Almost instantly, Jim's gaze was riveted on the newcomer. "She was beautiful," he recalls. "Five-foot-two, eyes of blue, with long, dark, wavy hair that broke over her shoulders, a captivating smile . . ." He was dancing to a different tune, but suddenly he couldn't keep the lyrics of the currently popular "My Ideal" from running around and around inside his head: "Will I ever find the girl of my mind, the one who is my ideal? Or will I pass her by and never even know that she was my ideal?" (Jim, who has been known to change key in the middle of a song, confesses that if his ideal had heard him singing those words, she most assuredly would have passed him by.)

> Jim's gaze was riveted on the newcomer. "She was beautiful," he recalls.

He tried bravely to keep his attention on his matronly partner, but he carefully choreographed each gyration to allow himself another glimpse of the lone figure sitting demurely beside the dance floor.

Anne's escort had thoughtfully arranged for her an official analysis of her dancing proficiency. The official analyst-interviewer? None other than Jim. "That's the worst mistake that fellow ever made," he chuckles.

Not too surprisingly, Jim found Miss Lewis to be the most promising dancer he had ever held in his arms, whereupon he immediately signed her up for ten hours of instruction at the bargain rate of one hundred dollars. At the conclusion of the introductory lessons, he sold her the five-hundred-dollar Bronze Medal Course, which meant she would have to come to the studio weekly for six more months. Because her continental tour had devastated her financial resources, and her new salary checks had not yet begun, Anne recalls floating a loan to pay for expanding her talent.

But she felt she was getting her money's worth. On December 28, 1952, Anne addressed a scented blue note card, decorated with swan and lily pads, to Mr. James Kennedy, Arthur Murray's Studio of Dancing, Lafayette Street, Tampa, Florida:

Dear Mr. Kennedy,

I just wanted to write you a note and wish for you the happiest new year ever.

I'm enjoying my lessons so much and consider myself extremely fortunate for having such an outstanding instructor.

Best wishes.

Sincerely,
Anne Lewis

With this ladylike, almost Victorian courtesy, began three-and-a-half years of intermittent correspondence between two young people from widely differing backgrounds. The frequency of letters exchanged between Tampa and Lakeland or Bartow rose steadily, as did the warmth of the messages. Studio rules forbade dating between instructors and their students, but as soon as the course was finished, Jim invited his ideal to a picnic with the other teachers and their friends. A casual reading of the complimentary closes at the bottom of each letter reveals an interesting progression from that original "Sincerely, Anne Lewis" to "Your No. One Girl, Anne" to "Love and Kisses, Anne" and a mysterious "88" borrowed from her secret ham radio code, which she was soon teaching Jim, who, like the Athenians, loved to learn any new thing.

As a case in point, note the message with which Anne (an extremely articulate and accomplished letter-writer) finished a communication to Jim on her office typewriter after sharing several months of practice on the Morse Code:

> I had a little trouble making out your code message at first because you put "w" for "u" every time. You had .-- instead of ..- I can't do it very well on the typewriter. I got the idea, though, and it was a mighty sweet message!
> ../ -- .. ../ -.-- --- ..-/ .- -. -../ .-.. --- --- -.- .. -. --./ ..-. --- .-.
> .-- .- .-. -../ - --- / - .... ./ .-- . . -.- . -. -../ .-.. --- ...- ./ .- -. -../ -.-
> .. ../ .. -./ -.-. --- -.. .. ../ 88, Anne

Perhaps that's enough invasion, in the name of research, into the private language of lovers. Their secret will remain with them and a few unscrupulous individuals who may do a little deciphering for themselves.

It was a beautiful and a beautifully expressed romance. However easily the distance between Tampa and Lakeland could be traversed by a three-cent stamp, the train ride was something else. Anne wrote in October 1954:

> I just figured up yesterday: I've ridden on that 5:30 train for five consecutive Saturdays. The conductor thinks I live in Tampa and just get home on the weekends. I feel like a regular commuter.
>
> I *do* wish you lived in Lakeland! Then, after we got married (!) I could keep this good job I have and we could save a lot of money and could get a house (and with my interior decorating book and pots and pans, we would be all fixed). It's so

exciting to think about, anyway!

I'll plan on taking the train Saturday if I get off from work in time unless I hear from you to the contrary. If I find I won't get off in time, I'll call you. In the meantime, write me, if you can.

How has your work at the studio been? Sometimes I want to talk to you about your long-range plans with Arthur Murray's. Do you expect to own some studios some day, or do you suppose you'll be managing a larger one, or what? I'm sure you have thought about it, but you've never talked to me about it. To use your question, "What is your goal?" I'm getting too serious, aren't I?

One more serious thought before I close—

../.-.. --- ...- ./-.-- --- ..-/ c

I've almost forgotten my code.

All my love,
"Yours"

They were not yet engaged, but this beautiful young girl (her friends said she looked exactly like Jeanne Crain, the movie queen of the 1950s), the veterinarian's daughter from the small town, was obviously smitten with the suave dance instructor in the big city. And like every young woman in love, she dreamed of a future that would not be too unlike paradise itself. In November 1954 she wrote:

The ideal situation came to me, but is impossible, I guess. I thought it would be just wonderful if you worked for Publix [a Florida grocery chain] or some place like that where it takes someone like you to really work up. That's what Speedy [her brother-in-law] has done. He's gone up and up just because he has that "something" that you have. . . . You could come home at 5:30 or 6:00; we could have Saturdays and Sundays to ourselves once in a while. It would just seem like heaven to me in so many ways.

May I dream a little more? I was just thinking if you

worked around here and we could live in Lakeland, I could keep my job (because there wouldn't be another opportunity in a hundred years where I could make the salary that I'm making here) and with our money pooled, your brains, ambition and abilities, and the things that we could do together—Utopia!!!!

Anne's sprightly letters provide a private insight into the progress of the romance. In one, written at her desk in Bartow, she confided to Jim: "I am writing this on the office typewriter so it will look like I'm working. I have typed forty-two letters today and have thirteen more to go!" Closing with another one of her passages of secret code, she added this at the bottom of the page: "Burn this after you have read it. Please don't leave it lying around." Her modest protestation might suggest to the intrusive reader that the code contained something downright scandalous, but it didn't—just some more perfectly innocent "love and kisses." Apparently her concern was that the boss might somehow discover that the company typewriter had been commandeered briefly for a secretary's love letter—a serious matter indeed!

The dream began to assume the proportions of reality when the studio gave Jim an unexpected three-hundred-dollar Christmas bonus. With that windfall, he rushed to a nearby jewelry store and picked out the very best half-carat diamond ring he could find. From there he dashed to his Pontiac and drove to Lakeland. Later in the evening, the big moment arrived at scenic Lake Hollingsworth, where Anne had performed in many water-ski shows. Jim parked the car, reached into his pocket, and presented her with the ring and his marriage proposal. The girl of his dreams accepted, and bliss reigned supreme. December 3, 1955, became a Kennedy date to remember.

Anne's very next letter mirrored the new excitement that filled her heart. From her trusted office typewriter she wrote of her double joy—being engaged to Jim and being able to tell her boss that she would be quitting her job:

Wednesday, Jan. 11, 1956

Dearest Jim,

This is another one of those weeks when I'm topsy-turvy at the office, but I wanted to take a moment to tell you how more than thrilled I am that we are "promised." I just feel so different, it's truly amazing. I feel more like a woman than I've ever felt before, and that might sound funny, but it's the truth.

I just can't wait to tell you all the comments about my gorgeous ring and all the nice things people have said about you. Everyone is so thrilled for us and is wishing us so much joy and happiness which I know will be ours. Your taste was so exquisite in choosing the ring, and I haven't seen one yet that even compares with its beauty.

Anne's very next letter mirrored the new excitement that filled her heart.

Mr. _____'s face dropped down a mile. And I even got brave enough to tell him just what I thought of him. It was constructive criticism and it did him some good, too.

All my love and kisses,

Anne

It was a traditional wedding at the First Presbyterian Church of Lakeland, with her sisters as bridesmaids and his brother as best man. They became husband and wife on August 25, 1956, and went off on a traditional Riviera honeymoon (Florida, not France). The vacation excitement was enhanced by a near-tragedy off Riviera Beach. Jim was teaching Anne scuba diving when her mask became filled with water. Because of the essential weights connected with the diving gear, she was unable to rise to the surface for air. Jim was able to use his lifesaving training to save his bride's life and tow her back to the security of shallow water.

How the ideal marriage can be achieved has been demonstrated by both partners for more than four decades now. Jim has articulated the principle many times in his public addresses and writings. Let us allow him to tell it in his own words:

"Marriage can be either a tremendously constructive experience or it can be unimaginably destructive in the lives of those involved. What makes the difference between a constructive and a destructive marriage? Let us consider the way things develop.

"Two people fall in love. What is more wonderful than two people in love! It is spring again! Bells are ringing and birds are singing! There is a time of great romance. At last the heart's desires have been met. The question is popped. The engagement comes. The big day arrives, followed by the honeymoon. Each has met the most wonderful person in the world—an angel, indeed; an Adonis in human form. My ideal! Do you remember? Each was a composite of the most magical charms. Flaws—why, the very idea! . . . not in my beloved! This is my ideal. If there are any flaws at all that some friends might have candidly pointed out, their words were received quite coldly. Certainly there were none worthy of notice and none that even began to compare with the over-whelming good that flowed from this dear one. Ah, the wonderful astigmatism of romance.

"Not only did you have such feelings about your beloved but, more than that, you shared them with this special person. He or she shared similar feelings with you and you were lifted right up out of this world into the heavenlies. Indeed, at last you had found someone who could look beyond the braces and the blemishes that had been there just a little while ago and see you for the wonderful person that you really were, someone who had true insight into real character. The person you had been looking for for years had at last come.

"And the constructive aspect of this was truly remarkable. Why, you began to improve on every side! What is more wonderful for a young man, they say, than to fall in love with a good woman? He becomes a better man. My hero! And you become braver by the moment. So it goes—you responding to her or his statements about the wonderful characteristics of your life. And so all who have ever fallen in love have noticed not only that their beloved had marvelous characteristics and qualities, but also that they themselves became better persons thereby. This is just an intimation of the potential for constructive betterment that exists in marriage."

This all sounds agreeable enough, doesn't it? But Kennedy's thesis contains a delayed-action bomb guaranteed to shake up his listeners and readers. A successful marriage, he emphasizes, is not built on love and romance! "It is based on commitment, commitment to believe that marriage is a permanent, indissoluble relationship between two who have become one and who no longer are two. Until we have that commitment we do not have fertile ground for the seeds of love to take hold in."

In 1956 neither Jim nor Anne claimed fully to understand that commitment. Her decision on whether to accept this man as her partner for life had already become involved in a far greater decision that had confronted Jim. Her commitment to him was inextricably linked to a vastly more profound commitment that he had just made—one that would affect both their lives, not until the end of earthly existence, but through all eternity.

In this marriage, there would be more than two persons living as one; already a third Person was present to guarantee a perfect and lasting union.

But how had Jim come to know Him?

THE
MAN
OF
GOD

TUNED IN AND TURNED ON

He that heareth my word, and believeth
on him that sent me, hath everlasting
life, and shall not come into condemnation;
but is passed from death unto life.
—JOHN 5:24

Early in their acquaintance, like any other couple, Jim and Anne talked about many things. Inevitably, Anne, a lifelong church-goer still addicted to the habit, got around to asking him, "Where do you go to church?"

"Nowhere," was his laconic reply. "You don't have to go to church to be a good person." Then, as if to strengthen his affirmation, he recast it in the positive mode: "You can be just as good a Christian without going to church."

Jim was not prepared for Anne's soft-spoken but firm rebuttal. Almost in a whisper, she said, "No you can't." That was all, but somehow, like a tiny dart of conviction, her simple, three word protest found immediate lodging in his brain.

"I was utterly taken back," he says today. "I had never had my little pet saying challenged before and I was amazed that anyone could have the audacity to say such a thing." Except for her, Jim really didn't know anybody who attended church or who considered it terribly important one way or the other.

The profound lesson Jim learned from that terse conversational exchange—one which he has repeatedly emphasized over the years—is the unknowable importance of any kind of spoken testimony, no matter how insignificant it may appear to be. "I had never had anyone witness to me at all about anything religious. I had never heard the Gospel. But I realized later that the least witness can be far more effective than we know. The slightest suggestion of concern about another person's spiritual condition may be the beginning of a change of direction in that person's life," he says today.

He recalls the unwillingness of his best friend in Tampa, a young musician whom he had known in high school and college, to bring him the Gospel. The young friend had been led to Christ by his own brother, but he never discussed salvation with Jim. Asked later if he had ever considered telling Jim of his need for Christ (at the very time that Jim was ripe for it), his reply was, "I thought about it, but I figured Jim would probably knock me down a flight of steps! That fellow is hopeless. He is a hopeless reprobate."

Jim Kennedy *was* a well-muscled six-footer who had been in a couple of major fights. In the first he was blindsided by a sailor who knocked him unconscious with an unsportsmanlike blow to the jaw. In the second Jim had gone to help an elderly man who was being set upon by a much younger pugilist. Witnesses saw two blows struck: Jim hit the assailant, and the assailant hit the ground. The musician-friend's failure to witness to Jim could have been a matter of misjudgment as well as timidity. But there was still the missed opportunity. That young man's word of witness might have redirected a "reprobate" toward a great ministry for God.

With Anne's gentle assertion still echoing in the remote recesses of his mind, Jim was aroused from a deep sleep one Sunday afternoon. He had wearily turned in just before dawn after an almost-all-night dance party, after instructing his clock radio to awaken him to music at the appointed time. But instead of being pleasantly massaged back to consciousness by Guy Lombardo and "the sweetest music this side of heaven," he was jarred wide awake by a voice that sounded as if it were thundering right out of Heaven. It was the weekly broadcast of Dr. Donald Grey Barnhouse, pastor of the Tenth Presbyterian Church in Philadelphia and one of the first great radio evangelists. "This was the last thing I needed in my bedroom, especially when I was a little hung over," Jim remembers. "I got out of bed to change the station and put on some good music. Before I reached the radio, this Presbyterian minister stopped me dead with a question that practically set me back on the edge of my bed."

In the stentorian tones for which he was famous, Dr. Barnhouse asked: "Suppose that you were to die today and stand before God and He were to ask you, 'What right do you have to enter into My Heaven?'—what would you say?"

In that electrifying moment Jim felt totally disarmed. He didn't have an answer. He would discover a few years later that millions of people do not have an answer, and Barnhouse's penetrating question, in modified form, would become the linchpin of Jim's worldwide Evangelism Explosion that would sweep literally thousands into the kingdom in the decades to come. But in 1955 the crucial dynamic change was taking place in the inner life of Jim Kennedy, who continued to listen to a radio preacher's explanation of the plan of redemption through faith in the Man of redemption—a message he had never heard before.

"I was completely dumbfounded. I had never thought of such a thing as that. As I sat there on the edge of my bed with my mouth hanging open, I groped desperately for some answer. I was a hundred million miles from being anything resembling a theologian, but I had enough common sense to realize that this was a very important question and that if I didn't have the answer to it I might be left standing on the dock when the ship set sail. I might even be left somewhere worse than that, but I didn't like to think about where that might be."

Jim was hearing the Gospel for the first time, and he was born again. Born again? This urbane, street-smart sophisticate who had never evidenced any interest in religion, who had devoted precious few seconds to the contemplative life? Why would somebody who was doing exactly what he liked to do and making it pay within shooting distance of $750 a week, a smooth operator who seemed to have the world by the tail, be so affected by a routine Sunday sermon from Philadelphia? Could it be a temporary delusion triggered by some thoroughly explainable stimulus that would wear off in a few days? Jim knew something about psychological phenomena; what he did not yet know was the power of the Holy Spirit to use spoken testimony to transform the heart of a person in need of Christ.

Consider the evidence. For the next few days, Jim did his work in a continued state of astonishment. Something undeniably miraculous had happened to him. The morning after the broadcast, as he was shaving, he found himself restating in wonder: "Jesus Christ says I am going to live with Him forever in paradise!" It seemed to be too good to be true, yet the certainty renewed his sense of assur-

Something undeniably miraculous had happened to Jim.

ance and joy. He was more convinced when he began to see a radical reformation of his own desires and habits. No more appetite for the occasional cocktail. No more inclination toward loose talk. No more promiscuity, as he recalled in a May 1988 reply to a reporter who said that young people today are "compelled" to engage in sexual immorality: "That is not true and it is not true that they have to. I was converted when I was almost twenty-four. I had been, and I say it to my own shame, promiscuous prior to that as a young, unregenerate, American heathen. I had lived as most of them do. But then, I saw Christ in all of His glory and His grace and His mercy, and I found His forgiveness and the transforming power of His Holy Spirit that changed my life. I lived for several years after that as a young single adult—continent, practicing sexual abstinence, and for thirty-two years, married, practicing fidelity to my wife. It is a lie that they have to do it."

For such a man to turn 180 degrees without the help of another person would require an act of God. Jim was now praying, confessing his guilt and his need. He had come through a heart transplant. He was suddenly curious about the Bible and what its unfamiliar pages had to say to him. Although he hadn't the slightest idea of where to start looking, he felt an overwhelming desire to investigate the fundamentals of Christian theology. He had a new sense of life, new purpose, new power, new affections, new destinations. It was as if he had sloughed off his old life like a worn-out coat. He had put on the new creature in Christ. Above all, he was filled with a strange and wonderful awareness that he had passed from death to life.

Jim described the experience in a book published in 1979: "To this day I have friends from twenty-four years ago who do not know what happened to me. One moment there was a young man managing an Arthur Murray dance studio, his heart and affections fastened entirely upon the things of this world. Then suddenly, overnight, something happened: a new person was born and an old person died. Those things which once to me seemed so desirable, so compelling, now seemed as filthy rags, dead men's bones, things of no interest to me at all.

"Other things, the things of the kingdom of God, those things that are invisible, those things that are eternal, which never occupied my thoughts at all and upon which my heart never dallied, have become exceedingly precious to me. Upon those things my affections have been fastened. There is no other solution than that twenty-four years ago I was born all over again.

"This is the only thing you must do during your stay on this planet—the only thing you must do. You don't even have to grow up. You don't have to succeed. You don't have to get married. You don't have to have children. You don't have to have a home, a car, and all of the things people think they must have. The only thing you must have is a rebirth, because your entire future depends upon it.'"[1]

In that Tampa apartment, on that remarkable Sunday afternoon, Jim made the transition from presumption to truth. He had presumed that if anybody else got into Heaven, he was good enough to make it; he didn't realize that he was calling God a liar—God, who says, "There is none good, no not one." He had presumed that because he respected the Ten Commandments, he would be entitled to enter the kingdom; he didn't know that Christ warned, "Moses gave you the commandments and none of you has kept them." He had presumed all along that by performing some good deeds and accumulating an acceptable record of good works, he could reach Heaven at least by a side door, or at worst, the back entrance.

But Barnhouse's uncompromising message was battering Jim's rationalizations into tiny, ineffectual pieces. In tones loaded with power and authority, Barnhouse was explaining that such reasoning was exactly like that of a man deciding to enter your home at three o'clock in the morning by putting up a ladder to your second-floor window. You would be inclined to shoot such an intruder, who obviously could claim no right to come into your house. "What do you think God is going to do," Barnhouse asked, "when you attempt to climb up through some back window, when He has already told you that Christ Jesus is the door, and that there is no other access? Jesus said 'Those who come to the Father must come by Me.' There is no other way into Heaven."

That was the Word of God speaking through a man, and for the first time in his life Jim began to look into the Bible he had never noticed before—looking with an inquiring mind, wanting to understand its message. Although he would later become thoroughly knowledgeable in the available Hebrew and Greek manuscripts as well as the many recent translations, his choice has never changed. From the first, he has liked the Authorized Version.

"The King James Version of the Bible," he says today, "perhaps uniquely, as it states in its foreword, was written for the purpose of being read in services of holy worship. That was the primary reason for its having been written. Secondly, it was translated at the height of the Elizabethan era [1611], in a time when the English language probably achieved its highest summit of beauty. I think it has been pretty well downhill since that time as far as the grandeur and the beauty of the language are concerned.

"In every translation, of course, you sacrifice something for something else. There are no doubt other translations that are more easily understood. There are some that are more exacting; this is especially true of the Greek texts. There are some based on older manuscripts that may have some advantage in the way of accuracy. But overall, I have preferred the King James Version because of its majesty and glory and grandeur. I have loved it from the beginning of my acquaintance with the Bible."

That love affair with the Word of God would require many years of ripening and maturing. The inspired youth hardly knew where to turn for guidance and instruction; he just knew that he needed both. After the radio message, a second influence made a lasting impression on him that memorable week. In the preface to a special edition of a familiar classic (he wrote this almost thirty years later) referring to his conversion:

"I visited a corner newsstand and asked, 'Do you have any religious books?' The owner said he had just one, and he handed me a copy of *The Greatest Story Ever Told*. I went home and read part of the book each night for the next several days. When I completed the book, it seemed as if the Cross of Christ had been erected right in my apartment and now I knew—for the first time—I knew why Christ was suffering there.

"I slipped out of my chair onto my knees and asked Christ to come into my heart and to forgive me and cleanse me of my sins. From that day until this, my life has never been the same. I shall be forever grateful for the radio broadcast of Donald Barnhouse and for this book by Fulton Oursler, both of which God used to bring me to a saving knowledge of His Son.

"It is, therefore, with great joy that I present to you this special edition of Fulton Oursler's classic, *The Greatest Story Ever Told*. May it bring to your life the joy unspeakable which it brought to mine.'"[2]

Jim readily acknowledges that his kind of conversion experience—the climactic, thunderclap revelation—is not necessarily the route by which all, or even very many, Christians arrive at a personal conviction of the need for a Savior. Indeed, most probably fit the illustration of the airline passenger whose plane takes off in Atlanta and lands in Miami. Perhaps the passenger dozes off along the way and can't tell anyone the details of time and circumstance at the specific moment when the plane crossed over the Florida-Georgia line. But the line was undoubtedly crossed because the plane is securely parked in Miami.

Perhaps the instantaneous conversion is more often documented than the gradual, prolonged-process type of salvation experience. The New Testament, for instance, gives us the most marvelous and inspiring examples: the man born blind, Mary Magdalene, Matthew the publican, the centurion's servant, the Gadarene demoniac, Zacchaeus, the thief on the cross, the Ethiopian eunuch, Cornelius, Paul the apostle, the Philippian jailer, and many others who came to Christ instantly. Augustine testified that, as he read one sentence from Romans 13:13-14,

> I did not choose to read more, nor had I the occasion. Immediately at the end of this sentence, as if a light of certainty had been poured into my heart, all the shadows of doubt were scattered.

For the poet William Cowper, it was Romans 3:25. He said,

> On reading it I immediately received power to believe. The rays of the Sun of Righteousness fell on me in all their fulness; I saw the complete sufficiency of the expiation which Christ had wrought for my pardon and entire justification. In an instant I believed, and received the peace of the Gospel.

And there was Martin Luther, the Roman Catholic monk who suddenly got up off his knees while climbing and kissing the Scala Sancta (sacred stairs) because a single verse of Scripture—"the just shall live by faith"— pierced his mind and con-

"**I** discovered that God was offering me eternal life and I wanted it."

vinced him that he could never earn his salvation by such foolishness.

There was John Calvin, whose testimony was, "God suddenly converted me unto Himself."

Also there was John Wesley, who wrote in his diary: "It was a quarter to nine, and for the first time in my life I knew that I trusted Jesus Christ alone for my salvation, and I felt my heart strangely warmed and knew that He had delivered me from sin and death unto eternal life."

There was Charles Spurgeon, who recalled his visit to a small chapel where an unlettered layman, substituting for the minister, pointed his finger at the young man and said, "You are going to be miserable forever unless you obey my text, 'Look unto Christ!'" Spurgeon later recorded: "In that moment my soul was flooded with the reality of the grace of God as I looked unto the cross of Jesus Christ. I knew that I had received eternal life! My soul was filled with joy. I could have danced all the way home."

The young man who was to be the future minister of Coral Ridge Presbyterian Church was drawn into an elite company as, all alone at the age of twenty-four, he felt his heart "strangely warmed." Some time later he said, "I found out what Jesus Christ had done for me. I discovered that God was offering me eternal life and I wanted it. Nobody ever twisted my arm. I had never met a Christian. I heard the Gospel only one time, but I wanted Jesus Christ. I have often said that if there had been six big men between me and Christ, they might have stopped me, but I sincerely doubt it."

The real life of D. James Kennedy had begun. It started with a question. It expanded from a question to a quest, a quest for more of the God he had never known. His quest would lead to conquests for Christ totally beyond his capacity to dream on that or any other Sunday afternoon.

FORWARD INTO BATTLE

Also I heard the voice of the Lord,
saying, Whom shall I send, and who
will go for us? Then said I,
Here am I; send me.
—ISAIAH 6:8

Jim's insatiable new hunger for spiritual nourishment drove him to a logical source of supply: a fellowship of believers. After checking out a church or two, he settled on a neighborhood Presbyterian church in Tampa. Right away he was drawn to a Bible class made up of young people who met on Sunday nights. During the week, alone in his apartment, Jim began to devour massive chunks of Scripture and to commit them to memory. In a very short time the class knew that here was no ordinary seeker of Bible information. He was out to acquire in-depth knowledge of the sacred book from Genesis to Revelation. Within months, Jim was teaching the class.

As every sincere Christian knows, the change of allegiance from the pleasures and preoccupations of this world to the demands of Christ is likely to involve the new convert in some embarrassing moments—at least, embarrassing to others. Jim had identified himself with the Christian Business Men's Club, which met in a hotel room off the main dining room. At the end of a session he came out into the open area with the others to pay the cashier, who happened to be a student at the dance studio he managed. With a look of disbelief, she blurted out, "I never thought I'd see you in a group like this!" Jim replied frankly, "Neither did I." Another time, while Jim was giving his testimony, three young women arrived a bit late for the service. They were Arthur Murray dance students. The trio tripped gracefully down the church's sloping aisle until the girl in the lead position suddenly caught sight of Jim and froze in her tracks before the girls behind her could check their momentum. The result was an undignified pile-up right in the middle of the congregation.

Jim did nothing to conceal his new identity, of course, but neither did he advertise it publicly. He was still pondering many things in his heart, among them the disharmony between his old career and his new faith. He had not even discussed the matter with Anne, but she was beginning to catch on. She was aware of a remarkable improvement in Jim's self-image and was delighted to learn that he was teaching a Bible class.

Without realizing the depth of his conviction, she complimented Jim on his church-going. But as he began to recount his conversion experience to her, and as she observed his behavior changes, she saw far more depth than she had at first suspected. Actually, as she listened to his testimony again and again over a period of months, she began to realize that she had never come that far herself, even though she was the one with a religious background. She could see it clearly now: what she had known all along was not fulfilled Christianity, but churchianity, and she wanted the reality that she saw in Jim's new faith. Eventually, without any of the finesse of an experienced evangelist, Jim prayed with Anne and led her to a personal knowledge of Jesus as her Savior and Lord. His first victory for Christ was the woman he loved.

After almost two years of slow but steady spiritual growth, it became apparent that a sense of call was growing in Jim's soul. At first he ignored it. Then he tried to rationalize it away. Finally he tried to fight it. His resistance mounted over the next twelve months until he found his conscience and his common sense locked in an intense struggle. His immediate concern was his job and self-preservation. The studio was paying better than ever, and he and Anne earned extra money at clubs as a professional dance team.

The pressure became unbearable. Late one afternoon, at the end of a busy week, Jim locked himself in his studio office and knelt in desperate prayer. His office seemed transformed into the ford Jabbock where Jacob wrestled with the angel of the Lord. "What do you want me to do, Lord?" he pleaded. No answer. He stretched out full-length, face on the floor. "Lord, do you really want me to quit this job? Are you sure you want to use somebody like me?" Jim had no visions and heard no voice, but he recalls every detail of that struggle. It was as if his right arm was being twisted behind his back and forced up toward his shoulder blades until he had no option except to cry "Uncle!" When he stopped fighting, he got to his feet and picked up the telephone. He could not believe it, but he was calling in his resignation.

When the conversation ended, Jim found himself without a livelihood.

As soon as his boss, who lived in Miami, heard Jim's voice on the other end of the line, he broke in with great news that couldn't wait—he wanted Jim to take over the studio in Sarasota, not only as manager but as half-owner. Jim felt close to weakening on the spot, but he couldn't forget that half-nelson the Lord had put on him. It was as if he could hear the hiss of the serpent, and he was able somehow to stammer out, "I'm quitting." When the conversation ended several painful minutes later, Jim found himself without a livelihood. It was Saturday night.

How did he feel now? Elated? Heroic? Filled with peace? Jim can tell you exactly how he felt. He felt that a heavy iron ball was lodged somewhere behind his solar plexus, weighing down his body as well as his spirit. He had by one willful act cut himself off from the only secure financial support base he had ever known. To make matters worse, his once substantial bank balance, which he had never bothered to keep close tabs on, now stood at thirteen dollars. Here he was—without a job, without money, without any prospect of support—and with this iron ball in the pit of his stomach.

Jim turned in his keys and left the studio. He went directly to talk with his pastor at Hyde Park Presbyterian, who was the current chairman of the Home Mission Committee. He had been impressed with Jim's zeal and teaching ability. He knew that tiny Bethel Presbyterian Church, located about twenty minutes out of Tampa across the causeway in Clearwater, could be losing its aged supply minister to retirement, possibly as soon as the first Sunday in February and that Jim might possibly take over at that time. But it was only December 3; the time lag was nicely calculated to permit Jim to die of slow starvation before opportunity just might decide to knock.

"But," Jim's pastor said, "why don't you go over there and deliver the sermon tomorrow morning at the eleven o'clock service?" Jim had no reason to decline, so he went to his apartment and began preparing a message. The prospect of preaching his first congregational sermon within the next fifteen hours was challenging, but Jim was not overawed; he had emceed too many dance programs to be tortured by stage fright. But he could certainly empathize with the reluctance of his Old Testament prototypes when God first handed them their marching orders. Like Moses: "O my Lord, I am not eloquent, neither heretofore nor since thou hast spoken unto thy servant: but I am slow of speech and of a slow tongue." Or like young Jeremiah: "Then said I, Ah, Lord GOD! behold, I cannot speak: for I am a child."

These heroes of the faith were overcomers, and so was God's new recruit. Like his scriptural predecessors, Jim sought out the Word of God, using as his text Jesus' parable in the twenty-second chapter of Matthew—the one about the man who showed up at the king's marriage feast without the required wedding garment. The subject was not chosen without forethought; it was a direct outgrowth of Jim's moving conversion experience, when his attention was riveted on Barnhouse's key question about one's right to enter God's Heaven. He could preach this text with conviction.

By eleven o'clock the next morning when Jim and Anne had located the little Bethel Presbyterian Church, which he remembers as "sort of cute," he was still bedeviled by that iron ball; even with his mind focused on the sermon he was about to offer, he had not been able to rid himself of that heavy reminder of his destitution. The taciturn old supply minister led Jim to a seat on the platform and conducted the first part of the service for the small congregation. After thirty minutes of rather uninspiring ritual and announcements, Jim was introduced.

Like a bolt from the blue, the host pastor told the flock that he had just come to an important decision. Since the board had sent this nice young man over to preach to them, he had decided not to retire in February—he was retiring right then and there! He presented Jim as the new preacher of Bethel Presbyterian Church!

Jim began his sermon. He was a bit nervous at the beginning and greatly excited under the skin. He may have maneuvered his feet conspicuously as a means of releasing pent-up energy—and a veteran dance instructor's movements could be suspiciously rhythmic in a pulpit setting—but Jim got through his first sermon under the patriarchal glare of the old man of the cloth. And his delivery was not without those surges of exhilaration experienced only by those who share the Word from a platform built on solid faith. He was thrilled to be taking up the torch and beginning in public the race that takes the faithful runner from glory to glory.

Best of all, that iron ball was gone, and Jim now understood its significance. God had simply used the fear that Jim picked up at the moment he had sacrificed his career to teach him one of the most marvelous lessons of his entire ministry: where God guides, God provides. At six o'clock the night before, Jim had no indication of any opening anywhere, not the slightest likelihood of a temporary supply position in the area, no assurance that he would be considered even if such an opportunity did develop by February. At 11:30 the next morning, he was on the payroll of the Home Mission Committee. Granted, 250 dollars a month isn't in the same class with the 750 dollars a week Jim had been pulling down at the studio, but it was adequate.

"That thing was resolved in such an incredible way," Jim recalls, "that it gave me tremendous confidence that God is able to supply my needs, which is something every preacher needs to have. If a minister can't trust God to supply his needs, then he has to trust the people in the church. And if he is looking to them for support, he is going to curb his message to be sure he doesn't step on their toes. That is what happens to many ministers. I see that experience in December of 1955 as a significant example of God's providence—which I think has helped me all along in my dealings with money in the pastorate. I discovered for the first time in my life what I would discover many times subsequently: that God was able to supply all my needs." Jim preached at the

Clearwater mission right on into August of the following year and then returned part-time in the summer of 1957. A dear little woman who played the church piano was his greatest encourager, opening her home every Wednesday night for the kind of prayer meetings vital to building the confidence of a new young preacher of the Gospel. After all, he had experienced—in a relatively short time—not only conversion, but conscription into the army of God; not redemption alone, but registration for the draft as well; not just an invitation to be saved, but a call to lifelong professional service.

What does a person do when called to preach? He or she does what every member of the service does:

(1) separates self from worldly affairs
(2) reports for duty
(3) enters training to learn how to fight

Step One: Jim deliberately took up the task of disentangling himself from all the pursuits that had occupied most of his waking hours. That had meant talking himself out of a career and separating himself from the lifestyle that went with it. This involved more of a soul-struggle for both Jim and Anne than either had anticipated; at times even their marriage plans appeared to be in jeopardy. In a letter dated June 13, 1955, with the waggish salutation, "Dearest D. James," Anne's remarks shed light on the turmoil through which they were passing at the time:

As you intimated in your letter of June 9 things do seem futile and "solution-less." If you feel the call to the ministry, you would never be happy or satisfied unless you answered it, so I see no other path for you to take. Your problem would be whether or not to get some education to prepare you for such a vocation or to become another kind of preacher that wouldn't require any more schooling. That would strictly be your decision to make.

After you left last night I tried to figure out why it was I felt the way I do. I think one reason is, I've always wanted an "8:30-to-5:00" husband because Mother never did have one. Daddy never knew when he was going to be able to come home and he didn't know when he was going to have to leave in the middle of the night. Carl [her brother-in-law, a preacher] is just about the same way. Many times on his vacations down in Florida, a member of his church would die, and he would have to go back to Virginia or Washington for the funeral. . . .

I firmly believe you should make your decision without considering me at all because if I influenced you to do something that you wouldn't be happy with, we would both go down in utter defeat. You'll just have to do what you think is right for you, and then I'll have to make my own decisions.

Oh, dear, I just don't know. . . .

When the word got out that Jim was actually giving up his lucrative Arthur Murray career to go into preaching, some of the folks around Lakeland were even heard to use the word *fanatic*. But Anne had staunchly defended his decision from the moment she perceived the depth and sincerity of his conviction. As a matter of fact, she wrote Jim excitedly in March of 1956 that she had found the courage to share her Christian testimony for the very first time in her life, an action which drew this immediate response from her husband-to-be:

Dearest, Dearest, Dearest, Dearest Anne,

Praise the Lord! I prayed that you would have the courage to give your testimony to someone this week. I prayed that prayer in my room—walked down the stairs, and read your letter. How wonderfully God answers prayer!

I love you more than I have ever loved you before! I just

want to go and tell everyone how wonderful you are. That's a big step, Anne, and you look bigger in my eyes than ever before.

It takes a big person to empty one's self and give all the credit to Christ. That's what Paul and Knox and Luther and Livingstone did. Now that you have "come all the way out" for Christ, you will have power that you never had before. Expect some people to misunderstand. That is bound to happen—but keep looking up. I pray the Lord will let you see some conversions soon. Pray—and you'll have them. Bill Kirkpatric, our deacon, raised his hand for salvation Tuesday. Mrs. Barnum and I prayed for him Monday night. Praise the Lord!

I feel like cords of steel bind us together now, Anne.

I love you completely,

Jim

That was the voice of a new creature in Christ—not of the old Jim Kennedy who had been in love with the world and its enticements. He had adjusted to a new life, and with his encouragement Anne was making the same adjustments. She was able to tell him in another letter, "You have evidenced to me a sincere desire to do what is right, and I certainly have all the confidence in the world that you will be an outstanding success as a minister. I think you have that 'something extra' that it takes to be great, and it makes me feel good all over." That kind of joint commitment enabled two people who loved and excelled in dancing, to give it up—along with other worldly pursuits—for the sake of their testimony.

Step Two: That was the introductory preaching assignment with the providential assist. As a Christian soldier, Jim reported for duty at the Bethel Presbyterian Church under the most unlikely circumstances, and God took care of all the rest. That doesn't mean, however, that from there on the Lord was going to change all the circumstances to provide Jim with a smooth and carefree path. Scarcely a month after he took the plunge into ministerial waters, Anne was hospitalized for tests which could have indicated the need for major surgery (which fortunately was not required). The extent of his concern for his future bride, as well as the depth and passion of his spiritual commitment, were eloquently expressed in a letter dated January 1, 1956:

> Dearest Anne—Dearest, Dearest Anne,
>
> I never realized just how much I loved you until I got your letter stating that you were in the hospital. I almost left my final exams and went to Durham. If I couldn't have phoned, I think I would have.
>
> Darling, you taught me more about fervent prayer today in one hour than I've learned in 2 1/2 years.
>
> I completely trust that the Lord Jesus will be with you and comfort you and guide the doctor's hand and bring you back safe and well to me.
>
> Anne, Darling, if anything ever happened to you, I'd be ready to die, for life would hold no joy for me if you were not here to share it.
>
> Oh how I thank God that you assuredly know Jesus as your personal Savior. Our faith, love, and knowledge of the Lord is often increased when we're flat on our backs in bed. I am sure that you will get both a physical and a spiritual blessing from your trip.
>
> My love and devotion grow with every hour that we are apart.
>
> Come home to me soon, Dearest.
>
> Jim

There were some uncertain times and even a few dark days for the new warrior for Christ, but he pressed ahead. Without realizing it, he was following Corrie Ten Boom's prescription: "Don't bother to give God instructions. Just report in."

Step Three: The final response to the call was to resume

the long and arduous process of preparation—to get an education. To make of himself the most effective minister he was capable of becoming, Jim would first have to return to undergraduate school and to do the necessary damage control there before he could move on to the larger challenge. Later on, he would need knowledge over a vast range of subject matter, specific training in the skills of communication, a mastery of the whole Bible from the Hebrew and Greek sources through modern scholarship, and exposure to all the disciplines of seminary instruction.

To begin with, it meant a return to the not-too-inspiring secular scene where his academic foundation of about five years B.C. awaited him. Under the rules, advanced seminary work could be taken without the baccalaureate, but the awarding of the higher degree would be conditional on the completion of the lower. This academic red tape meant that Jim would be allowed to start his seminary training in the fall of 1956 but would have to return to the University of Tampa for two more summers.

Accordingly, he hit the campus running in the fall semester of 1955 with his sights on a bachelor's degree in English. In gratifying contrast to his earlier performance at the university, he began to rack up A's and B's—demonstrating to those who might remember him as a C learner that the potential had been there all along. It had simply never been tapped. As teachers often comment, all the student needed in the first place was proper motivation. Jim's introduction to the Master Teacher was sufficient to galvanize all the compo-

All the student needed in the first place was proper motivation.

nents of his being—a brilliant mind, a trusting heart, and an eager will—to accomplish great things for the Lord.

It might be helpful to retrace the chronology of events during this major turnaround in the lives of a young couple, events which seemed to be piling on top of one another at times. On that memorable evening of December 3, 1955—the day that Jim had come to grips with himself and had made his final decision—he drove from Tampa to Lakeland with an engagement ring in his pocket. Anne was not fully prepared for the triple round Jim fired in one dizzying salvo:

(1) I have quit my job at the studio, which means I'm almost flat broke.

(2) I am going into the ministry, and I know you always said you wouldn't want to be a preacher's wife.

(3) Will you marry me?

But Anne was close enough to the Lord to recognize the dictates of duty that led Jim to that watershed in his life. Her faith enabled her to sacrifice her personal desires on the same altar and to place her future, along with his, in divine hands.

Making such monumental decisions did not mean the end of the young couple's search, but only the beginning, and the next mountain to climb came into view: seminary.

C H A P T E R • 6

CULTIVATING THE GOOD SEED

Study to shew thyself approved unto
God, a workman that needeth
not to be ashamed . . .
—2 TIMOTHY 2:15

[Seminarium (Latin): a seed plot; a controlled environment
conducive to embryonic growth and development; a nursery]

Seven miles east of downtown Atlanta, nestled in the gently rolling landscape of old Decatur, is the fifty-seven-acre campus of Columbia Theological Seminary. Jim Kennedy decided on this institution as the logical place to seek training "that the man of God may be thoroughly furnished unto all good works." It was logical because of its location—the closest Presbyterian center of learning to his home base in Tampa, where he still had those two summers of undergraduate course work to complete. Also, the Atlanta economic boom offered excellent job opportunities for his new bride. Sure enough, before long Anne's qualifications landed her a top-rated position as executive secretary in one of the city's major brokerage houses. That job would provide a predictable and workable family budget for Jim's three years of intensive graduate study.

Columbia also offered academic excellence. It had a long-standing reputation for uncommon quality. Its faculty was known for superb scholarship, a passion for teaching, a strong commitment to the Church, and a pastoral concern for the students. Its students, with enrollment limited to never more than five hundred, were likewise known for their eagerness to learn and to become faithful and effective leaders. Its curriculum combined traditional disciplines with creative innovations to prepare men and women for useful service.

But Jim's initial interest in Columbia stemmed from a printed sermon he came across in the seminary catalog while he was a student at the University of Tampa. He was in the library exploring the offerings of various "divinity schools" when the message written by Dr. Cecil Thompson, professor of evangelism at Columbia, caught his attention. The simple plea emphasized the necessity of preaching the Gospel to bring lost souls to Christ; too many sermons, the professor argued, were not drawing the needed response from congregations. Those who delivered themselves of such sermons, he said, might as well be firing a machine gun into a mud bank—a figure of speech that etched a permanent niche in Jim's memory. Here, he decided, was a man who had a heart for God, the kind of teacher he was looking for. His choice was made.

The institution achieved national attention first, perhaps, because of what happened to Woodrow Wilson there. In the little chapel, formerly a carriage-house, the future president of Princeton University and occupant of the White House, was "reborn for eternity," as he expressed it. The little chapel was also the scene of the writing of the historic *Book of Church Order* (Presbyterian Church U.S.).

In Wilson's day, of course, the school was located in Columbia, South Carolina. Established in 1828, it was first known as "The Classical, Scientific and Theological Institution of the South"—an unambitious title. By 1925 it was more simply and more accurately named Columbia Theological Seminary, and two years later its books and equipment, its students and faculty, its ministry and traditions were moved lock, stock, and barrel from South Carolina to Georgia. The reasons for the move appeared sound. The synod was aware that the population of the Southeast and of Presbyterians was shifting, and the centers of influence were shifting with it. Leaders of the seminary, along with prominent Atlantans, were convinced of the city's leadership of the New South. In a spirited fund-raising campaign, Atlanta's 14,193 Presbyterians from 74 churches responded by quickly oversubscribing a half-million-dollar goal. Columbia had found its permanent home, where the potential for growth was assured as the Greater Atlanta Presbytery went on to expand to 116 congregations with more than 45,000 members.

Adding luster to the image of Columbia Theological Seminary during its first few years in the new location was a young Scotsman who had come to the United States for advanced study. Peter Marshall entered the seminary not long before Jim Kennedy was born. The famous Washington minister and chaplain of the United States Senate, whose poetic prayers and devotional messages have been read by millions, was immortalized in the popular book and motion picture, *A Man Called Peter.*

Columbia's roster of prominent alumni has continued to expand in recent decades with names like Leighton Ford and Calvin Thielman, who was Billy Graham's pastor at Montreat, North Carolina; and Ben Haden, founder of the widely viewed television evangelism ministry, *Changed Lives.*

But just three weeks after their marriage, Jim and Anne had more practical things on their minds as they drove up to the campus in separate cars loaded with housekeeping paraphernalia. First Jim disposed of his car to get some cash in hand (remember the $13 bank account?). Then they found the home they would live in for the next three years—years

First Jim disposed of his car to get some cash.

that Anne remembers as "the hardest and the happiest" of their early life together.

"Home" was a garage apartment about half a mile from the campus. Hand-built by the owner, it made an indelible impression on the young couple: the entire structure vibrated rhythmically when they walked up or down the outside staircase, and they could get a clear view of the garage below by peering through the cracks in the floor. Their landlord also made a lasting first impression. They found him in one of the rooms sitting near the center of a freshly varnished floor, brush in hand. But he gave them a cheery greeting: "I think I've made me a mess!" Particularly unforgettable was the plumbing. Jim was advised to leave the water running in the bathtub when the weather turned cold. It did—the temperature hit ten above in Atlanta's first cold snap. Jim's morning trip to the bathroom disclosed an ominous mound of ice in the tub, with a solid column leading up into the faucet, like a crystal stalactite. The toilet, of course, was rendered totally dysfunctional. But the apartment was in their price range, and they stayed.

Jim immersed himself in his ministerial studies. He welcomed Old Testament Hebrew, New Testament Greek, systematic theology, homiletics, hermeneutics, and all the other "-ologies" and "-ic"s that equip the accomplished man of God. He noticed right away that students tended to choose favorite professors, usually by how "orthodox" or how "liberal" the teachers appeared to be. The one instructor for whom most students seemed to develop great respect and affection was the well-known Ph.D. who built his own famous radio ministry—Manfred George Gutzke. Jim's description: "He was built like a gorilla, bald as a rock, bushy brows that seemed to be growing straight out at you, enormous hands and a heart to match." In younger days, Gutzke had been heavyweight fight champion in the Canadian army. He was still physically powerful, but even more so spiritually. As professor of English Bible, he was almost a legend at Columbia Theological Seminary for his ability to inspire a student . . . and to entertain. Whenever you heard uproarious classroom laughter, chances were it was one of Dr. Gutzke's classes.

The Kennedys, who both tend to extract the best out of every experience, made the most of the three years at Columbia. Jim excelled academically, earning his master of divinity degree with *cum laude* distinction and winning one of four graduate scholarships that he would use later. Atlanta's musical and cultural programs, opportunities for campus fellowship, "intern" preaching in various churches, and research and study made the time go by swiftly and profitably. Outstanding ministers came to the region and provided inspiration, especially Dr. Donald Grey Barnhouse, who conducted a series of meetings. When Jim met the veteran evangelist and told him how a Sunday afternoon broadcast had changed his life, Barnhouse had him give his testimony at the next service in Peter Marshall's former church, Westminster Presbyterian.

One of the unanticipated advantages of seminary life was the erasure from Jim's mind of a haunting encounter he had shortly before he entered Columbia. While he was still at the Arthur Murray Studio and had just answered the call to preach, one of his students, a middle-aged woman, said to Jim, "Before you go into the ministry, I want you to talk to a doctor friend of mine." Willing to comply, he went to the doctor's office, which was located in his rambling, gloomy, forbidding Tampa home.

Inside, Jim suspected that something was very strange.

He had already noted that the woman's friends were unusual—even "weird." The house was dark, with heavy drapes and large overstuffed furniture, reminding Jim of the depressing home of the television Addams family. Soon a door opened back in the dim recesses of the house, and the doctor came out—a tall, gaunt gentleman with a sepulchral expression—dressed in a black suit. It was like something right out of a Hollywood horror film.

"I'll never forget what he said to me," Jim recalls. "He said, 'Young man, I understand that you are thinking about going into the ministry.'

"Yes, sir. That's correct."

"Young man," the doctor said menacingly, "people need more than to be talked at." With that, he turned and left a totally confused young man standing there.

"That shook me up terribly," Jim says. "I thought: 'He's right. People do need a lot of things—doctors and carpenters and engineers—all sorts of things.' But the Lord did not allow that to dislodge me from my calling. Then, when I got to seminary, during the first year I read a book. The title just leaped out at me: *Jesus Came Preaching*. It was a book about the power of preaching and what it has accomplished through the centuries.

"That book was an incredible relief and a blessing to me, to see that although people do need other things, they desperately do need to hear the preached Word of God to get the other things they're doing into proper perspective for all of life. That man who made such a sinister impression on my thinking was a naturopath, and I think that he and all of that woman's friends were into some form of the *occult* at the time. I didn't even know what the word occult meant; I had never seen or heard of such a thing. And, although I didn't understand what was going on, I knew there was something strange, something evil, about these people. I am sure now that it was an occult group of some sort and that he was doing his very best to dissuade me from going into the ministry."

As the end of seminary days came into view, Jim gave serious consideration to the next step. He did not feel a specific call to the foreign mission field, but he was convinced by a sermon on the subject that it was best to go ahead and enlist. If God did not want a person to pursue that course, the sermon argued, He would close the door. That made sense to Jim, so he formally applied to the World Mission Committee as a candidate for missionary duty in what was then the Belgian Congo (today, the Democratic Republic of Congo). How did his wife take this news? Anne was totally supportive; whatever God's will for Jim turned out to be, that was what she wanted. He busied himself studying the African interior.

With the final six months before graduation counting down to two weeks, Jim was advised to send out letters to the stated clerks of five presbyteries inquiring about pulpits that might still be unfilled until he heard from the World Mission Committee. This close to commencement, the most desirable opportunities were all gone. The only response to his inquiries came from Fort Lauderdale, May 11, 1959—just days before his graduation.

The Home Mission Committee of the Everglades Presbytery was testing the waters for possibly organizing a new church in the underdeveloped northern section of town. Members had been taking turns meeting with whatever volunteers they could lure through advertisements and word of mouth. Jim was welcome to come down to Fort Lauderdale and look the situation over. He had been recommended by the pastor of Atlanta's Westminster Presbyterian Church and by the president of the seminary. These two represented the extremes of the divergence that by now had become rather pronounced at Columbia, where there was an unabashed shift toward liberalism. Such a double recommendation was most unusual, and therefore the committee was interested in hearing from James Kennedy.

When the candidate arrived on the scene, there was not a

whole lot to give him encouragement in the way of a building, a budget, an organization, or a congregation. But the committee did have a nice name picked out: the Coral Ridge Presbyterian Church. Jim wondered at the sign erected on a sandy plot on 50th Street—a little-traveled road destined to become Commercial Boulevard in future years. The sign announced: "Presbyterian Church To Be Built On This Site." All Jim could see was barren space in all directions. Plenty of weeds, but no people—almost no houses—in his prospective parish. "Looks like a good place to have a church for field mice," he quipped to his hosts. Seriously, where was the church to meet? In a small cafetorium of an elementary school located outside of Fort Lauderdale, north across the line in Pompano Beach.

"Looks like a good place to have a church for field mice."

For all the young preacher knew, this could be a temporary slot, for he was still waiting to hear from the World Mission Committee, and he was committed to leave for the Congo when the call came. He accepted the schoolhouse church offer on that condition.

Three months after his graduation, when the word did come from the mission board, he was turned down. Because of an asthmatic condition showing up on Jim's physical, he wasn't appointed as a foreign missionary.

It was God's will, and it was all right with Jim Kennedy. He had spent enough time baiting the hook. He was casting his line in Fort Lauderdale.

A
PLACE
TO
GET
STARTED

*As my Father hath sent
me, even so send I you.*
—JOHN 20:21

ort Lauderdale, from the very outset, was a place
that could use a little help. It was a real fort, all right, built of
palmetto logs along the bank of the New River in 1838 by
Major William Lauderdale and his famous Tennessee
Volunteers, U.S. Army. It would be difficult to understand
modern Fort Lauderdale without knowing about the New
River, a freshwater ribbon twisting from the Everglades east-
ward into the Atlantic Ocean.

The New River provided early settlers with the only
direct access from the beaches into the jungle-like interior.
Major Lauderdale located his fort strategically inland a short
distance to separate the understandably inhospitable
Seminoles from their principal food source, the arrowroot
plant they called *coontie.* They had learned to extract flour
from its starchy roots.

That was the beginning of civilized life along the New

River—but not too civilized. The fort itself eventually rotted away in its steamy swamp environment, but not before it had been visited by such military notables as William Tecumseh Sherman and Robert E. Lee in happier decades before the Civil War. Following that national catastrophe, a census taken in what was now the municipality of Fort Lauderdale revealed that there were only eighty-five white people hardy enough to co-exist with the unfriendly Indians, the too-friendly alligators, the gargantuan mosquitoes, and the devastating hurricanes that struck without warning. A sort of token consolation was provided by the government-sponsored "houses of refuge" erected at five locations along the coastline of Southeast Florida. Here shipwrecked sailors and other survivors of the elements might hope to find temporary shelter, and possibly some food and water.

Once again Fort Lauderdale found itself in desperate need of outside help when the scourge of yellow fever began to ravage the South in successive waves of misery and death. Help arrived in the unlikely person of five-foot-three inch Thomas S. Kennedy, affectionately known as "the little doctor." Although no relation to D. James Kennedy, "Doc" also had a mission. He ministered to Indians and whites alike. Without benefit of medical training, he was known to perform surgery with a pen-knife and at least one successful amputation with a carpenter's saw. And he never lost a patient.

Once again Fort Lauderdale found itself in desperate need of outside help.

All Doc Kennedy had to do to get transportation across the New River on his errands of mercy was to yell; somebody would always send a boat over to pick him up. H. M. Flagler, whose railroads were putting Fort Lauderdale on the map, was so impressed with "the little doctor" that he gave orders to all his engineers to stop and give him a lift to anywhere down the line he needed to go. Doc Kennedy's folk-medicine preventatives, widely pre-scribed by word of mouth, are today credited by historians with staying the murderous hand of "yellow jack." Fort Lauderdale was the only community in South Florida to sur-vive the epidemic without a fatality.

A bit more substantial and much more spectacular help was on the way for thousands of dwellers on the periphery of the Everglades—a neat euphemism for the almost impen-etrable bogs and swamps that constituted most of the terrain. When Napoleon Bonaparte Broward became governor in 1904, he brought an imaginative engineering plan to pull the plug out of the southern part of the peninsula and drain it of much of the water that had reserved it to wildlife. A veritable navy of dredge boats appeared to begin the herculean labor of converting the tangled landscape into geometric patterns of inviting islands bordered by clean-cut canals in every direction. Broward seemed to have taken his text right out of Genesis 1: "and let the dry land appear."

It didn't take private developers long to sense the possi-bilities. They carved their own canals, all boasting direct access to the open sea, wherever homesites could be imag-ined. On esthetic appeal, promoters advertised scenic Fort Lauderdale as "the Venice of America," pointing with pride to the fact that while the hometown of Titian and Veronese had only sixteen miles of navigable streets, its brash new American namesake would offer more than 150!

When men of foresight, like Hugh Taylor Birch, chief legal counsel to Standard Oil in Chicago, decided to forsake all for a more placid environment, the impact was felt across the country. Exploring the coastline for a likely place to settle down, Birch put into the calm lake at Bahia Mar Marina to avoid a storm and found just what he was looking for, the beach at Fort Lauderdale, "the most beautiful spot on the face of the earth."

Birch quickly bargained for a plot of this desirable land and bought 180 acres on the strip between the ocean and the Intracoastal Waterway, just north of what is today Sunrise Boulevard. The primitive, densely wooded paradise, formerly tenanted by the Seminoles, was almost a mile of golden beach, a botanical wonderland filled with banyan, mangrove, sea grape, and palm trees.

Birch paid seventy-five cents an acre in the Gay Nineties, a total of $120. By contrast, when the Galt Ocean Mile— considerably north of Birch's property and restricted to the beach—changed hands about the time Jim Kennedy moved to Tampa, the multimillion-dollar transaction was in its time the largest ever recorded in American real estate records.

But Birch, wanting others to enjoy the Florida he had discovered, left the virgin tract as a preserve and park open to the public. To this day it provides Fort Lauderdale with one of the most envied original woodland strips along the overdeveloped coastline and waterway.

There was no doubt about it, Fort Lauderdale was emerging as one of the Gold Coast's brightest jewels. With such favorable publicity leaking out to the chilly North, the land boom was predictable. Owning a piece of Florida real estate became a national fantasy, and real estate sharks came up with some sure-enough fantastic frauds as the boom-and-bust cycles generated bewildering chaos for the state's economy. Tourism became big business, competing with citrus for top position among local industries.

Through it all, Fort Lauderdale, like Topsy, just "growed." No longer was it merely a place between other places—the plush Palm Beaches above and world-renowned Miami below—but a metropolis in its own right, manifesting a unique identity. In fifty years' expansion, Fort Lauderdale made the transition from the status of suburb to that of cosmopolitan population center of one million souls in the "greater" context.

It was still a city that could use some help when Jim Kennedy came upon the scene with his M.Div. and a heart for ministering to the needs of people. He knew the area and understood that it wasn't exactly like Tampa, which was a bona fide vestige of the Old South, with a healthy dash of Spanish flavoring stirred into Bible Belt morality. Actually, in its spiritual heritage and historical background, Fort Lauderdale was more like a southeastern version of the Old West—a sort of Dodge City-by-the-sea. In both settings the relentless wind blows free most of the year, indifferent to whether it carries prairie dust or beach sand.

Gambling and rum-running from the islands had always flourished just outside of Miami's often more deliberate attempts at law enforcement. Such activities, along with the kinds of entertainment usually sought by the miscreants involved, had given Fort Lauderdale a reputation as a "wide-open town." After all, America's number-one gangster, Al Capone, had flagrantly operated his palatial gambling casino for underworld cronies scarcely a stone's throw away in Hollywood, and nobody had complained. Illegal booze flowed in such volume during Prohibition that surrounding communities, fairly or not, hung the unflattering, sobriquet of "Fort Liquordale" on their lusty neighbor. But the townspeople themselves were as disturbed by such carryings-on as a later generation would be when drug traffickers from all over the hemisphere would target their city because of its highly strategic location.

By whatever standards it may be measured, the territory to which the divine casting of lots led Jim could never be called uninteresting. It is home to a population that appears to double during "season" along with the traffic. Its potpourri of humankind seems to include every conceivable ethnic, economic, and cultural or subcultural group in the catalog. The young and the restless are intermixed everywhere with the old and the helpless. You'll see at the same intersection the ostentatious tycoon and the downright scruffy drifter. The great working hordes who have too little chance to relax rush past the great reveling hordes bent on celebrating the rites of spring, summer, fall, and winter. There are the introverts who are afraid they will be noticed and the extroverts who are afraid they won't be. High above are the condo sun-worshipers keeping a wary eye on the transient crowds below and wondering where in the world they all come from (which frequently turns out to be the same place they came from themselves). As in every American city, people watching is an ongoing attraction in Fort Lauderdale.

As for self-image, it has never been better. An ad in the real estate section of the daily newspaper, *The Sun-Sentinel*, exudes pride and optimism:

AT LAST, A SOUTH FLORIDA HOME
FOR THE ULTIMATE URBANITE

Suddenly, there's a brand new city-by-the-sea in South Florida. A city of great buildings, open-air plazas, river-front parks, art galleries and a cornucopia of cultural events. It is a city that is the realization of the dreams and plans of visionary developers. A city that has grown, in a few short years, from humble beginnings as a suburb, into South Florida's most desirable community. It is a city known as Fort Lauderdale.

Such are the general historical and demographic backdrops against which Jim made his ecclesiastical debut. His arrival with a mandate to start up a church might remind one of the apostle who found himself in the bustling maritime city of Corinth in ancient Greece. It, too, was an urban giant dominated by twin principal drives: a zeal for commerce and a devotion to the pursuit of pleasure. Set against these strongly secular influences, however, were active communities of believers. Paul must have been surprised when the

Lord reminded him in a night vision, "I have much people in this city." Similarly, Fort Lauderdale has always enjoyed the ameliorating leaven of aggressive Christian forces, dating back to the earliest days when the Methodists brought organized church life to the New River settlement.

One of Jim's very first items of business was to check out the little cafetorium of McNab Elementary School, which was actually located clear outside of Fort Lauderdale, north of the McNab Road city limit line in Pompano Beach. It really wasn't much, but he was eager to get to work. This was his parish—his very first. The fields, sure enough, appeared to be white unto harvest, and there was plenty of fallow ground where he had been commissioned to sow new seed. It looked like a place where anything would grow, and Jim felt prepared.

But he was not prepared for the disastrous crop failure that awaited him.

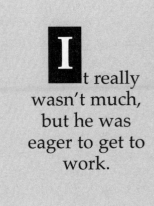

It really wasn't much, but he was eager to get to work.

PART THREE

THE
MAN
OF
VISION

NOBODY SAID IT WOULD BE EASY

Fear thou not; for I am with thee: be not dismayed; for I am thy God: I will strengthen thee; yea, I will help thee. . . .
—ISAIAH 41:10

What happened to young Jim Kennedy during the first ten months of his Fort Lauderdale ministry was not only humiliating and disheartening; it had the makings of a tragedy. He experienced enough anguish and pain to drive a lesser person right out of the ministry. Since that baptism of fire beginning in 1958, the story of how he got started has become something of a legend documented in magazine articles, newspaper interviews, television presentations, videotapes, books, and film—and in Jim's own testimony delivered from pulpits all over the world.

But because of what he allowed that first excruciating

year to teach him, because he held on long enough to realize that Christ only wanted to make His strength perfect in human weakness, Jim today can look back on that time as the greatest blessing of his formative ministry. And in that odd way in which the passage of years enables us to look back on the once-frightful experiences with a mellow, kindly, even amused perspective, Jim now sees rich humor in the events that introduced him to full-time preaching.

In 1981 Jim himself delivered one of the most delightful tales of those tough times to a global gathering of colleagues and some lay persons for a clinic at Coral Ridge Presbyterian Church. They were there to hear from him about a miracle that had occurred at Coral Ridge twenty-two years earlier and that had vitally affected their own ministries. Jim was in rare form as he took his audience back to the very beginning of his trials and tribulations. The entire transcript follows in all its hilarious good humor. It offers intensely personal insights into the mind and emotions of Jim Kennedy and into audience response.

"I don't know about the rest of our pastors here, but I always sort of had the idea that whenever I heard of a minister who was noted for evangelism, I formed a sort of stereotype in my mind of what that person was like. He was a bold, extrovertive type who went up and grabbed people by the lapels and said, 'Brother, are you saved?' And I want you to know that, like many of you, that is about as far from a description of myself as I can possibly imagine.

"I've always considered myself to be shy, though I must confess I have a little difficulty convincing some of our church members of that fact, but it's absolutely the gospel truth. And this manifested itself particularly when it came to witnessing. I found that it was extremely difficult for me to do. In fact, I had a problem going up and saying, 'Good morning' to a complete stranger, much less talking to him about something as personal as religion.

"I had a lot of excuses as to why I didn't witness. But I had felt the call into the ministry. I went to the seminary and graduated with all the requisite courses in preaching and came down here to Fort Lauderdale to start a new church. I was full of vim and vinegar. I was a veritable Daniel come to judgment, and I preached everything I had in every sermon, and that wasn't a whole lot. But nevertheless I gave it what I could. We put an ad in the paper and we gathered together about forty-five people into an un-air-conditioned school cafetorium about 8:30 on a Sunday morning.

"They were what I might describe as about forty-five heterogeneous pagans. Maybe some of you didn't know how we started Presbyterian churches. [*laughter*] I see some of you suspected that's how we started Presbyterian churches. [*laughter*] How do you think we get them in the shape they're in if we don't get them started right? [*laughter*]

"And so I gathered these forty-five people together, and I preached to them with everything I had. In fact, I preached to them the greatest sermons that have ever been preached in the history of the Church. No, I would like to be humble about it, but I feel it important that I be honest. So I say it again, I preached to them some of the greatest sermons that have ever been preached: Spurgeon, MacLaren, Luther, Calvin. [*laughter*]

> "They were what I might describe as forty-five heterogeneous pagans."

"In fact, so powerful was that preaching that in the space of some ten months I had taken that little band of forty-five people and had built it up into a mighty army of—seventeen! [*laughter*] In Presbyterian circles, that is what is called a

Scottish Revival [*much laughter*]. Now, you know, in ten months I had gone from forty-five to seventeen, and a little bit of extrapolation made it clear that, any way you looked at it, I had about two and-a-half months of ministry left [*much laughter*] until I was going to be preaching to my wife, who was threatening to go to the Baptist church down the street [*much laughter*].

"It was about then that I decided I'd better try something different—change my tactics. I figured that if the mountain wouldn't come to Muhammad, Muhammad would go to the mountain! I decided that I would visit somebody and would proclaim the Gospel to them right where they were. As I said, I had a very good reason why I didn't do that sort of thing. Unlike the excuses that so many other people had, I had a valid reason. You see, I have always suffered from a very serious back ailment: I have this broad yellow stripe that goes right down my back [*laughter*], and somehow it connects to my jawbone. It has rendered me absolutely silent in many circumstances where the less circumspect would no doubt have opened their mouths and would have said who-knows-what?

"But in spite of that back defect, I determined that I had best go and visit somebody anyway. I got a card, a card that looked like it had been signed by a little old lady, from the shaky handwriting. I figured that if I couldn't outtalk her, I could certainly outrun her—even with my back problem [*laughter*]. I had a second brilliant idea: I would take somebody else with me, and that person could learn how to do it from watching me. Now, that was brilliant because I didn't have the faintest idea how to do it, which fact was to come very painfully home to me shortly.

"So, I knocked on the door of this home and waited for the little old lady with her gray hair to open the door. The door opened and I found myself staring at—a belly button [*laughter*] of someone who was not vastly different in size from the gentleman you heard earlier on this program; he was about that big. As a matter of fact, he has his own television program now. It's called *The Hulk*, I think. [*laughter*]

"There he was, in an undershirt. He had a can of beer in one hand and a cigar in his mouth. Now, he was just my sort of person, the kind I had really been looking for to begin my witnessing career with. So I said to him, 'Is Mrs. Jones home?' And he said, 'N-n-yah!' [*laughter*] I said, 'Thank you very much' and started to leave [*much laughter*]. Then he added, 'Whadja want with 'er?' 'Nothing at all, I assure you. Uh, the fact of the matter is, I'm the pastor of this little church down the street. It's a very little church—wouldn't hurt anyone [*laughter*]. And, er, the truth is, your mother visited us last Sunday, and I was just returning the compliment. You can just tell her that we dropped by.'

"And then this guy said one of the nastiest things that I have ever heard come out of the mouth of any human being. Some of you pastors here know that people can be downright ugly to preachers at times—and this man really did it. I want you to understand that I had done nothing to provoke this fellow—I mean absolutely nothing. You can bank on that. Well, right out of the blue he said to me, 'Come in' [*laughter*]. Can you believe that? I mean ugly [*laughter*].

"Evangelism Explosion International started right there, with me walking into that living room with my knees knocking together. We sat there, and we had a very enlightening and edifying conversation—about the weather. And we progressed from there to sports. He was a Golden Gloves fighter; we got off that in a hurry [*laughter*]. We moved on to the news, and there wasn't much new. And back to the weather; it was getting much warmer [*laughter*].

"When my layman who was with me said, 'Sic 'em,' I said, 'Hush, man! You'll get us both killed!' [*laughter*] I said, 'I'm working up to it.' I had been working on it for years—I just wasn't up to it [*laughter*] any way you look at it. And finally, with great chagrin, I told this man (God forgive me) how much I had enjoyed the visit. We excused ourselves and left. And you know something? I couldn't even look at that layman all the way back. Not only had the mountain not come to Muhammad; Muhammad couldn't even climb a molehill! It was a very embarrassing situation.

"I got back to my home, and I want you to know I prayed earnestly, 'Lord, what am I doing here? Surely this is all a big mistake. Surely you didn't call me into the ministry to fail miserably like this.' I really wondered if I shouldn't leave the ministry and take up something else.

"About that very time I got a letter from a preacher up in greater Atlanta where I had gone to seminary. I had attended his church several times. He wanted me to come up to Atlanta and, believe it or not, conduct ten days of evangelistic services! That's right. This fellow who had just decimated one church—now he wanted me to ship it across states lines! [*much laughter*] Have Plague, Will Travel [*laughter*].

"So I packed up some of 'our sermons,' [*laughter*] and I headed north. I was very happy to get away from my Fort Lauderdale fiasco. I showed up, and I told this fellow, 'Well, here I am; I'm ready.' He said, 'That's great. You'll be preaching every night.' 'That's wonderful,' I said. Then he added something: 'However, that's not the most important thing.' And I suddenly had a cold chill that went right down my yellow stripe. I said to myself, 'Oh, Lord, don't let this guy say what I think he's going to say next. Lord, he looks like that type.' [*laughter*] And sure enough, he was, and he did. [*laughter*] He said, 'The most important thing is that we are going to go out every morning, and the same thing in the afternoon, and sometimes at night after the services. And you're going to have an opportunity to witness to these people eyeball to eyeball and toenail to toenail. And I have saved all the tough nuts for you.' [*laughter*] 'Thanks a lot,' I said to myself. But aloud I said, 'That's great.' You know, we professional evangelists don't like to fool with anything but tough nuts. To be perfectly honest, in my own ministry I've never dealt with anything but tough nuts [*laughter*]. There's just one problem, however; I came up here to Atlanta to tell you that I wasn't going to be able to come [*much laughter*]. There's a funeral you're going to have here in town if I don't get out of here quickly!' [*laughter*]

"No, I didn't really say that. I was trapped, and I didn't know what to do. I went back to my hotel room that night, got down on my knees, and I prayed, 'Oh, Lord, what am I going to do? I don't know how to witness to anybody.' I felt like an M.D. just graduated from medical school—they slap a scalpel in my hand the next morning, and I haven't the faintest idea how to cut anybody open. I said, 'What am I going to do? This preacher is going to be sitting there looking at me and, Lord, what am I going to do?'

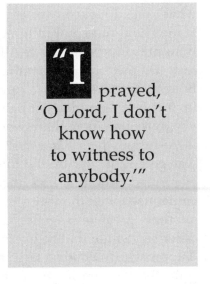

"You know what happened? Nothing. So I got down on my face on the floor. I mean I was flat out on my face on the floor. I prayed for hours. I said, 'Lord, you've got to help me! I can't do this. I am absolutely desperate! I don't know what to do. This fellow's coming to get me in the morning, and I don't have any idea what I'm going to do. You've got to do something!'

"The most amazing thing happened: morning came. [*laughter*] And the preacher came shortly thereafter and picked me up. We went to a home and knocked on the door. The door opened. Remember that big hulk of a fellow in Florida? He'd moved to Atlanta! [*laughter*] Well, not really—it was his bigger cousin, I think. [*laughter*] We went in, and I was going over in my mind what had been the latest thing in the news, sports, and weather when this preacher blew the whole morning. He said, 'Well, Hank, I've brought this professional evangelist out to talk to you about your soul.' [*laughter*]

"There I was. He pointed to me. I gulped a couple of times real hard. I was in such a state of panic I didn't know what to do. I looked over at the preacher, and I looked over at the Hulk, and I looked up to the Lord, and I tried definitely to grasp for something. All of a sudden I remembered a text: 'Do the thing that you fear.' I think that's from Second Ecclesiastes 3:2 [*laughter*]. 'Jump right in.' So, I jumped right in, feet first. You may not believe this, after what I just told you, but in no more than twenty minutes, I had that big fellow—furious [*much laughter*]! He was getting redder and I was getting whiter by the minute. In fact, the only thing I ever read where I had the feeling that anybody ever empathized with the way I felt at that time was in a book by another great evangelist, Mark Twain [*laughter*]. He described a fight that he got in when he was a young fellow: 'I approached my adversary stealthily, and I placed my nose squarely between his teeth, and threw him heavily to the ground on top of me.' [*laughter*]

"It was while I was lying there in the middle of the living room floor, breathing between his teeth, that I suddenly realized what the whole problem was [*laughter*]. It came like a flash, an illumination right out of Systematic Theology 302b, I believe [*laughter*]. Suddenly everything was clear. The problem was simple. Any theologian with an ounce of sense would certainly understand what the problem was. The problem was that this man was evidently non-elect [*much laughter*].

"Very simple. I felt so much better immediately [*much laughter*]. You know, it's a funny thing. I told that story at Calvin Seminary and nobody laughed [*laughter*]. I told it at Asbury Seminary, and they carried three people out on stretchers [*much laughter*]. Well, my pastor friend had come to a very different conclusion. The problem, indeed, was simple. The problem, as far as he was concerned, was that I was a non-evangelist [*laughter*].

"So he took over the conversation, and in no more than fifteen minutes he had this man on his knees accepting Christ. I want to tell you, that was a very traumatic experience for a budding young theologue, to see the non-elect converted right before his very eyes [*much laughter*]! That'll shake you right out of your T-U-L-I-P tree! No, I really believe it—for my friends here. I was just obviously abusing it. And during that week—those ten days—some fifty-four people came forward in those meetings. However, on any given evening, I could have told you who it was that would be coming forward because I had seen that pastor lead them to Christ during that week.

"I want you to know that that was an amazing experience for me. I said to the pastor, 'This is absolutely incredible. I saw a murderer accept Christ. I saw an adultress accept Christ. And all sorts of people in between. How in the world did you ever learn to do this?' He said, 'A year ago, I didn't know how.' 'You're kidding,' I said. 'What happened?' He replied, 'It was at the very same evangelistic crusade last year. Last year, we really had an evangelist.' I said, 'Oh.' [*laughter*] The pastor continued: 'He took me out with him; then I learned from watching him.' Well, I learned from watching this fellow.

"I came back to Fort Lauderdale, and I was really enthusiastic. But there was one question that was buzzing around in my mind as I was flying back, and I want you to know what it was. Yes, this worked in Atlanta, the heart of the Bible Belt, but will it work in Fort Lauderdale? That was the question. I found out that it worked in Fort Lauderdale; it worked anywhere it was tried—in the inner city and in the outlying rural regions. It works in America and Canada and Africa and England and Hong Kong and Singapore and Australia. It works because it is nothing other than believers carrying the Gospel of Jesus Christ to others, just as Christ said we should. It carries with it a written guarantee that His Word will not return unto Him void.

"I began to do in Fort Lauderdale exactly what I had seen this fellow do. Fact of the matter is, I even began to sound like him—even developed a southern accent there for awhile. I picked up some of his idiosyncrasies. I always knew when he was going to get into the Gospel because he had this idiosyncrasy: he would always slap his knee before he would go into the Gospel. So I would run up the hill and get right up to the point of getting into the Gospel, and I would always sort of get stuck. I would screw up my courage to the sticking place, and then I'd slap my knee and I'd go over the hill and be into the Gospel—just as simple as that.

"So that, my friends, is the key to Evangelism Explosion International! Everybody together, right hand on the right knee, let's see it! [slap] Beautiful! [*prolonged laughter*] Now, aren't you glad you came all the way around the world to this clinic to learn that amazing trick of evangelism? [*much laughter*] Well, that helped me the first year, and by the grace of God I even got to the place where I didn't have to slap my knee [*laughter*]. I have told many clinics that fact; then I made a videotape of presenting the Gospel to someone, and I saw the videotape. I couldn't believe my eyes—I came to the place of getting into the Gospel and, sure enough, I slapped my knee [*laughter*]. I thought I had gotten over that. No, I really have, and I pray now that it won't be long before the Lord will enable me to leave my blanket at home [*much laughter*].

"So I started running around. I was busier than a one-armed paperhanger with the itch. I started witnessing to people everywhere, and, sure enough, people responded here just as they did up there. People began to accept the Lord. I could look out right here in this sanctuary and see several people who accepted Christ in those first few months when I came back from Atlanta twenty-two years ago. God is still working in their lives, and I praise the Lord for that.

"After about a year, I stopped long enough to get over panting breathlessly, and I said to myself, 'There's only a certain number of people that I can reach alone.' And then I had an idea! Why don't I train some others to do the same thing? That's where Evangelism Explosion really began. So I took a man out with me—an elderly gentleman who had been a Christian for about sixty years. He always wanted to lead someone to the Lord and never knew how. I took him out for months and months—thought I'd never get rid of him. Finally, I put both feet in the small of his back and pushed him out of the nest [*laughter*]. He went out and began to lead a lot of people to Christ. Then there was another man I took out for a month or so. Then I went away on vacation, and he called me up the next week and told me he had led somebody to Christ.

"I said to myself, 'Lord, maybe this is it. Maybe this is the way.' And I will report that from around the world there come stories of the fact that this is the way, because this is what Jesus did. He called the disciples that they should be with Him. It wasn't until somebody took me by the hand and led me out that I began to overcome that blinding fear that so silences so many people in the Church.

"Dear friends and pastors, may I say that Christ said to you that you are to equip the saints to do the work of the ministry, and that's a great thing. To those of you who are lay people, I say to you that the greatest privilege and the greatest responsibility you'll ever know is the privilege of being able to lead another person to Jesus Christ."

DAY
OF
SMALL
BEGINNINGS

And [I] will do better unto you than
at your beginnings: and ye shall
know that I am the Lord.
—EZEKIEL 36:11

Lest the preceding chapter with its warm overlay of nostalgic good humor leave the impression that the beginning of Coral Ridge Presbyterian Church was a barrel of laughter, those first ten months need to be retold in the cold light of fact.

In the first place, starting up a church from scratch—without benefit of facilities, staff, choir, predictable income, established routine, Sunday school support, or even a dwelling place for the pastor and his wife—is a formidable undertaking for which no seminary courses can prepare the new minister (and for which none are offered). Any kind of church program requires a certain amount of administration, voluminous record keeping, some correspondence, regular and occasional publications of all kinds, serious music production, active recruiting, promotion, publicity, and the physical preparations that attach to the conducting of public meetings. All these activities precede and undergird the real business of ministering to the spiritual needs of people.

For the pastor, it all adds up to one thing: work—lots of work, exhausting work, sometimes thankless work. It means the untimed expenditure of energy—physical, emotional, mental, spiritual. From Day One, Jim Kennedy's approach has been that of the old pastor who was asked whether he favored the concept of the forty-hour week. "Oh, absolutely," was his reply. "I think it's a fantastic idea. I am so thoroughly sold on the forty-hour week, I've been putting in two of them every week for the past thirty-seven years!"

The precisely defined "job description," which has become an integral part of modern-day employment considerations, is something with which Jim has never had any personal involvement. "My job description," he says, "is whatever has to be done." He will confess that, like Dwight L. Moody, he has gotten bone-tired in the work time and time again, but never once has he been weary of the work.

But what of that inauspicious job awaiting him at the little McNab schoolhouse? After all, one of the committee members had actually whispered to Jim, in what could only be termed indiscreet candor, "I couldn't believe you would accept this job at $4,800." This was the work to which God had called him, the work that the Lord had opened up for him, the work for which he had studied and prepared and prayed all these years. And now he was actually here! He was excited about God's work and eager to get on with it. The notion of seeking some other place, once he learned that the door to the Congo mission field was permanently shut, never crossed his mind.

The Kennedys arrived in Fort Lauderdale in early June and took two rooms at a motel on Highway A1A, right down on the tourist-crowded beach. They lived in one of the rooms and stored all their household belongings in the other. This was to be their "manse" for the next six months. At the close of such improvised living, Jim would follow the lead of ancient Jeremiah, who, in the face of uncertainty of the worst kind, "purchased a field" in a heroic act of faith. In this way the prophet signified his belief that Israel's future was in God's hand.

Jim and Anne had no assurance of permanence in their new place. Until the mission to which they had been assigned could show evidence to the Presbytery that it had the support of at least fifty full-time communicants, there was no guarantee of official recognition of enduring church status. Thus, when they raised the down payment for a lot on 19th Avenue (with a generous assist from Anne's father) and plunged into debt for the construction of a home of their own where only one other house was being built, it was a testimony of their faith in the future that God had placed before them. And the very same word that came to Jeremiah came to them: "Behold, I am the Lord, the God of all flesh. Is there anything too hard for Me?" They had already discovered the answer to that question.

But first on the agenda was the matter of getting things in order for the Sunday morning worship services. Unfortunately, Jim's little group of about forty-five was compelled to meet at the unaccustomed time of 8:30; another struggling mission group from a different denomination had the school cafetorium already sewed up at 11:00. This was destined to change within a few weeks because that group apparently was doomed to extinction. It seems that the pastor played hooky one Sunday, and the following week the entire congregation failed to show up. Thus by the hapless default of their cafetorium co-tenants, the Presbyterians gained a firm grip on prime time.

As for the "sanctuary" itself, the eye-catching seats were several rows of wooden cafeteria tables which, with the release of a spring, converted into bulky benches. Somehow they didn't look like pews. They looked more like—well, like overturned cafeteria tables. Supplemented by a number of carved-on, child-size chairs, total seating capacity would be strained by 150 souls. But at the time overcrowding was no problem.

A rather nice little stage was built into one end of the room, and around a veteran piano Anne began to build a music program. She gave solo performances until she could get a vocal trio together and form a small choir. Anne took the challenge seriously, driving to a distant church to practice each week because the schoolroom was not available on weekdays.

Somehow they didn't look like pews. They looked more like overturned tables.

McNab Elementary School's air conditioning system was manifestly heaven-sent—that is, if the east windows were opened and the wind was right. When the ocean breeze prevailed it could be quite comfortable, and it was nearly unbearable otherwise, particularly in South Florida in the summertime. Another environmental nuisance was presented by the occasional land crab invasions of the building; they crawled right over the shoes of unsuspecting worshipers. A genteel touch was provided for those early services, however, by a faithful member who never failed to pick up a bunch of gladioli from the produce department of a nearby grocery store and drop them artfully in a vase in front of the lectern on the stage.

In this setting, Jim took up his appointed work on Sunday, June 21, 1959. Someone on the committee had thoughtfully typed and mimeographed four dozen copies of a bulletin, and had distributed it to the fewer than four dozen people there. It included this item: "We are happy to have Mr. James Kennedy, who, by appointment of the Presbytery of the Everglades, has come to be our Pastor and to lead us toward an organized Presbyterian Church in our community."

The pastor-to-be eased right into his first sermon at Coral Ridge Presbyterian Church with confidence and enthusiasm. He was truly thankful for the quarters that had been provided and especially for the opportunity they housed—the opportunity to ascribe glory to God. His message was an exaltation of the amazing love that sent Jesus Christ into the world—not merely as a preacher, a teacher, an example—but as the Savior. That first sermon was conspicuously biographical because Jim was still filled with astonishment that God loved him enough to send His only Son to die that he and every other sinner might, by grace alone, enter into Heaven to live eternally. Charter members (a few of them are still in the church) remember that the new preacher spoke with the same zeal and conviction that characterize his sermons today. They were impressed then, as listeners are now, by the sound doctrine, the cogent persuasiveness, the flawless delivery, and the deep reverence of his messages. The infant church seemed bound to show immediate and rapid growth.

Attendance began an unexplainable decline as the months went by.

But it didn't. Attendance, instead of inching up past the fifty-mark, began an unexplainable decline, which became a downslide as the months went by. Jim and Anne worked harder at the sermons and the music and the fellowship, but the heart-wrenching plunge continued. At the end of ten months of pure Gospel presentation, the original attendance of about forty-five each Sunday now stood at a staggering low of seventeen! The carefully nurtured mission church effort appeared to be succumbing to some sort of "McNab Jinx" that had eliminated the previous 11:00 occupants.

But Jim would not accept that. He knew that something obviously wasn't working the way it was supposed to. And suddenly he put his finger on it. It had to be, of all things, the "invitation" that he had been using at the close of his sermons. In the Bible Belt the closing invitation to "stand up" or "come forward" and make a public profession of faith in Christ was a standard church service fixture. Jim had used it many times while interning as a seminary student in pulpits across Alabama, Georgia, and South Carolina, where the congregations would have been shocked by its omission.

But the worshipers who came to McNab cafetorium were transplants from Pennsylvania, Ohio, New York, Illinois. They might tolerate the stock invitation in a Billy Graham crusade, but they were extremely uncomfortable with it in their own church. Jim recalled the shocking lack of response when, on an early occasion, he went into the fixed pattern: first, a closing prayer; then, "every head bowed and every eye closed"; and finally, "if you wish to accept Christ as your personal Savior, just slip up your hand." When he opened his eyes and looked up, every member of the congregation was sitting there with head erect and eyes wide open, staring disconcertingly back at him. He almost lost his composure for a moment. But gradually it dawned on Jim that, with the possible exception of one or two native Floridians, the people of his congregation were not accustomed to this time-tested Old South procedure and simply did not know how to respond.

Most of his parishioners were too genteel to complain about the preacher's invitation methodology, but one or two let it be known that they were highly offended. One outraged dowager went so far as to make her exit in a huff, drawing her mink stole about her shoulders and demanding to know: "What kind of cult is this?" As Jim made a home visit, the occupant opened the door, recognized him, blurted, "We don't want anything to do with that sawdust trail religion!"

and slammed the door in his face.

Such extreme responses were rare indeed, but Jim realized that something else was needed. If simple invitations couldn't be relied upon to build up the numbers, what else? Home visitation certainly was essential and was being pressed vigorously, yet it was not producing the desired results. What was lacking? Then, when Jim was at the very nadir of his ministry, a letter arrived, by providential "coincidence," from a fellow preacher he had known at the seminary. (This was that dramatic turning point related by Jim in his monologue of the previous chapter).

Kennedy Smartt wanted Jim to come to his church, Ingleside Presbyterian in Scottdale, Georgia, to conduct a ten-day series of evangelistic services. There, in the Greater Atlanta area, he would discover the missing key that was to unlock his problem at the McNab schoolhouse church. There and in Fort Lauderdale, the Lord would reveal fully to Jim Kennedy the vision for which He had been preparing and which he was now ready to receive—a vision that he would label "Evangelism Explosion."

It was not until the discouraged young preacher was led to visualize the total impact of the revelation he had stumbled upon, the effect it would have on Coral Ridge Presbyterian Church and on more than 100,000 thousand other churches around the world, that he could shout in victory: "This is the Lord's doing, and it is marvelous in our eyes."

THE
ATOM
EXPLODES

. . . do the work of an evangelist,
make full proof of thy ministry.
—2 TIMOTHY 4:5

When Jim Kennedy returned from that totally unanticipated indoctrination at Kennedy Smartt's church, he brought a gift for his decimated flock. He had acquired something so "exceeding great and precious" and of such inestimable value that he could hardly wait to share it with his faithful remnant. What was this gift? It was a knowledge, a skill, an ability that he had not possessed just ten days before.

Simply put, he now had the secret of witnessing, of effective, productive, personal witnessing. He had learned how to deactivate the paralyzing fear that had thwarted all his previous feeble evangelizing efforts. He had discovered the sure way to lead a person to Christ in a one-to-one situation. And he had been shown, beyond all doubt, that this was the route to certain Church growth.

Most importantly, he had faced the shocking revelation

that the first problem confronting a pastor in the evangelism challenge is the pastor himself! Without knowing how to do personal soul-winning, a pastor can only stand in the pulpit Sunday after Sunday berating the congregation for not getting the job done. Personal soul-winning cannot be considered an extra or incidental—it is an essential: the pastor must be accomplished and successful in evangelizing individuals. If he finds he is not, then he must learn precisely how to do it from someone who does know how to witness fruitfully.

The proof that Jim knew what he was talking about came quickly. As he began to put into practice in Fort Lauderdale what he had seen and tried in Atlanta, souls were led into the kingdom, and new members joined the little church in the McNab Elementary School. The pain of the old downward spiral was forgotten as attendance spurted from the "Stalwart Seventeen" up to sixty-six, more than enough to charter a fully organized church. The official ceremony took place on May 22, 1960, just eleven months after the birth of the doubtful new mission.

It was a time of excitement, of fresh confidence, and of joyful fellowship as the charter total almost doubled the following year to a healthy congregation of 122. The little cafetorium was actually beginning to present seating problems. Sunday school classes had also been started, with small groups meeting in clusters in corners of the room and up on the stage, each trying not to eavesdrop on the class nearby. The school principal was prevailed upon to allow classes in the library, and the first-aid dispensary was converted into a nursery for younger families.

The Kennedy's newly finished ($19,300) home virtually became "the Church" except for Sunday mornings. Anne developed needed expertise at setting up and putting away folding chairs for evening services twice a week on the terrazzo patio, at preparing sack lunches in her kitchen for youth groups, and at having things ready for Session deliberations. Her mother, back in Lakeland, generously shipped the family piano to meet the need at the new house on 19th Avenue.

With that much going on, it is not difficult to understand how the recorded installation program of July 31, 1960, bequeathed to the archives of church history for all the world to see—a monumental error. The text declares that "James D. Kennedy was duly installed as pastor of Coral Ridge Presbyterian Church." A single such instance of misnaming could surely be forgiven, but five more times the printed page consistently refers to "the Rev. James D. Kennedy!" The Presbytery of the Everglades had not installed the wrong man—only the wrong typist.

Jim had found the right answer, but the remarkable results led to a new question about how much one man could do. He pondered the possibilities for a long time as he continued to bring new converts in, one at a time. Then, like a bolt of lightning, it hit him. What he needed to do, he realized, was not just to win souls, but to train soul-winners. Jesus had been careful to make that requirement explicit and imperative in His instruction to go and make disciples, "teaching them to observe all things whatsoever I have commanded you." In biblical terms that is known as "equipping the saints" by transferring to them the techniques that work for you.

Jim had found the right answer.

Jim explained it simply: "If I lead you to Christ and then her and then him, that's addition. One plus one plus one equals three. The world, on the other hand, is not adding, but multiplying its own; by the time we have gained three, it has

114

gained ten. What the Church must do is to get the process of spiritual multiplication going on a worldwide scale. We can do this by training witnesses to train witnesses. That was the way the original disciples turned the world upside down in their day. One of the most bitter opponents of Christianity, a man named Celsus, wrote in the second century that what made the rapid spread of Christianity so outrageous was that it was being accomplished, not by the recognized clergy, but by 'fishermen and fullers and all sorts of commonplace people.'"

Warming up to one of his favorite areas of research and study, Kennedy gave this lucid historical explanation: "In the first three centuries, Christianity grew enormously because it was accepted naturally that a person who became a Christian did not just retire to a closet and keep the conversion a big secret.

"Now, I lived to be almost twenty-four years old in America without being a Christian, and never, ever, had anyone spoken to me about Christ. Never. If I ever met a Christian, it was a well-guarded secret. We should have guarded the atom bomb secrets half as well as all the Christians I met kept the secret of their Christianity.

"After the persecutions of Christians in Rome ceased and Rome was officially declared a Christian nation, millions of people were swept into the Church without ever really being converted. Instead of being a missionary force, the Church became a missionary field and became filled with people who never evangelized because they had never been evangelized.

"This continues right down to this day. The vast majority of people who are members of churches in America today are not Christians. I say that without the slightest fear of contradiction. I base it on the empirical evidence of twenty-four years of examining tens of thousands of those people on what they are basing their hopes of eternal life, and it's not Jesus Christ. It is merely their own morality, their own piety, their own goodness. They are not trusting in Christ for salvation; yet that faith in Christ is the essence of Christianity.

"Today there are thousands of churches in America where there are absolutely no professions of faith. That's why we have so many members who have never been trained in how to witness and situations where the preacher himself doesn't know how to witness and therefore does not provide any training. It would be practically a miracle in such a church if you found any people who were actually sharing the Gospel."[3]

Convinced, then, that the Church faces the alternatives "evangelize or fossilize," Jim made the requirement of witness-training a bedrock essential of his ministry within his first year out of seminary. It had been an excruciating lesson for him, but he testifies that the struggle at McNab proved to be the wellspring of greatest blessing in his ecclesiastical career.

The struggle at McNab proved to be the wellspring of greatest blessing.

That doesn't mean that from there on everything ran smoothly. Quite the opposite. The first effort at training others to witness consisted of a series of classes of intense instruction that ran for six weeks. Then the trainees were sent out into the community to try their wings. The results were absolute zero. In a second approach, the preparation time was extended to twelve weeks in order to include more detailed suggestions on what to say to prospects and more specific answers to objections that might be met. The plan still was not producing the expected response. Even a twenty-five-week-long training session accomplished no tangible results to count.

Jim, who was used to head-on confrontations with abortive projects in this field, wasn't about to surrender to this new baffler. Along with his praying he mixed in a good deal of cogitating. Once again, that friendly bolt of lightning flashed with the clear answer: take your trainees out of the church rooms and into the living rooms. You don't teach a teenager how to drive a car by discussing it in the garage; you get him or her behind the wheel out on the streets and highways. The lecture is fine, but the laboratory is also essential. Jim understood early on that the one overlooked but indispensable ingredient was on-the-job training. Only by having the would-be witness go out with an experienced trainer as long as necessary—to observe, then to participate, and ultimately to become part of a training team, teaching another newcomer how to do it—would any evangelism training program really work the way it should.

It was that simple, yet it appeared that nobody was doing it in an organized, systematic, thoughtfully structured way. Jim knew that such a program would literally explode the growth patterns of churches, once it was faithfully and intelligently tried. His little group of followers hardly understood what he was talking about when he told them, "We can change the world!" Some who were there recalled: "He had this vision, and while some of us didn't have the foggiest notion of what he meant, he was so sincere and so convincing that we believed him. We know now, as we see these people coming to our church from around the world, how their lives have been changed by Evangelism Explosion."

That was the logical name for Jim Kennedy's inspired idea. Actually, he first thought of calling it "Lay Evangelism," but by great good fortune, another group was already using that rather prosaic label. Jim thought of the expression that was so popular in the 1960s—the "population explosion" fed by the baby boom in America and all around the globe—and the perfect title came to his mind. Evangelism Explosion describes not the detonation of dynamite, but the explosion produced by nuclear fission, the multiplication of an infinite number of atomic particles, mushrooming and accelerating in all directions.

The original test site was the cafetorium at McNab schoolhouse, which by 1962 was trying to accommodate twice the number it had held the year before. With attendance now running in excess of two hundred, it was packed each Sunday. Church income for the year was up from zero to $11,000 (only a shadow of the $60 million that comes in each year now to fund the ministries emanating from the church, but nonetheless a substantial start). It was time to begin planning for the building site over on Commercial Boulevard that the Presbytery of the Everglades had hopefully set aside for the Coral Ridge Presbyterian Church of the future.

COMMERCIAL SUCCESS STORY

*The Lord shall increase you more and
more, you and your children.*
—PSALM 115:14

W hen a well-intentioned representative of the presbytery—a Dr. Larson, whose first name has been forever lost to historians—persuaded the Home Mission Committee to cough up $50,000 in the 1950s to buy a two-acre sandlot a mile and a half from the ocean in the wilderness that was North Fort Lauderdale, virtually nobody thought it made sense. Except for Federal Highway a few hundred yards to the east, there was absolutely nothing for miles around. So undesirable and so overpriced was the site considered to be that members of the committee were stricken with buyer's remorse.

One bitter opponent of the transaction tagged it "Larson's Folly." The forlorn vacant lot lived under that opprobrium for several years. But wasn't the paying of $24 for Manhattan Island lamented as "a typical Dutch treat"?

Wasn't the Louisiana Purchase from Napoleon, which doubled the continental territory of the United States for $15 million, referred to in Congress as "Jefferson's Blunder"? And wasn't the acquisition of Alaska for $7.2 million (2 cents an acre) derided as "Seward's Folly"? All have been exonerated by history as fantastic real estate "steals." So also was the good name of the much-maligned Dr. Larson redeemed when Jim Kennedy appointed a building committee in 1961 to make all necessary preparations for the construction of a

One bitter opponent of the transaction tagged it "Larson's Folly."

five-hundred-seat sanctuary on what was now Commercial Boulevard, to house the fast-growing Coral Ridge Presbyterian Church.

Since the once-adequate McNab schoolhouse was bursting at the seams, the building committee moved swiftly, engineering a fund drive that netted $112,500 for the initial outlay for a new meeting place. It was to be a rectangular, single-gable structure of antique brick with vertical panes of tinted glass (stained glass was preferred, but simply too expensive). And it would be deliciously air-conditioned.

Despite the growth in numbers, the church budget was still modest enough that robes for the expanding choir were considered an unaffordable luxury. That problem was solved, however, when the First Presbyterian Church of Lakeland donated its used robes to the Kennedys' church. Though slightly faded from years of service, they looked fine enough for the new building after they were run through washing machines full of maroon dye.

It was apparent from the beginning that a 500-seat facility wasn't going to measure up to the needs of this church. As the numbers kept galloping out in front of the space available, the busiest group in the organization was the building committee. It implemented the addition of an attractive Sunday school wing fronting on Commercial Boulevard for $61,500. It designed and built a neat little annex to the sanctuary on the west side of the pulpit at a cost of $40,500. This boosted the total auditorium capacity to 800.

The committee decided that a fire station, complete with brick training tower, was the next logical expansion step to the east. To get the adjacent property, the board rather ingeniously offered to build the City of Fort Lauderdale a brand new fire station several doors to the west. This deal was consummated for $127,000, and the church converted the former firefighters' quarters into administrative offices, more Sunday school rooms, and a youth center. The fortress-like tower was left intact and named "Teen Tower."

The pressure was directly on the preacher, who drew ever larger crowds as his reputation spread. The inevitable solution was to go to multiple Sunday morning services: two to begin with, then three during the winter months, and four on special occasions like Easter. Meanwhile, an inexpensive fellowship hall was added behind the education wing; here, three hundred more could participate in the morning worship services by closed-circuit television. All in all, such improvisations meant that eleven hundred could attend services. And still the numbers grew.

Few had realized the miraculous growth potential their pastor had envisioned in the new lay-visitation training program that was just beginning to crystallize as Evangelism Explosion. By 1967 Coral Ridge was singled out as the fastest-growing church in the denomination and one of the most rapidly expanding in all of America. After the church left the McNab Elementary School, with approximately two hundred communicants, the year-end figures continued to change dramatically:

```
1962 . . . . . . . . . . . . . . . . . . . . . . . . .246
1963 . . . . . . . . . . . . . . . . . . . . . . . . .426
1964 . . . . . . . . . . . . . . . . . . . . . . . . .665
1965 . . . . . . . . . . . . . . . . . . . . . . . . .903
1966 . . . . . . . . . . . . . . . . . . . . . . . .1,114
1967 . . . . . . . . . . . . . . . . . . . . . . . .1,339
1968 . . . . . . . . . . . . . . . . . . . . . . . .1,660
1969 . . . . . . . . . . . . . . . . . . . . . . . .2,005
1970 . . . . . . . . . . . . . . . . . . . . . . . .2,313
1971 . . . . . . . . . . . . . . . . . . . . . . . .2,296 (roll purged)
1972 . . . . . . . . . . . . . . . . . . . . . . . .2,512
1973 . . . . . . . . . . . . . . . . . . . . . . . .2,762
1974 . . . . . . . . . . . . . . . . . . . . . . . .3,134
```

Kennedy's faltering flock multiplied by more than fifteen times in a dozen years! And it was only the beginning!

Other pastors from all over the United States were taking note of the rocketing records at Coral Ridge and were writing to ask, "Jim, how do you do it?" At first, he tried to respond to each letter that came in, sharing in minute detail the evangelizing secrets that had been revealed to him. But the sheer volume made the letter writing impossible. Still, he wanted to help his fellow pastors get their stagnant churches off dead center and into healthy growth patterns.

The solution, Jim decided, was to conduct an Evangelism Explosion clinic. Announcements were sent out, and almost forty ministers came to Coral Ridge Presbyterian for instruction in this unique, chain-reaction method of people training people. The first clinic opened on February 20, 1967. The visitors were subjected to a week of how-to-do-it talk sessions followed by on-the-job visits in homes each evening with the church's lay witness teams. The lay people were petrified, Jim recalls, when they learned that they would be accompanied by professional clergy on their weekly rounds—that is, until they discovered that the pastors themselves were even more terrified. On the final night the visiting pastor on each team presented the Gospel under the scrutiny of the lay soul-winners.

An incident at one of the early clinics underscored the E.E. ministry's program assumption that paralyzing fear is the chief obstacle to effective witnessing. The same procedure was followed, with the visiting pastors scheduled to make the presentations on the final night. One of the visitors was staying in the home of a Coral Ridge trainer. On the morning before that final date with the unregenerate prospects, his hostess knocked on his bedroom door to announce that breakfast was ready. There was no answer. She knocked again: "Breakfast is ready, Reverend." After several more unsuccessful attempts to summon the guest, she entered the room to find the bed hastily made and no sign of the preacher or his belongings. Panicked, he had silently packed his bags and crept out of the house in the still of night. "For all we know," Jim says, "he is still running." As one who had been victimized by that same fear just a few years earlier, Jim could empathize with his unfortunate colleague—and he could have helped him to conquer that terrible handicap to a fruitful ministry.

Toward the end of the church's dozen years of expansion at the Commercial Boulevard site, a separate organization, Evangelism Explosion International, was set up. The ministry had jumped across the border into Canada and over the Atlantic into Great Britain. Inquiries arrived from churches in other countries on six continents. The multiplication principle gained momentum, necessitating the translation of Kennedy's textbook, *Evangelism Explosion* (Tyndale House, 1970), into more than 95 languages, with more than one-and-a-half million copies in English alone distributed through three subsequent editions.

The nonprofit corporation, established in 1972 with the

Coral Ridge pastor as founder and president, today occupies an entire floor of the Knox Center on Federal Highway, plus additional staff members all over the world. One pastor wrote, "I would have E.E. in my church even if we never saw a single convert added because of what the training does in the spiritual growth of our people." Inevitably, as individuals grow in spirit, the church grows in size.

What makes the program unique in ecclesiastical history is the fact that it is not a "para-church" organization. That is, nothing is done with this ministry outside of the local church. E.E. is purposefully designed, right down to the workbook materials, so that it will never supplant any denominational distinctions or ministries. More than 400 denominations use it in their churches. The training is built entirely around the New Testament example of on-the-job training.

From all points of the compass come excited reports of phenomenal growth through E.E. training. One institution in Argentina experienced an expansion of ten times its original membership in two years. In Manila and Seoul the most rapid growth patterns were recorded in E.E. churches. And in the United States, seven of the fastest-growing Southern Baptist churches were enrolled in the program. The president of the Christian and Missionary Alliance indicated in one annual report that 75 percent of all professions of faith in that denomination were directly attributable to E.E. churches.

The global scope of the operation has become mind-boggling. The idea that Jim Kennedy tried out in near

> The global scope of E.E.'s operation has become mind-boggling.

desperation in his little church now flourishes in more than 100,000 churches worldwide. Over 500 new training clinics are held annually. In one recent year, E.E. saw 1.4 million people come to Christ on a budget of just $2 million. In March 1996, Evangelism Explosion reached an unprecedented milestone when it became the first ministry to actively reach every nation of the world—211 countries in all. Jim joined leaders from the four corners of the globe in Fort Lauderdale for a celebration at Coral Ridge Church. In a moving ceremony, representatives from every nation of the world carried flags into the sanctuary to mark the milestone. "There were more flags in our sanctuary than are represented at the United Nations," remarked Jim.

Coinciding with this historic event, the fourth edition of Evangelism Explosion was published. The new subtitle, "Equipping Churches for Friendship, Evangelism, Discipleship, and Healthy Growth," expresses how E.E. has grown and expanded its vision to reach out in the 21st century. "We have adopted a four-fold emphasis," says E.E. Executive Vice President Tom Stebbins, "that recognizes the importance of establishing friendships as the foundation of church-based evangelism efforts." Next comes E.E.'s clear presentation of the Gospel message and a commitment to disciple new believers and train lay people in evangelism. Finally, as a church-based ministry, E.E. seeks to promote healthy growth in the local church. "Not just numeric church growth, but healthy, growing individuals in those churches," says Stebbins.

E.E. is diversifying, as well, to reach even more people with the tools of evangelism, discipleship, and healthy church growth. "Youth E.E. is really exploding," says Stebbins. This program for teens is going international, as is its "sister" program, Kids E.E. In 1999, the first Kids E.E. clinic was conducted. In Columbia, a ten-year-old named Monica led 80 adults to Christ by sharing the Gospel using E.E. every day on the bus. A nine-year-old Vietnamese girl who overheard her parents using the E.E. outline, caught on and led a 26-year-old businessman to Christ.

E.E. is also going into the prisons. The aim is to train inmates to share their faith with their "captive" audience. In one Tennessee prison, 400 of 1,000 inmates have come to Christ through this outreach. A prisoner serving a life term is the teacher/trainer coordinating the effort. This prison received Tennessee's top award for good behavior.

All this is in line with Jim's original vision for Evangelism Explosion. In fact, E.E. continues to be central to the work of Coral Ridge Church, where the pace has never slackened. Leadership training clinics continue, with pastors and lay people coming in from far and near to get the careful instruction and hands-on experience that are the key to E.E. The church conducts two full semesters of thirteen-week courses for its own membership, and the pastor who started it all still teaches and goes out with his trainees on Thursday evenings. Anne Kennedy is the trainer with the all-time record for longevity in witnessing; she started going out with Jim at the very beginning.

It is little wonder, then, that Coral Ridge has been listed almost every year since the mid-1960s as the fastest-growing Presbyterian Church in America and one of the fastest-growing in any denomination. Gospel Films decided to produce in 1970 a dramatic motion picture depicting the story of E.E. *Like A Mighty Army* has been shown in more churches than any other film ever produced," says Billy Zeoli, president of Gospel Films.

For many years, Billy Graham had Kennedy bring the message of his unique equipping ministry before the Billy Graham School of Evangelism three times a year—before a total of more than forty thousand ministers. While the Coral Ridge Church remains totally separate from the E.E. structure, its recognition in *Decision* magazine as "one of the five great churches in North America," unquestionably stemmed in part from the spectacular achievements of the evangelization ministry.

And so the commercial success story continues. With every nation reached, E.E. has set its sights on new goals: Reach every territory of the world, and then reach every people group with the Gospel. Since people groups are much more numerous than nations (Vietnam, for example, has approximately 100 people groups), E.E. has an ambitious workload already laid out well into the 21st century. Such a goal envisions the personal evangelizing of more than 100 million people.

There is virtually no way to measure the impact of this one ministry as conceived in the mind and the heart of one man. Jim finds the explanation in Jeremiah 33:3, which is probably the Scripture verse he most frequently quotes: "Call unto me, and I will answer thee, and show thee great and mighty things, which thou knowest not."

TELLING THE OLD, OLD STORY

*And the things that thou hast heard of me
among many witnesses, the same commit
thou to faithful men, who shall be
able to teach others also.*
—2 TIMOTHY 2:2

The heart of Evangelism Explosion, of course, is the presentation of the Gospel. Nothing is accomplished until a lost person hears, understands, and accepts the Gospel. Just how to make that presentation in the most natural, gracious, and convincing way has been the mental preoccupation and the heart passion of Jim Kennedy from the earliest days of his ministry. Once he discovered the way, he began putting the step-by-step process down on paper—first in note form, then as a workbook for trainees, and eventually in his famous book *Evangelism Explosion.*[4]

First published in 1970, with revisions in 1977, 1983, and 1996, this textbook for soul-winners provides unquestionably the clearest explanation of how to be saved. In his foreword to the third edition, Billy Graham quotes a Canadian

Nothing is accomplished until a person hears, understands, and accepts the Gospel.

pastor who calls Kennedy's plan "the most revolutionary technique for personal evangelism to mobilize the sleeping giant of our laity to be discovered in the Twentieth Century."

The presentation itself, in extended outline form, is reprinted here for its significance, sheer interest value, and engaging readability. The focal point of the interview begins with the "two diagnostic questions" (E), whose biographical import should be apparent.

I. INTRODUCTION

A. Secular life

(A knock at the door.)
Good morning, Mrs. Tucker. I'm Dr. Kennedy from the Coral Ridge Presbyterian Church. May we come in and visit with you a while?

Why, hello. Please do come in.

Thank you. This is Mary Smith and George Simon from our church. We were so happy to have you visit with us and wanted to become better acquainted with you.

That's real nice of you.

May we sit over here?

Fine.

Thank you. This is a lovely home you have. That painting is most interesting. It seems to radiate peacefulness and contentment. Did you paint it yourself?

Oh, no. A friend did it for me just before we moved here. We have enjoyed it.

Where did you move from, Mrs. Tucker?

Virginia.

Virginia! I thought I noticed a bit of Virginia accent.

I don't doubt it.

Do they really say "aboot the hoouse" up there?

Yes, they do.

Do they really? Let me hear you say "about the house."

Lookoout, there's a moouse in the hoouse!

That's delightful. I've always enjoyed listening to people with Virginia accents. Tell me a little more about yourself. How did you happen to move down here?

We vacationed in this area several times and just loved it. When my husband retired we came down and looked around one summer and settled in Fort Lauderdale. We just love it here.

It is a beautiful city, isn't it?

Yes, it is.

B. Church background

What church did you attend back in Virginia?

Baptist.

The Baptist church? Well, I knew there was something nice about you. I have many friends who are Baptists.

Thank you. I was a charter member.

You had the joys of seeing a new congregation born and you helped it grow.

Yes, some of those days were pretty trying, but we got our problems ironed out and it is a large church now. I was president of the Women of the Church for two years and taught a Sunday school class for awhile.

Wonderful! It's good to meet someone who is really active in the life of her church. We are truly delighted to have you here in Fort Lauderdale with us now. **How did you happen to attend our church?**

C. Our church

We were looking for a church in the neighborhood and while driving around we saw your building.

How did you like the service?

Oh, we liked it very much. The people seemed so friendly and made us feel at home. The singing is wonderful. You people seem to really enjoy singing. Somehow the spirit was different.

You noticed something different about the congregation?

Yes, we did.

Do you have any idea what causes that difference?

No, but I'd like to know.

D. Testimony

1. Church (as here)
or
2. Personal
Let me share with you what I think it is. You know, many people have mentioned to me that they sense something different about our church. They noticed the singing, as you did. They saw something different about the expression on people's faces—as if they were happier. Is this the sort of difference you were thinking of?

Yes.

The secret of that difference is really rather simple when you look at it closely.
Jesus Christ came that we might have life and have it abundantly. The Scriptures were written that men and women might know that they have eternal life and yet we have found that a majority of people that go to church, even those who have gone all of their life, aren't really sure that they have this abundant life, and they're not really sure about what will happen to them when they die. They have hopes, but they don't know for sure that they would go to Heaven. For many years I felt that same way. I was striving but I wasn't really sure. How about you, Mrs. Tucker?

E. Two diagnostic questions

1. Have you come to a place in your spiritual life where you know for certain that if you were to die today you

would go to Heaven?

Why, I don't think anyone can really know.

You know, that's just the way I felt about it. For many years I didn't know. I wasn't even aware of the fact that anybody knew. But let me tell you some really good news: I discovered that it is possible to know and there are a great many people who do know.

Really?

That was an amazing discovery to me! In fact I even learned that that was the reason the Bible was written! The Bible says: "These things have I written . . . that ye may know that ye have eternal life" (1 John 5:13).

Why, I never knew that!

I didn't either. Isn't that a fantastic thing! Think how wonderful it would be if you could go to bed tonight and lay your head on your pillow knowing for certain that if you don't wake up in your bedroom, you will wake up in Heaven with Jesus Christ. Wouldn't that be a wonderful thing to know?

Yes, it really would.

Would you like for me to share with you how I made that discovery and how you can know it too?

Yes, please do.

All right. I'll be happy to, for it is the greatest discovery that I have ever made. It really has changed my whole life. I wouldn't trade everything else in the world for this wonderful assurance and the joy of sharing it with other people. You know, it's amazing how many people are hungry to know! I talk to people in all strata of society and everywhere there are men and women eager to know, and yet no one has taken the time to explain these things to them.

I've never heard it.

Before I get into it, let me ask you another question which, I think, really crystallizes our thinking on the matter. This was a question that was very helpful to me. A minister asked me this one day:

2. Suppose that you were to die today and stand before God and He were to say to you, "Why should I let you into my Heaven?" What would you say? That's a pretty good question, isn't it?

It certainly is.

It really makes you think. What would your answer be?

Well, I never thought of anything like that. I've gone to Sunday school and church all my life. And I try to be as good as I know how. Of course, I know that I haven't always been perfect, but I don't think I've ever intentionally hurt anyone. And I try to love my neighbor. I don't think I've been too bad.

All right. Anything else?

Well, I visit the sick and I do the very best I can to live according to the Golden Rule.

Well, thank you, Mrs. Tucker. It's Rene, isn't it? May I call you that?

Yes.

(Good news)
You know, Rene, when I asked you if you knew for sure if you had eternal life and you said that you didn't, I thought I had some really good news to tell you. And after your answer to that second question, I know that I do! In fact, I would say that in the next few minutes you are going to hear the greatest Good News that you've ever heard in your whole life. That's quite a statement to make, isn't it?

It certainly is.

II. THE GOSPEL

A. Grace

1. HEAVEN IS A FREE GIFT
Well, let me see if I can back it up. You know, all my life I felt exactly like you did. I thought that Heaven was something I had to earn; something that I had to merit by keeping the commandments and following rules and sometimes I almost despaired of the whole thing. Then I discovered something that absolutely amazed me. I discovered that Heaven is not something that you earn, or that you deserve, or that you work for, but that, **according to the Scriptures, Heaven— eternal life—is absolutely a free gift!**

Free?

Absolutely free! Isn't that amazing?

Yes, it is.

2. IT IS NOT EARNED OR DESERVED
It's unearned, undeserved, and unmerited. It's free. You know, we sort of think there's nothing in this life that's free. We always look for the price tag. And we are probably right.

But thank God that the greatest thing that man could ever have—eternal life—is free! Of course the idea that we have to pay for everything is something which is ingrained in us from our earliest days. This is the way which seems right to every man. In fact, most people think they're going to get to Heaven that way.

Yes, it is.

(Man's ways are not God's ways)
The Bible says this: "There is a way which seemeth right unto a man but the end thereof are the ways of death" (Proverbs 14:12). God says that His ways are not our ways and as high as the heavens are above the earth, so high are His ways above our ways and His thoughts above our thoughts. **God's way is the way of grace.** He is the God of all grace. Rene, let me show you a Scripture verse in the New Testament. This is found in **Romans 6:23.** You see what it says? "For the wages (wages, of course, are what we earn, what we deserve) of sin (and we're all sinners) is death (physical death, spiritual death, eternal death); BUT (and here's the Good News) the gift of God is eternal life through Jesus Christ our Lord." "The gift of God is eternal life." Isn't that amazing, Rene?

That's wonderful!

Why, it's the most wonderful thing that I've ever heard in all my life!
I'm sure that this raises many questions in your mind. "How can these things be? How can God do this and still be just? And who gets the gift, after all? Everybody?" Not at all. In fact, **Christ said that few there are that find the way and many there are which go in to destruction (Matthew 7:13-14).** Well, if everybody doesn't get the gift, who does get it? How do we get it? And how can we know if we have it?
Now, Rene, let me see if I can answer these questions for

you. In fact, I think I can show you not only that this is the way, but when you understand what the Bible teaches concerning man and concerning God, I think you will see that this is the only way it could be.

B. Man

1. A SINNER

The first thing I came to understand was what God says about man in the Bible—that is what God says about us, you and me. This is a practical place to begin because it brings us face to face with the predicament in which we find ourselves—and a real predicament it is! **According to God's Word, we have made a colossal mess out of everything we have our hands on.**

If we were to get away from this planet and look at it objectively, we would appreciate the truth of this statement. We have wars and riots; we have crime and delinquency; we have murder and hatred and envy and strife. According to the Bible, **all of these are the result of sin.**

This is the fatal malignancy which infects the soul of the entire human race. The Bible says, "There is none righteous, no, not one . . . for all have sinned and come short of the glory of God. There is not a just man upon the face of the earth that doeth good and sinneth not. We have turned every one to his own way" (Roman 3:10, 23; Isaiah 53:6). The Bible teaches that all of us have sinned, right?

I know that.

(Word, thought or deed)
This is a very black picture. In fact, the Bible paints it even darker. It is against this backdrop that we must see the glorious picture of the Gospel. Sin is a cancer destroying the human race and cannot be dealt with effectively until it is openly acknowledged.

In thought, word, and deed we have all come short of the

standard God has set for us. **Jesus said that sin in thought is the same as sin in deed.** "Ye have heard it said . . . whosoever shall kill shall be in danger of the judgment . . . but I say that whosoever is angry with his brother without a cause shall be in danger of the judgment. Ye have heard that it was said . . . thou shalt not commit adultery; but I say . . . whosoever looketh on a woman to lust after her hath committed adultery. . . ."

Christ said further, "Ye have heard that it hath been said, thou shalt love thy neighbour . . . but I say unto you, love your enemies, bless them that curse you, do good to them that hate you, and pray for them that despitefully use you . . . that ye may be the children of your Father which is in Heaven" (Matthew 5:21-48). Jesus made it very plain. He said, "Did not Moses give you the law, and yet none of you keepeth the law?" (John 7:19).

(Omission or commission)
The Bible teaches that we have not kept God's commandments but have violated them all; if not in deed, at least in thought and word. We have not lived by the Golden Rule all the time. We have not really done the best we can. **There are not only sins of commission,** in word, thought, and deed, but according to the Bible, **there are also sins of omission:** those things which we should have done that we have not—failing to pray or to read the Bible, or to truly love our neighbor, or to go to church. The Bible says these are all sins.

Sometimes I wonder just how many times a day the average person sins. I imagine it's fifty to one hundred times or even more. John Calvin said no one knows the one-hundredth part of the sin that clings to his soul. Today a psychologist would tell us that we have forgotten 99 percent of all those things we have ever done wrong. We suppress them because we don't like to think about the unpleasant.

Just suppose that a person sinned only ten times a day or even five—or even just three. Why, he would practically be a walking angel! Imagine, if not oftener than three times a day did he think unkind thoughts or lose his temper or fail to do what he ought toward God and man—he would be a pretty fine person, would he not?

Even if he were this good, he would have over 1,000 transgressions a year! If he lived to the average age of seventy, then he would have 70,000 transgressions. Think what would happen to an habitual offender in a criminal court with 70,000 transgressions on his record!

2. CANNOT SAVE HIMSELF

This impresses us with man's predicament. **According to the Bible he is a sinner.** He has broken God's Law.

The Bible goes on to teach that our predicament is compounded by another factor that is understood by even fewer people. Because man is a sinner, **he cannot save himself**, he cannot earn his way into Heaven. That is, he cannot merit eternal life by doing good things. The Bible states this clearly. "Not by works of righteousness which we have done, but according to his mercy he saved us" (Titus 3:5). "By grace are ye saved through faith . . . not of works, lest any man should boast" (Ephesians 2:8-9).

There was a time when I thought I could get to Heaven by keeping the Ten Commandments, living according to the Golden Rule, and helping people less fortunate than myself. However, occasionally I would wonder just how well I would have to do all these things to get into Heaven.

It was sort of like wondering in school, what is the passing grade in my classes? Did you ever wonder about how good you would have to be to make it, Rene? Well, **God has told us how well we have to do these works to get into Heaven.** He has revealed the passing grade in His class of life. **Do you know what it is?**

No.

All right. Hold on to your chair! Are you ready? Here it

comes! Jesus said, **"Be ye therefore perfect,** even as your Father in heaven is perfect" (Matthew 5:48).

Perfect?

There it stands! That's the passing grade! The amazing thing I discovered is that **God doesn't grade on a curve.** God says, "Be ye . . . PERFECT" (Matthew 5:48).

This is not an isolated text that might be interpreted in some other way, but something that is taught throughout the Bible. For example, Paul said, *"Cursed is every one that continueth not in all things which are written in the book of the law to do them"* (Galatians 3:10). If we don't continually do everything that we are told to do, then we are under the curse of God.

James put it another way: **"If we offend in one point we are guilty of all"** (James 2:10). If we commit just one sin we step outside the realm of the law and become an outlaw. You don't have to break every law in the book to be a criminal and have the police looking for you; just one crime is all it takes to have a lot of policemen looking for us. One sin is all that it takes to make us guilty and to make us an outlaw. Just one sin! Satan thought just one evil thought and because of that he was cast out of Heaven (See Isaiah 14:12-15).

Well, then, no one's going to be able to go to Heaven!

It would look that way, wouldn't it? You see, what we have said is that your understanding (which is the same as mine used to be) is simply that a person gets to Heaven by trying to be good enough. Now, boiling it all down, that is what you've come to understand all your life, right?

Yes.

(None good enough)
Just like I did. But the problem is: **What is good enoug**h? The

Bible makes it plain that **good enough is perfect!** There is no doubt about that fact.

This presents a problem, doesn't it? It does look as though nobody is going to Heaven.

That's right.

(Impossibility of salvation by works)
Well, that would be right—if this was the way that you get to Heaven! Martin Luther said that *the most damnable and pernicious heresy that has ever plagued the mind of man was the idea that somehow he could make himself good enough to deserve to live with an all-holy God.*

We couldn't make an omelet out of five good eggs and one rotten egg and serve it to company and expect it to be acceptable! Well, even less can we serve up our lives to God, which may have many things in them that men would call good, and yet are filled with deeds and thoughts that are rotten, and expect them to be acceptable to God.

If we want to get to Heaven by our good works, then all we have to do is be perfect. God's standard is complete obedience to him at all times—and all of us have fallen short of this. We just don't have the wherewithal to pay for eternal life.

Queen Elizabeth I of England offered her doctor half the British empire for six months of life when she was dying. Of course, the doctor couldn't give her six seconds. How much less, then, can we buy eternal life from God by our good works.

(An entirely different way)
If anybody is going to be in Heaven, then there must be some entirely different way of getting there.

The Bible, of course, says that there are going to be people in Heaven. Might I add that Jesus seemed to indicate that the number of people in Heaven will be a minority of those who have lived upon the earth. "Strait is the gate, and narrow is the way, which leadeth unto life, and few there be that find it . . . for wide is the gate, and broad is the way that lead-eth to destruction, and many there be which go in thereat" (Matthew 7:14, 13). This "few" is a great multitude that no man can number, but seemingly it is the lesser part of mankind, which makes us realize that we can't just take it for granted.

Trusting in our own efforts to be good obviously will not get us to Heaven. This was the religion of the Pharisees. Do you remember? Jesus described them in this way: "They trusted in themselves that they were righteous" (Luke 18:9). Many people have this belief today. In talking of these matters with literally thousands of people, we have found the vast majority indicate they intend to enter Heaven on the basis of their own good works. The Bible teaches, "There is a way that seemeth right unto a man" (Proverbs 14:12). It would appear that this is the way that seems right unto man. But the Bible continues, "the end thereof are the ways of death."

So then there must be another way. What is it? Well, to understand it we have to move on from our consideration of what God has said about us to what He says about Himself. About us, He has said we are sinners and we can do nothing to remedy our sinful condition.

C. God

1. LOVING AND MERCIFUL

One of the most amazing and most difficult facts to learn about God is that *He loves* us in spite of what we are. He loves us, not because of what we are, but because of what He is. For the Bible tells us that "God is love" (1 John 4:8).

This love of God becomes all the more incomprehensible when we have come to see ourselves as we truly are. Then we feel like crying out with the great hymnist, Charles Wesley:

> And can it be that I should gain
> An interest in the Savior's blood?

Died He for me, who caused His pain?
For me, who Him to death pursued?
Amazing love! how can it be
That Thou, my God shouldst die for me?

How vast! How measureless is this love of God for us!

2. JUST—THEREFORE MUST PUNISH SIN

But the same Bible that tells us that God is loving and gracious also tells us about this same God that He is just and righteous and must punish sin. God tells us, "I am holy and just and righteous. I am of purer eyes than to behold evil. The soul that sinneth it shall die" (Habakkuk 1:13; Ezekiel 18:4). We are looking at man's problems now through the magnifying glass of God—as they are seen by an all-holy, sin-hating God who says He is angry with the wicked every day. Because He is a just Judge, He must punish our sins. His law declares that our sins must be punished: That He will by no means clear the guilty (Exodus 34:7b). He threatens to visit our transgressions with the rod and our iniquities with stripes. There is no doubt about this—**God will certainly punish all sin.**

In our hearts we would view with contempt a judge who is overly lenient with offenders. If one were to "slap the wrist" of his friend who was guilty of a heinous crime, we would cry, "Impeach him. Justice must be preserved." So it is with God. "Shall not the Judge of all the earth do right?" (Genesis 18:25).

I thought God was mostly love.

He is both holy and loving. It is interesting to note that for many centuries before He revealed the real height of His love in Jesus Christ, He established that His throne is a throne of righteousness. He is the thrice-holy One who will deal with sin. Throughout the Old Testament His justice and holiness are clearly manifested.

If He were only justice we would all be condemned. However, He is loving and merciful. **Although He must punish sin, He loves us and therefore doesn't want to punish us.** If He were only loving, there would be no problem. If He were the grandfather figure, as most Americans picture him, He could just take us all to Heaven—all of us: Dillinger and Capone, Nero and Judas, and the devil himself. He would simply say, "Come on, fellows I didn't really mean it when I said, 'But every one shall die for his own iniquity'" (Jeremiah 31:30). *No! Any love dealings that God has with us must be consonant with His justice.*

The teachings that God emphasizes about Himself are: **He is holy and just and must punish sin; but He is also loving and merciful and does not wish to punish us.** In effect, this created a problem which He has solved in Jesus Christ.

D. Jesus Christ

1. WHO HE IS—THE INFINITE GOD-MAN

Now, what is the answer to that problem? God in His infinite wisdom devised a marvelous solution. *Jesus Christ is God's answer to our predicament.* He sent him into the world and, as you know, we celebrate His birth every Christmas.

Rene, I would be interested in your opinion about Christ. Who do you think He is? What kind of a being was He?

Well, He was probably the best man that ever lived. He was a wonderful teacher and I believe He is supposed to have worked miracles.

Fine! Jesus was a great teacher and miracle-worker. And He was good. Anything else?

Well, He was the Son of God.

Yes, He was. But I am also a son of God. Is He any different from me?

I don't really know.

The Bible teaches that Jesus Christ—Jesus of Nazareth, the Carpenter of Galilee—**was and is God!** He is the Creator of the world! He is the One who created the whole universe! Jesus is God Almighty, himself!

This comes as a real surprise to many people. They don't realize that He is God the Son—that God is Father, Son, and Holy Spirit, and that the Trinity is one God. Yet we sing this truth every Sunday morning in the Doxology: "Praise God from whom all blessings flow . . . praise Father, Son and Holy Ghost." Or, as the Westminster Confession puts it, "In the unity of the Godhead, there be three Persons of one substance, power and eternity."

2. WHAT HE DID—PAID FOR OUR SINS AND PURCHASED HEAVEN FOR US, WHICH HE OFFERS AS A GIFT God the Son became man! This is what we mean by incarnation. This is what we celebrate at Christmas. God became man for a grand and noble purpose. He left His home in glory and was born in the filth of a stable. He lived a perfect and spotless life. He taught the world's greatest teachings! He worked its mightiest deeds. Finally He came to the end of His life—to **that hour for which He had come into the world.** In that hour we see the **great transaction** about which the whole Bible is written—the great transaction which is the central fact of the Christian religion.

What is it?

Let's imagine this book in my right hand is a minutely detailed account of my life. It includes everything I have ever done. Every word I have ever spoken, every thought that ever crossed my mind. Someday, the Bible says, the books are going to be opened and everything about our lives will be brought to light. "The hidden things of darkness will be made manifest. That which has been whispered in the ear will be shouted from the housetop" (1 Corinthians 4:5; Matthew 10:27, paraphrased). Everyone will know all about us—all we've thought or done; all our hidden motives; all the sins—most of which we have forgotten. How many thoughts can you remember from twenty years ago?

None!

(The multitude of our sins)
Psychologists tell us 10,000 thoughts go through the human mind in one day. That's 3,500,000 per year! To remember only 1 percent from 20 years ago you would have to come up with 35,000. Someone has well said that a clear conscience is quite often the result of a poor memory.

If we must give an account of every idle word, how many would that be? We speak millions every year. Who knows? God does! They are all written down in His book. And one day the books will be opened. I am utterly convinced of one thing: that **if any man is judged according to the things recorded in the book of His life, he will be condemned.** I am certain that this is true of my own life.

Here then (hold up the book) is the problem—my sin. God loves me (point at fingers of right hand) but He hates my sin (point at book) and must punish it.

To solve this problem He sent His beloved Son into the world (lift up left hand parallel to right hand). The Scripture says, "All we like sheep have gone astray; we have turned everyone to his own way; and the LORD hath laid on him the iniquity of us all" (Isaiah 53:6). (As you say the words "laid on him," transfer the book in one distinct motion from the right to the left hand and leave it there.) God has laid to the account of Christ all of my sin and guilt. All of my sin which

God hates has been placed on His beloved Son. Christ bore our sin in His own body on the tree (1 Peter 2:24).

Then I read something which, as a parent, astounded me. It was that Christ was "smitten of God and afflicted. It pleased the LORD to bruise him; he hath put him to grief" (Isaiah 53:4b, 10a). What does it mean to suffer infinitely? Whatever that means, I realized that Christ had done that for me.

> We may not know, we cannot tell
> What pains He had to bear,
> But we believe it was for us
> He hung and suffered there.

(It is finished)
On the Cross Jesus endured the wrath of God, the infinite wrath of God. Even the sun hid its face as the God-man descended into Hell for us. Finally, *when the last sin had been paid for, Jesus said, "It is finished!"* (John 19:30).

This is an interesting word in the original text. It is *"Tetelestai,"* a commercial word which means "It is paid; the debt is paid." "The wages of sin is death" (Romans 6:23), or the wrath of God. Jesus said, *"Tetelestai. It is paid!"* Further, He said, "In my Father's house are many mansions. If it were not so I would have told you. I go to prepare a place for you" (John 14:2). *"Tetelestai."* It is paid. It is purchased. With His own passion on the Cross, Jesus secured a place in Heaven for His own people. Christ then rose triumphantly from the grave.

We do not worship a dead Christ, but a living, glorious Savior. The most important fact in the history of mankind is that **Jesus Christ rose from the dead** and is the **Lord** of life. Not only is this the most important fact, beside which all others pale into insignificance, but also it is the **best-attested fact of human history.** For almost six weeks, Christ showed himself alive to hundreds of people after His passion by many infallible proofs.

For centuries men have tried to disprove the Resurrection of Christ. But every effort of the skeptic has been discredited by another skeptic until the entire endeavor lies in a heap of rubble before the irrefutable fact of the empty tomb. Through His incredible victory over death He now offers us life everlasting.

(The gift of God)
Most of my life I thought as you. If ever I was to go and dwell in Heaven, I would have to deserve it. My life would have to be good enough. In other words, I would have to pay an admission price of good works to enter the door of Heaven. I was amazed to learn that it's not so!

I don't have to pay for it. Jesus has already paid for it and I can have eternal life as a gift. Listen: "The wages of sin is death but the gift of God is eternal life through Jesus Christ our Lord" (Romans 6:23). That is the Gospel, the Good News of the Christian faith: **God offers Heaven to us as a gift.** Heaven is free to us because it was paid for by Christ. The Gospel is not "do," but it is "done." Jesus paid it all.

The Bible says, "By *grace* are ye saved . . . not of works lest any man should boast" (Ephesians 2:8, 9). What is the meaning of grace? The Chaplain to the Queen of England at a meeting of world leaders once gave this acrostic: G-R-A-C-E: God's Riches At Christ's Expense. God's riches: forgiveness, Heaven, eternal life, peace, joy, and a sense of the love of God—**at Christ's expense.** The expense of the scourge, Gethsemane, the mocking, the plucking of His beard, the crown of thorns, the nailing of His hands, the piercing of His side, the wrath of God, and Hell itself. "Jesus paid it all. All to Him I owe." He offers us eternal life as a gift by grace.

Who receives this gift? Everybody? No. The Bible says that few find the way to life and that many go to destruction.
How then can we have this gift?

E. Faith

This brings us to the fifth and last thing we need to understand: **We receive the gift of God by faith.** The Bible says, "By grace are ye saved *through faith*" (Ephesians 2:8).

Faith is the key that opens the door to Heaven. You know, you could have a key ring with a lot of keys on it, like this; they all look somewhat alike. But I'll tell you something. If you go to the front door of my home, you could try all of these keys except the right one, and they would not open that door. The right key to Heaven is called **faith, saving faith.** That is what will open the door to Heaven. There is nothing else in the world that will open that door.

1. WHAT IT IS NOT—MERE INTELLECTUAL ASSENT

Let me tell you what saving faith is not. Many people mistake two things for saving faith. If you were to look at these keys you would find that several of them look very similar. In fact, you might not be able at first glance to tell which was which. So it is with faith.

Now, **the first thing that people mistake for saving faith is this: an intellectual assent to certain historical facts.** You believe in God, don't you?

Yes, I always have.

You always have believed in God. So have I. But that type of belief is not what the Bible means by saving faith. I believed in God all my life but for about twenty-five years I was not truly saved.

The Bible says the devil believes in God. Did you know that? The Bible says, "Thou believes that there is one God; thou doest well, the devils also believe, and tremble" (James 2:19). **So believing in God is not what the Bible means by saving faith.** The demons in the Gadarene demoniac said, "What have we to do with thee, Jesus, thou Son of God? Are thou come hither to torment us before the time?" Even the demons believe in the deity of Christ! But they evidently weren't saved! That's one thing people mistake for saving faith; an intellectual assent to the historicity of Christ, but that's not what the Bible means by faith.

   . . . *(nor temporal faith)*

Let me give you one other thing that people mistake for saving faith. You have prayed to God many times, haven't you?

Oh, every day.

You've had problems that you've committed to the Lord, right? You've trusted him for some things.

Oh, yes. I couldn't have gotten through life without prayer.

Rene, for example, what did you trust Him for?

Well, when my children were sick, when our finances were low and our business was bad—why, I've always prayed to the Lord for those things.

You see, you had more than intellectual assent. You have actually trusted Him for some things, right?

Yes.

Your children were sick. Your financial situation and your business were bad. I could probably add other things. You probably trusted Him for decisions which you had to make; you probably even prayed that He would keep you safe while you traveled on a long trip. Perhaps you had an operation. You prayed to Him to bring you through that safely. Things like this.

Yes.

Now, all of these are good and you should trust in the Lord for all these things. But, you see, **even this is not saving faith.** We might say that when you trusted in the Lord for your finances—you had a financial-faith. You trusted in the Lord to take care of your family—you could call that family-faith. You trusted in the Lord to help you with your decisions—you might call that deciding-faith. On trips you had traveling-faith.

There is one element all these things have in common. They are temporal, aren't they? They are all the things of this life, things of this world that shall pass away. Now many people, I find, trust the Lord for all these temporal matters. But **saving faith is trusting Christ to save you**—to save you eternally.

2. WHAT IT IS—TRUSTING IN JESUS CHRIST ALONE FOR SALVATION

I never thought of it that way.

Why, neither had I. You see, I trusted the Lord for this, and that, and for the other, but to get right down to what I was trusting in for eternal salvation—I was trusting in myself. I tried to live a good life. I tried to keep the Ten Commandments. I tried to live by the Golden Rule. *I, I, I, I*—you see? It was "I!"

What did I ask you—"What are you trusting in for eternal life? What are you trusting in to get into Heaven?" Do you remember what you said? "I try to do the best I can. I try to live a good life according to the Golden Rule. I try to do all these things." Do you see?

Saving faith is trusting Jesus Christ *alone* for our salvation. It means resting upon Christ alone and what He has done rather than upon what I have done to get me into Heaven. As the Scripture says, "For God so loved the world that He gave his only begotten Son that whosoever believeth in him should not perish but have eternal life" (John 3:16).

This is illustrated very clearly in the life of John Wesley who started the Methodist Church. He went to Oxford Seminary for five years and then became a minister of the Church of England where he served for about ten years. Toward the end of this time he became a missionary from England to Georgia, in approximately 1735.

All of his life he had been quite a failure in his ministry though he was, as we would count men, very pious. He got up at four o'clock in the morning and prayed for two hours. He would then read the Bible for an hour before going to jails, prisons, and hospitals to minister to all manner of people. He would teach, and pray, and help others until late at night. He did this for years. In fact, the Methodist Church gets its name from the methodical life of piety that Wesley and his friends lived.

(Wesley's experience)

On the way back from America there was a great storm at sea. The little ship in which they were sailing was about to sink. Huge waves broke over the ship deck and the wind shredded the sails. Wesley feared he was going to die that hour and he was terrified. He had no assurance of what would happen to him when he died. Despite all of his efforts to be good, death now for him was a big, black, fearful question mark.

On the other side of the ship was a group of men who were singing hymns. He asked them, "How can you sing when this very night you are going to die?" They replied, "If this ship goes down we will go up to be with the Lord forever."

Wesley went away shaking his head, thinking to himself, "How can they know that? What more have they done than I have done?" Then he added, "I came to convert the heathen, ah, but who shall convert me?"

In the providence of God, the ship made it back to England. Wesley went to London and found his way to

Aldersgate Street and a small chapel. There he heard a man reading a sermon which had been written two centuries earlier by Martin Luther, entitled "Luther's Preface to the Book of Romans." This sermon described what **real faith** was. It is **trusting Jesus Christ only for salvation—and not in our own good works.**

Wesley suddenly realized that he had been on the wrong road all his life. That night he wrote these words in his journal: "About a quarter before nine, while he was describing the change which God works in the heart through faith in Christ, I felt my heart strangely warmed. I felt I did trust in Christ, Christ alone, for salvation; and an assurance was given me that He had taken away my sins, even mine, and saved me from the law of sin and death."

There it is. That is saving faith. **Repenting of his sins**, he trusted in Jesus Christ alone for salvation. Now, would you say that Wesley had not believed in Jesus Christ before this night? Of course, he had. He was a biblical scholar and had studied about Christ in English, and Latin, and Greek and Hebrew. He had believed in Christ in all these languages. But he trusted in John Wesley for his salvation.

After this he became the greatest preacher of the eighteenth century. But it all began when he put his trust in Jesus Christ alone for his salvation and received him as his Lord.

(Resting on Christ)
Let me illustrate. You see this chair here? A lovely chair, isn't it?

Yes.

You believe that chair exists?

Yes.

Do you believe that it would hold you up?

Yes.

But, you see, it's not holding you up for a very simple reason: you're not sitting on it. That is the way I was with Christ. I believed Jesus existed. I believed He was divine. I trusted him for finances and for health, as you have done too. But, you see, saving faith is trusting in Christ for my salvation. Some people will trust the Lord for their protection when they go out at night. They wouldn't think of putting out the garbage at night without trusting the Lord to take care of them. But as far as their eternal welfare is concerned, they are trusting in their own efforts because they have never understood what the Bible teaches.

Saving faith is putting our trust in Jesus Christ alone for eternal life. Years ago I **repented of my sins** and transferred my trust from myself to Jesus Christ; from what I had been doing for God to what He has done for me on the Cross. By a simple act of faith I transferred my trust from what I had done to what Christ had done for me. Just as I am now transferring my trust from this chair that I have been resting on (representing my good works) to this one representing Christ. Now I'm resting on only one thing: that is, Jesus Christ. No longer am I trusting what I have done; rather, I trust what He has done for me.

We've sung this in many hymns, such as, "On Christ the solid rock I stand,/All other ground is sinking sand" . . . "Nothing in my hands I bring/[**good works, prayers, church-going, loving my neighbor—nothing in my hands**], Simply to the cross I cling." Did you ever sing this?

Just as I am without one plea,
(Just as I am—a sinner, unworthy, undeserving,
   without one plea)
Except Thy blood was shed for me,
And that Thou bid'st me come to Thee,
O Lamb of God, I come, I come.

How amazing is the love of Christ that He is willing to

receive us just as we are and to cleanse us, forgive us, and give us eternal life.

(Right actions, wrong motives)
Let's say that this pen in my right hand represents eternal life. There are only two relationships you can have to it. Either you have it, as this hand does, or you haven't, as my left hand doesn't. Now if you don't have it and you believe it exists, you are going to want to get it. So you do the best you can; you love your neighbor, go to church, read the Bible, pray, give money, and then you say, "Lord, here are all the things I've done. I hope I've done enough to get into Heaven."

But you see, in this case it becomes evident that everything you've done has been for the motive of *getting* eternal life. There is this *selfish motive* underlying everything and so you couldn't possibly get it.

Furthermore, the problem is something like that old song: "Sixteen tons and what do you get?/ Another day older and deeper in debt." Sixteen conscious hours and what do we get, another day older and deeper in God's debt because every day we sin.

We could never earn eternal life. The Bible says that God came to earth and on the Cross in the Person of His Son He paid for eternal life—an infinite price. By His graciousness He offers it to us freely as a gift. (Move pen in right hand over to the left hand.) It is received by faith: "Faith is the hand of a beggar receiving the gift of a king." (Reach out with left hand and accept the pen from the right hand.)

This beggar reached out an unclean hand over twenty years ago and received the gift of eternal life. I didn't deserve it then and I don't deserve it now—nor will I ever deserve it. But I have it! By grace!

(The right motive for living a godly life)
Why, then, should I try to live a good life? The reason for living a godly life is gratitude. That's the motive for godly

living. I'm not trying to gain something I don't have by my efforts to be good; rather, I'm saying "thank you" for the gift of eternal life that Christ has given me.

A former president of Princeton put it this way in a book. He said that as a young man he accepted Christ and the gift of eternal life. All the rest of his life was simply a P.S. to that day, saying, "Thank You, Lord, for what you gave to me then." The motive for all is gratitude for the gift of eternal life. "The love of Christ constraineth us" (2 Corinthians 5:14).

III. THE COMMITMENT

A. The qualifying question

Rene, **does that make sense to you?**

Oh, yes, that's beautiful!

B. The commitment question

Rene, you have just heard the greatest story ever told, about the greatest offer ever made by Jesus Christ, the greatest person who ever lived. It's called the "Good News," the Gospel of Jesus Christ.

Now, Rene, the question God is asking you is simply this: **Do you want to receive this gift of eternal life?** This gift that the Son of God left His throne and went to die on the Cross to procure for you—would you like to receive it?

Oh, yes, I would.

C. The clarification of commitment

(Transfer your trust?)
Wonderful! Let me clarify just what this involves. It means, first of all, that you are going to transfer your trust, that is, your hope of eternal life from what you have been doing to

what Jesus Christ has done for you on the Cross. He takes our sin and we receive His righteousness. This means that though we have failed to keep God's commandments and to live consistently by the Golden Rule, Christ perfectly obeyed all the laws of God. He has lived the perfect life.

(Receive the righteousness of Christ?)
That perfect life of Christ is imputed to us the moment we believe. It is reckoned to our account—placed to our account—so that in the sight of God we are then accounted as perfect. It is as though the spotless white robe of Christ's perfect character and obedience were placed upon us, and in that robe we stand faultless before God. Only in this way can we ever acquire that perfect standing that God requires of us. **Do you want to stop trusting in Rene and start trusting in Christ?**

Yes, I do.

(Receive the resurrected and living Christ?)
You receive eternal life by receiving the Person of Jesus Christ. "He came unto his own and his own received him not. But as many as received him, to them gave he the power to become the sons of God" (John 1:11-12). We can receive and know the most exciting person in the history of the world because He is alive!

(Receive Jesus Christ into your life as Savior?)
Christ is alive! He says, "Behold, I stand at the door, and knock: [at the door of your life] if any one hear my voice, and open the door, I will come in to him, and will sup with him, and he with me." This means that He will have intimate communion daily in your life. He will come in to forgive you and to cleanse you and to give you eternal life. He will come into your life and make you **His child** and an **heir** of an eternal fortune **if you receive Him.** Rene, **would you like to ask Jesus Christ to come into your life as your Savior today?**

Oh, yes.

(Receive Jesus Christ into your life as Lord?)
Let me say one thing. I'll say it very plainly. When Christ comes into a life as Savior. He comes to do something for you: to forgive you and give you eternal life. But, also He comes as Lord. He comes as Master and King. He comes to demand something of you. He says there is a throne room in your heart and that throne is rightly His. He made you. He redeemed you. He bought you. He says that He wants to take His rightful place on the throne of your life. **Are you willing to yield your life, to surrender your life, to Him, out of gratitude for the gift of eternal life?**

Repentance is a complete change of mind about life and death.

Yes, I would like to.

(Repent of your sins?)
He also commands us to repent of our sins. **Are you willing to repent of your sins and follow Him?** That means a willingness to turn from what you have been doing that is not pleasing to Him and follow Him as He reveals His will to you in His Word. Repentance is a complete change of mind about life and death, and about God and this world. It is wrought by His Spirit working within us and it leads inevitably to a transformed life.

Rene, are you willing to repent of your sins and become a responsible member of God's forever family and follow Him and serve Him as a member of His body, the Church?

Yes, I am.

D. The Prayer of commitment

All right, Rene. **The Lord is here right now.** We can go to Him now in prayer and we can tell Him that you want to **cease trusting in your own strivings,** and you want to **put your trust in Christ** the Lord for your salvation and receive Him as your personal Savior. Is this truly what you want?

Yes.

All right. May I point out to you, Rene, that the Lord is **looking at your heart more than He is listening to your lips.** He says, "Ye shall seek me and find me, when ye shall search for me with all your heart" (Jeremiah 19:13). If this is really what you mean, then the Lord will hear your prayer and grant you eternal life. Let us pray.

(Preparatory prayer)
Father, I pray that Thou would grant to Rene the gift of eternal life. May Thy **Holy Spirit** draw her unto Thyself. Grant her faith to believe Thy promises. Grant her **repentance** to turn from her sins. **Reveal unto her Christ crucified today.**

(Prayer together)
(Heads still bowed.) Rene, the Lord has said, "Where two or three are gathered together in my name, there am I in the midst of them (Matt. 18:20). He is right here. You are not talking to me now but to Him. If you really want eternal life, will you say to Him aloud:

Lord Jesus, I want you to come in and take over my life right now. (She repeats each phrase.) I am a sinner. I have been trusting in myself and my own good works. But now I place my trust in You. I accept You as my own personal Savior. I believe You died for me. I receive You as **Lord and Master** of my life. Help me to turn from my sins and to follow You. I accept the free gift of eternal life. I am not worthy of it, but I thank you for it. Amen.

(Continuing in prayer with heads bowed.)

(Assurance of pardon)
Father, you have heard the prayer Rene prayed, and I ask that in this quiet moment Thy **Holy Spirit** will grant unto her the assurance of life eternal; grant unto her the certainty that her sins are forgiven. Grant that she may hear in the depths of her soul Thy voice saying, "Thy sins be forgiven thee. Go in peace." Grant, O Christ, that she may hear Thy voice saying, "As far as the east is from the west, so far have I put thy sins from thee, never to remember them against thee anymore. He that believeth on me shall not come into condemnation. He that trusteth in me is passed from death unto life. He that believeth on me shall never perish but has everlasting life (paraphrased from Psalm 103:12; John 3:18; 5:24; 3:16). In Jesus' name, we pray. Amen.

E. The assurance of salvation

Rene, you have just prayed the most important prayer you have ever prayed in your life. I want you to see now what Christ says about what you have just done. In **John 6:47** the Lord says something very significant. I would like you to read this. "Verily, verily, I say unto you, he that believeth on me hath everlasting life." (Have her read aloud.)

All right, Rene, in our prayer you didn't hear any angel choirs; or see any visions. However, by a simple act of faith you have placed your trust in Jesus Christ for your salvation. Is that correct?

Yes, it is.

In whom are you now trusting, Rene, for your salvation?

Jesus Christ.

He says, "he that believeth," that is, he that trusteth "in me has eternal life"—that doesn't mean an intellectual assent, for you have believed in Christ all your life in that way. This doesn't mean trusting Him for temporal affairs. You've done that all your life. **Saving faith means trusting Christ alone for eternal salvation.** Is this what you have done today?

Yes.

Jesus says that the person who does that has everlasting life. Do you believe Him?

Yes, I do.

Rene, if you should die in your sleep tonight, where would you wake up?

In Heaven.

And if God asked why you should be in Heaven, what would you say?

I am trusting Christ.

The angels are rejoicing! God said it. That settles it. Rene, if you meant in your heart what you just said with your lips, then you have the promise of Christ that He has forgiven your sins, adopted you into His family, and given you eternal life. Praise the Lord! We may rejoice in it. **Welcome, Rene, to the family of God.**

TRUTH: STRANGER THAN FICTION

*Go out into the highways and hedges,
and compel them to come in, that
my house may be filled.*
—LUKE 14:23

After two or three hours of on-the-job training, all Evangelism Explosion teams return to the church to report on their experiences so that all may share, for purposes of inspiration or instruction, the best and the worst of what they have encountered. While the great majority of visits are quite similar in nature, there have been some reports of not-so-usual confrontations—and a few in the believe-it-or-not category.

The procedure to be kept in mind is that a typical team of three persons—an experienced trainer and two trainees—is calling on a prospect who may have been attending church services. In such a situation, the outcome may be more predictable than when the prospect has not been "softened up" in advance by hearing the Word of God from the pulpit. After the trainer has established a relaxed conversation and a receptive frame of mind, he or she eases into the presentation of the Gospel with the two diagnostic questions: (1) Have you come to a place in your spiritual life where you know for certain that if you were to die today you would go to Heaven? (2) Suppose that you were to die tonight and stand before God and He were to say to you, "Why should I let you into My Heaven?"—what would you say?

Then, after careful explanation of the Gospel in its five phases (grace, man, God, Christ, faith), the trainer presses for commitment and the assurance of salvation. As trainees mature, of course, they are given the opportunity to give part or perhaps all of the Gospel presentation.

If that is what goes on during a typical E.E. contact, how could the results be anything memorable or even out of the ordinary? Let's just look at a few of the case histories reported at Coral Ridge Church alone:

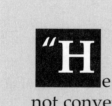

"He was not converted," the pastor told the workers, "but I was."

ITEM: At one report session, a visiting pastor who was the secretary of evangelism for an entire denomination announced that the team he had gone out with had failed to convince the prospect. "He was not converted," the pastor told the assembled workers, "but I was." Born again during the visit, he returned to his church and denomination with that same confession. More than a dozen cases involving the conversions of pastors at E.E. clinics have been reported.

ITEM: A trainee who had not yet memorized the presentation received a wrong-number call on her home telephone, began to read the outline directly from her E.E. workbook to the party on the other end of the line, and led the person to Christ right there on the telephone.

ITEM: At the conclusion of each clinic, the participants are asked to witness to someone within twenty-four hours to confirm to themselves what they have learned. One trainee, who was a pastor, decided that the person sitting next to him on the plane was a likely prospect. The friendly conversation was easy to get into; the shift into spiritual matters received a warm response; and just as the pastor got ready to pop the first diagnostic question, 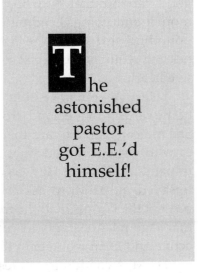 his intended target looked him in the eye and asked, "Have you come to the place in your spiritual life where you know for certain that if you were to die today you would go to Heaven?" The astonished pastor, thinking he was about to E.E. his first prospect, got E.E.'d himself.

ITEM: A converted Jewish woman who worked in E.E. headquarters in the Knox Center dialed the number of a Jewish unbeliever with whom she had previously made contact. He listened to her testimony but hung up without making any commitment. About ten minutes later he called back. "I was in the very process," he told her, "of committing a grossly immoral act. Your telephone call prevented my carrying through with it. I believe the Lord had you call me at that moment for a purpose." He responded to the Gospel and became a Christian.

ITEM: An experienced trainer got into a casual conversation with another woman while both were standing in waist-deep water at the beach. The surf was heavy enough to lift both of them off their feet and drop them down again with every wave, but the trainer began her Gospel presentation under those circumstances in order not to break the good rapport that had been established and to keep the momentum going. Leading that person to salvation in the pounding surf made the trainer realize that effective witnessing requires no special setting or props but only a receptive heart.

ITEM: A woman visiting Coral Ridge Church signed one of the cards provided and dropped it into the collection plate. She indicated on the card that she needed help. An E.E. trainer who visited learned right away that the problem was an impending divorce. He was able to get the attention of the unsaved husband, to ask the diagnostic questions, and to present the Gospel, and the man was dramatically saved, the marriage relationship was restored, and the couple became active and loyal workers in the church.

ITEM: A condominium resident watched the Coral Ridge service on television. When the logo showing the church building came on, the man thought, "I've seen that church somewhere," walked out on his balcony, and looked across Federal Highway. Sure enough, there it was. Later, an E.E. team called on him and invited him to accept Jesus as his Savior. He decided he ought to get a Bible, so he went down the street a few blocks to the Christian Bookstore, which happened to be operated by a Coral Ridge Presbyterian Church elder and his wife, who urged the man to visit the Greenhouse—another lay outreach program established by yet another elder and his wife. First attracted to the church via a far-reaching satellite television broadcast, the man was brought into it by a veritable net of providential contacts. He became a Christian, a church member, and a deacon.

ITEM: A New Englander visiting in Fort Lauderdale responded to an E.E. visit with a profession of faith in Christ. She returned to the Northeast where, for five years, she had no real association with Christian influences. She then moved to

Florida, and those on the E.E. team who had made the contact five years before were delighted to find that she had nevertheless grown spiritually during her absence and was ready to take her place as a mature Christian church leader.

ITEM: A trainer, waiting in a hospital for her father to be returned from surgery, encountered another patient in his mid-eighties. She talked to him about his spiritual condition and discovered that he lacked assurance of his salvation. Leading with the diagnostic questions, she brought the old man to a full and complete commitment. Sharing the hospital room with her father, the elderly gentleman shouted like a child enjoying his first Christmas. "I'm going to Heaven!" he told anybody who would listen. He never left the hospital alive.

ITEM: A veteran trainer was witnessing to a group of rather worldly types (a questionnaire approach is used in such instances where regular E.E. appointments have not been made). The entire group showed little interest in the presentation of the Gospel that follows up the questionnaire and moved on down the beach. The trainer happened to have a very strong voice which carried far enough for a lone "hippie" to eavesdrop on the entire interview. The young man immediately walked over to the trainer as the others left and said, "I want to hear more." The result was a glorious conversion and consequent change of lifestyle for a dropout from society.

ITEM: A pastor attending one of the clinics (apparently against his will) displayed an openly hostile attitude at the kickoff banquet and at the first all-day session of instruction. Nevertheless, he went out that evening with the team to which he was assigned and saw the trainer convincingly win two souls to the Lord. He was so affected by the experience that he called the clinic director for a private appointment in his office the following day. The pastor got on his knees and poured out all the bitterness of spirit that was locked up inside, confessing that he had been a preacher for seventeen years without really knowing Christ. As a new man in Christ, he repeated his confession to the fully assembled clinic and returned to his own Methodist church to report the experience to his bishop. The denominational publication later carried an article about the pastor and his "John Wesley experience at the E.E. clinic at Coral Ridge."

ITEM: A pretty young trainee was getting into her car at a shopping mall when a man suddenly appeared, knife in hand, and pushed her into the car ahead of him, threatening her not to resist. He drove her car out onto the street and in a direction leading out of the city while she sat on the passenger side in near panic. Seeing her Bible on the dashboard, she asked her sullen captor if she might read; he didn't object, and she began reading aloud from the Gospel. Then she began to go through the E.E. presentation from the very beginning, asking questions and supplying imaginary answers as if she were reciting a monologue. Strangely enough, her kidnapper remained silent and appeared to be listening intently. As she proceeded through the diagnostic questions, he seemed to melt and, almost in tears, he asked her forgiveness for what he was doing. She persuaded him to turn the car around and head for her local church. There she introduced her assailant to her pastor, who reinforced her testimony, and the man surrendered his life completely to the Lord. No charges were pressed, and the E.E. trainer rejoiced that both her life and his soul had been saved by the hearing of the Gospel.

ITEM: An elderly woman who was extremely ill was called upon by a team who rang the doorbell and were about to leave when they heard a faint "wait a minute" from inside the house. The team had another fifteen-minute wait while she struggled to get herself from bed to wheelchair and to the door. Finally they were admitted to the house and found her so weak that she had to be lifted back into the bed. She encouraged her visitors to go ahead with the Gospel presentation, and to their amazement the elderly woman visibly grew stronger as she listened intently to everything that was said. By the time the prayer of commitment was reached, the sick woman was able to proclaim the assurance of her salvation in a firm voice. Although death came within a few weeks, relatives reported that she was more vibrant and alert than she had been for many months.

ITEM: (Buckle your seat belts for this one.) As an E.E. team left a small efficiency apartment where, for an hour and a half, they had led a young woman to a profession of faith, the trainee said excitedly to her trainer: "Did you see them?"

"See what?"

"The man's shoes under the chair?"

"No, I was too busy to notice."

"You didn't see the pair of trousers over the top of the chair?"

"No."

"And didn't you hear the closet door crack open three or four times while we were there?"

"No, I was concentrating on the presentation."

What the trainer had missed and the trainee had detected was an unfolding plot that sounds like a theme out of Chaucer or Boccaccio. When the team knocked on the door, the young woman's gentleman caller had jumped hastily into the closet, minus his shoes and pants, and had been forced to stay there for an hour and a half to avoid an even more embarrassing predicament. And, to make matters worse, when he finally was able to leave his uncomfortable hiding place, he had a new, born-again Christian to deal with. You might say the E.E. team rained on his parade.

ITEM: Back on the beach, a teenage girl fell into a drunken sleep and awoke about four o'clock in the morning to sense a man crouched over her. She screamed, managed to escape and, realizing she needed help, put in a call to Coral Ridge Presbyterian Church. The minister of evangelism, who directs the E.E. training clinics, listened to the woeful tale of an alcoholic since the age of fourteen and the mother of an illegitimate child. After making contact with her at a beachfront restaurant where she worked, he had her come to his office at the church. There, as she heard the Gospel explained, she wept profusely, shook violently as if she, like Mary Magdalene, was being torn by the departure of demons, and had a dramatic, scriptural conversion. She began a totally new kind of life, involving herself in the church outreach programs and never taking another drink of alcohol. She became the housemother, eventually, at the church's home for unwed mothers; and as an E.E. trainer herself later on, her testimony was understandably effective in reaching many a lost young woman in the same terrible circumstances as those from which she had been delivered.

ITEM: A trainee who had not yet left the church prayer group was very eager to go out with a team rather than to remain behind praying for those who were out making contacts. When the call came for volunteers to join an incomplete team, he wanted to speak up, but felt utterly powerless to do so. A woman at the end of the row volunteered to go, leaving the trainee most unhappy with himself for not visiting prospects when he had the chance. His discontent was heightened when he learned at the report-back session later that two persons had been led to Christ by that team. Then it was announced that one of those two was an alcoholic and that he had responded only because the woman volunteer who went along was herself a former alcoholic. The trainee then realized that he had been restrained from making that particular visit, just as Paul was forbidden to go into Bithynia by the Holy Spirit because there was a more pressing work of salvation that needed to be accomplished.

ITEM: A woman trainer was assigned two ministers at a clinic. One was extremely pleasant; the other, a "cold fish." She dreaded working with the individual, but went ahead with the visit, pausing to pray in her car with the two pastors that somehow the love of Christ would be shown in their experience with the prospect. As she presented the Gospel, the trio were witnesses to a beautiful and impressive conversion. Afterward, the sour colleague was like a different person. "I was really turned off by this program," he confessed, "and I thought it was a bunch of canned garbage until I saw what happened. Truly the love of Christ did manifest itself, and I saw His power transform that person's life tonight." He returned to his church in Canada and built a lively E.E. program there.

ITEM: Visiting a Kentucky couple in their condo, the team was told enthusiastically of a year of intensive Bible study the couple had just completed with their pastor. But when the first diagnostic question was asked, "Do you know for certain that, if you died tonight, you would go to Heaven?" it was embarrassingly clear that neither one had the faintest idea that anyone could know such a thing—despite a year of "in-depth" Bible study. Seeing they had missed the whole point of the scriptural message, both made full professions of faith in Christ.

ITEM: During a questionnaire approach to a pair of young people in a shopping center, the two seemed interested and responsive until the trainer began the presentation of the Gospel. Then one, who apparently spoke for both, practically screamed, "Oh, you sound just like my mother!" With that, the pair backed away and actually broke into a full run to "split the scene." It was a saddening experience for the interviewer until his trainee saw a young man she knew in the same shopping center and was successful in winning him to the Lord.

All the foregoing examples occurred in the vicinity of the local church. But on the international fronts of this globe-circling outreach, events of a more spectacular nature are reported at clinics conducted by E.E. International.

ITEM: A charter member of Coral Ridge Presbyterian Church considered herself too shy to take part in the budding program, but finally decided that her shyness was really inverted pride—simply an over-concern for what other people would think of her. She didn't know what to do about shyness, but she did know what to do about pride. She confessed it, repented of it, and went through the E.E. course, later becoming a trainer. It happened that the very first Australian minister ever to come to a Coral Ridge clinic was sent out with her team. After she taught him how to train others, he returned to his pastorale, an Anglican church near Sydney, and began teaching the E.E. program to his parishioners. After training about eighty people, he conducted the first clinic on that continent. With representatives from more than forty churches attending, E.E. spread throughout Australia and from there to Tasmania, New Zealand, New Guinea, Indonesia, Fiji, the Solomon Islands, and many other parts of Oceania. All this was the result of one person overcoming her shyness and discovering not only how to witness, but also how to train a soul-winner. Her story demonstrates the multiplication factor that distinguishes E.E. from most other evangelization programs.

ITEM: From far-off Kenya came a Christian minister who had been converted from his tribe's pagan beliefs by a missionary. He was from a desperately poor area and had arranged a special purchase of a pair of shoes, in order to make the trip to Fort Lauderdale to attend the E.E. clinic. He completed the training, and with great enthusiasm, he returned to his native land. It was time for the annual fair in Mombasa. He set up his own booth; what he had to display and give away was the Gospel. He gave the E.E. presentation to anyone in the milling crowd who would stop and listen. His excitement was so contagious that before the fair was ended he had personally led about one hundred fifty souls to Christ at his one-man booth. A year later he had four trainees to share the booth with him, and literally hundreds of new converts were brought into the kingdom. The same man later worked with an E.E. team made up of Southern Baptists who had come to Kenya from the state of Texas. A major revival erupted and mass conversions were reported in the thousands.

ITEM: In Manila, E.E. spread to one hundred eighty churches over five years. A young woman, who worked as a developmental specialist in a large office building, received the training at her church. Held to a very rigid work schedule, she began to use her lunch hour each day as an opportunity to witness to one other person. Over a period of time she was able to train other Christians who worked in the same building to do on-the-job soul-winning. She experienced the satisfaction of seeing twenty-nine professional people saved in one month. The testimony of this faithful Filipino disciple: "I tell the Lord, 'God, I can die now. I have reached the highest peak of my Christian life.'"

BUILDING
FOR
ETERNITY

Through wisdom is an house builded . . .
and by knowledge shall the chambers be filled.
—PROVERBS 24:3-4

The resounding explosion on Commercial Boulevard was making one thing clear to Jim Kennedy: his church, after just a few years at its new dwelling place, was facing another move.

This time, to sidestep the patch-and-add-on approach of church construction, planning began a full eight years before the target date in 1973. A site search led to the selection of ten choice acres of land facing east on thriving Federal Highway, one of the principal arteries of Fort Lauderdale. The location, close to midpoint on a north-south axis between the first and second church homes and about half a mile east, was comfortably within the boundaries of the old familiar neighborhood.

A very real difference was that the new thoroughfare, with its upscale shopping and professional buildings that included some of the city's more impressive glass-sheathed towers, was definitely a more prestigious address for a growing church. But Jim was not interested in prestige; the exposure on Federal Highway (US 1) meant an opportunity to reach more people for Christ. Nevertheless, Billy Graham wrote Jim shortly before the dedication, "What a gorgeous and glorious church you are going to have—physically and spiritually."

The purchase price for the new real estate, $676 thousand was in itself a bold statement of just how far this fledgling church had come in the mere eight years between 1959 and 1967. The statement was punctuated in 1971 with an Easter Sunday groundbreaking ceremony on Federal and by the purchase of an additional five acres adjoining the site on the north. After all, twenty-five hundred seats, as compared with eight hundred maximum at the Commercial Boulevard quarters, would mean three times as many cars needing parking spaces.

A structure of classic proportions would require, first of all, the services of an architect of recognized ability and stature. The newly-appointed building committee needed to consult only briefly before engaging Harold Wagoner of Philadelphia. He had designed the stately National Presbyterian Church in the high visibility setting of Washington, D.C. Wagoner was engaged to draw the plans for a worship center that was to become one of the most beautiful and most inspiring church facilities in the country.

What exactly does a top-rated architect offer in the way of a monumental-class building at a predetermined cost estimate of $4.5 million. Let's begin with one of the tallest church towers in the United States at 303 feet. This hollow, poured concrete form, thirty stories high, became Florida's third high-altitude marker between Cape Canaveral and Miami. The top ninety feet consist of a fourteen-ton stainless steel spire and Cross, topped by an aircraft beacon known to boaters and fishermen far out at sea as "the mariner's light."

Combining utility with its awesome beauty, the spire houses the transmitting antenna for an FM stereo radio sta-

It became Florida's third high-altitude marker between Cape Canaveral and Miami.

tion, WAFG, which broadcasts religious programming around the clock. At the top of the tower, a carillon sends out the familiar melodies of faith on Flemish bells and a harp-celeste. From the spire down to the ground, faceted glass windows are illuminated at night and add the excitement of brilliant color—mostly reds and blues—to the landmark. These are the tallest glass windows in the world. A twenty-seven-foot figure of Christ stands at the base of the tower, directly above the main entrance, where the words "Come Unto Me" are engraved over the door.

The total tower structure, weighing in at a staggering thirty-nine hundred tons, provides the external visual focus; inside the building and through the grand narthex (lobby), the exquisitely-crafted sanctuary commands all attention. First-time visitors may feel they have stepped into an immense swept-wing jet. The illusion is the result of combining the two basic types of church buildings into one—which is what Wagoner achieved here. The traditional pattern, used in the medieval cathedral, is a long rectangle with transepts at the altar end, forming the shape of a cross. The more recent square or church-in-the-round model was developed to cluster the congregation more closely around the speaker—a concept popular with the Reformation churches, which emphasized preaching the Word.

An aerial view of the Coral Ridge church suggests the long lines of a cathedral, with the roof in the shape of a fish, the earliest symbol of Christianity. But inside, the nave or longitudinal dimension of the auditorium is offset by transepts set at forty-five degree angles on either side of the chancel (platform area), thus giving the roomy, swept-wing impression. At the rear of each transept an airy, suspended spiral staircase rises with its own small fountain, multicolored chandelier, and planter filled with lush foliage; a local newspaper article referred to these delicate ascents to the balcony as "pure serendipity." Eight balconies encircling the walls on three sides are so arranged that none is directly below another.

The chancel itself is a wide, open stage, which can easily seat a one-hundred-piece orchestra. Behind it rises a choir loft, a dream come true for Anne Kennedy. She could remember how difficult it had been to get a trio of vocalists together when the church was at the McNab schoolhouse. She could also remember Jim's optimistic promise that "there's no reason in the world why we shouldn't have as fine a choir as the Mormon Tabernacle because ours will be singing the praises of Jesus Christ." Today nine full choirs use the loft, which seats 150, with the side balconies allowing an increase of fifty more singers for a performance.

Ten-foot forms of vertical split travertine marble encase the entire sanctuary, providing a sand-colored base for the ivory-tinted plaster walls that soar to a ceiling height of sixty feet. From all directions, light streams in through eighty-six recessed windows of faceted glass (not painted or stained, but actual one-inch chunks of pure-color glass produced by Willett Studios of Philadelphia). These thousands of fragments are held together in an epoxy in swirling visual mosaics. As in the tower area on the other end, the colors in the chancel are predominantly blue and red; toward the center of the church, the hues gradually blend into soft tones of gold, green, and yellow. The ceiling was planned with ample lighting facilities for television five years in advance of their first use, and more than two hundred speakers insure perfect acoustic balance. Circuitry for future TV also was built into the walls.

The centerpiece of worship, as far as pure elegance is concerned, is the 117-rank Ruffatti pipe organ, the largest European-built instrument in the United States at the time. Constructed in Padua, Italy, on specifications drawn up by Coral Ridge's celebrated organist, Diane Bish, who served as senior organist from 1971-1991, the sixty-six hundred burnished silver pipes—ranging from forty feet long to the size of a small pencil—are not hidden in chambers but are ranked in white casework with gold leaf trim. "Fountains" of smaller pipes stand in the center of the facade to symbolize Christ as the Fountain of Life.

Highlighting the installation are four sets of *en chamade* (horizontal) trumpets on long stems projecting straight out toward the congregation. A special feature is the cymbelstern, which crowns the center section of the organ. When the cymbelstern is activated, the entire star turns visibly, while tiny bells of different pitches play in accompaniment to choir or instrument. An antiphonal organ in the rear loft of the sanctuary and a massive rosewood and ivory console of five keyboards complete the installation. Demand for concerts by Miss Bish—who is widely known for her original compositions, awards, and both live and televised performances throughout Europe and the United States—has been constant since she first introduced the Coral Ridge congregation to the wonders of the Ruffatti organ.

And what of the congregation? Was there a danger associated with the delicate beauty and the impressive grandeur of their new modern cathedral, which they occupied on December 23, 1973? Billy Graham thought so, and he warned in his dedicatory sermon on February 3, 1974, "Don't get too proud." He gently ribbed his audience, alluding to an anonymous clergyman who was supposed to have said, "If I ever see a humble Presbyterian, I'll be like Moses—I will turn aside and see this great sight."

"I hope that this congregation will not forget," Graham continued in a serious vein, "that it was born just a few years ago, forty-five or fifty people, as your minister has reminded you—people who loved the Lord, who believed in prayer and believed in evangelism. And you went out, and you have done something that has become a twentieth-century phenomenon in the kingdom of God. The example of this church is being followed by churches all over the world, and your responsibility is so much greater than the average congregation."

In the years that followed, the congregation has never broken stride. Overflow crowds of eight thousand and eleven thousand were present for that first service and for the dedication ceremonies, suggesting that as many visitors attended as did regular members. But a glance at the membership records reveals that Coral Ridge Presbyterian went right on as the fastest growing church through the 1970s and into the 1980s—doubling itself within eight years and closing in on a communicant roll of ten thousand toward the end of the year 2000.

Without the benefit of a bevy of professional philanthropists and "big donors," the congregation took the financial risks and faithfully gave their tithes and offerings to pay off the bond programs and purchase the handsome four-story Knox Center at 5554 North Federal Highway (just across the street from the church at 5555) to house the offices of the burgeoning programs of the overall ministry of Coral Ridge Church.

The congregation also nurtured the growth of the Sunday school Jim had started with two classes in 1960, with Anne as the first teacher. Under the more descriptive label of "The Church School for Christian Living," the number of weekly classes soared above seventy; the attendance grew from fewer than ten to well over one thousand after the first decade in the new facilities. The challenge of Christian education was supplemented by a Midweek School of the Bible and a host of other study groups. A greatly expanded library undergirded this work.

The focus, in other words, has never shifted away from

the vision Jim Kennedy brought with him to Fort Lauderdale in 1959. To help his congregation keep the vision centered not on the esthetics or the externals, but on Jesus Christ and the Word of God, Jim preaches from an eye-riveting pulpit on one side of the chancel and projected high above the pews, which somehow all seem to be close to the speaker. Richly carved in Bible symbolism, the African mahogany pulpit is in itself a stunning attention holder. Its most commanding feature is a towering cast-concrete "tester," which twists gracefully and arches high above the pulpit like a giant arm and hand overshadowing the speaker, who appears to be securely positioned under its divine protection. The outside of the free-standing form is ivory-tinted, and the side next to the pulpit is laminated from bottom to top with ribbed mahogany for a striking contrast.

In the medieval church the tester had a twofold purpose. First, it was intended to project the speaker's voice out over the congregation; actually, this one is deadened to avoid interference with the electronic acoustics. More importantly, the tester was designed to be a beacon directing all attention to the sharing of the Bible message. As with the churches of the Reformation, nothing at Coral Ridge Presbyterian Church is permitted to supersede the giving out of the Gospel. Physically and spiritually, the Bible message holds the place of highest honor. As worshipers leave the sanctuary, the last reminder they see—in bold lettering over the main exit—is "Go Ye Into All The World."

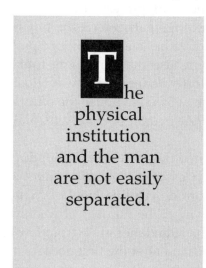

The physical institution and the man are not easily separated.

For those who spend a reasonable amount of time

observing both, it becomes apparent that the physical institution on Federal Highway and the man in the pulpit are not
easily separated from one another. The building and the life
are too closely intertwined for most people who know the
man to picture him apart from the inanimate structure. The
cornerstone, for example, is inscribed with large black letters
cut into ivory-tinted marble: "This church is built to the
glory of the Triune God and is dedicated to the service of
mankind through the fulfillment of the Great Commission of
our Lord and Savior Jesus Christ. EXCELLENCE IN ALL
THINGS AND ALL THINGS TO GOD'S GLORY."

It sort of reminds you of someone you know, doesn't it?
The words were written by D. James Kennedy.

CHAPTER • 1 5

LENDING WINGS TO THE WORD

What I tell you in darkness, that speak ye
in light: and what ye hear in the ear,
that preach ye upon the housetops.
—MATTHEW 10:27

Jim Kennedy's entire ministry could be graphically summarized in the form of a triptych—a three-paneled carving or painting, each panel depicting a different aspect or historical phase in the life of the same subject. In the course of his single pastorate over forty years (a recent study indicates that the typical tenure of the average pastor today is near three years), God has been dealing with him in an almost chapter-like progression: three church locations, each presenting special problems and challenges and each setting the stage for a major breakthrough in his service to Christ.

First, of course, was the bitter discouragement of the new pastor at the McNab schoolhouse site; through such testing the Lord brought Jim to discover the secret of personal witnessing as God's guarantee of church growth. At the second location, on Commercial Boulevard, he was frustrated by the woeful limitations on unilateral, pastor-centered soul-winning; through his repeated and disappointing efforts to break out of such restrictions, God revealed to him how to send out a global army of Christians equipped to do the same thing he had been taught to do—the Church militant under a banner labeled Evangelism Explosion International.

The third buildup of pressure and eventual breakthrough came in the magnificent "new" location on Federal Highway and centered on that peculiar charge, that highly specialized function closest to the heart of the true preacher: preaching the Word. "It is not reason," the first apostles told their converts, "that we should leave the Word of God and became too involved with the other necessary business of the church. Let us appoint elders and deacons to handle those things. But we will give ourselves continually to prayer and to the ministry of the Word." Any person whom God has called to preach desires above all else to be doing just that. And when he is preaching with the unction of the Holy Spirit and with power, he longs to reach the widest possible audience with his inspired message. As John Wesley boldly declared, "The world is my parish."

The immediate problem is that the typical pulpit is hemmed in by the four walls of an auditorium that seats a few listeners and shuts out the rest of the world. Multiple services may increase total listenership a fraction, but the traditional handicap of the local church remains—it attracts the attention of a very small portion of the local community, which may be made up of thousands of people who never attend in person, even though they might pass the church regularly while worship is in progress. The Coral Ridge Church, to be sure, had been successful in slowing down traffic on Commercial Boulevard. On one occasion, when the curiosity of drivers was piqued by the long lines they saw between services—people standing outside the main entrance in a queue three or four persons deep and stretching for several hundred feet down the sidewalk—an inquisitive motorist pausing in the traffic could be heard to remark,

"They must be giving away something free inside!" When the comment was passed on to Jim, he agreed in great amusement that yes, that was exactly what was happening inside the church; and he soon had a new sermon entitled "Giving Away Real Estate in Paradise." The driver couldn't have been more correct.

"Still, how to reach more people for Christ was a question that continued to echo in my mind," Jim says. "This led to the formation of Coral Ridge Ministries, whereby today I have the opportunity of preaching the Good News to thirty-five thousand cities and towns in America and one-hundred seventy-six other nations and territories by television and radio."

CRM—that was the new venture of faith that catapulted Coral Ridge Presbyterian Church into the mushrooming communication conduits of the mass media in 1974, when its preacher appeared over the airwaves of Channel 45 in Miami and on Channel 38 in Chicago. For the very first time, millions were watching the services and hearing the sermons which previously had been restricted to an audience of thousands.

The airborne Gospel was the inevitable solution to the problem of containment, especially to one who could trace the very hour of his salvation back to that 1953 message that was picked out of the electromagnetic spectrum by his radio receiving set. Until the age of almost twenty-four, Jim was an alien and a stranger to the Gospel because he avoided the places where the Gospel was shared. But by the mechanical miracle of voice transmission via broadcast frequencies, and by the grace of God, the Gospel invaded his apartment, his privacy, even his sleep—and his life was transformed.

From that time on, Jim never questioned the immeasurable value of a broadcast ministry. He explains: "I believe there are basically two things I can do to fulfill the Great Commission. The first one is what I do personally, whether I witness to an individual or couple or family, or I preach to a congregation. Or I can take a 'megaphone' and make that into a radio program—locally or nationally or worldwide—

or a television program or a tape or motion pictures or books or tracts or magazines. All of those are just 'megaphones,' which enlarge my personal witness and enable me to reach more and more people myself. To change the metaphor, in warfare that would be like going from hand-to-hand combat, to a pistol, to a rifle, to a machine gun, to an artillery piece, to a bomber, to an atomic bomb, to a hydrogen bomb.

"All of those are just 'megaphones' which enlarge my personal witness."

"On the other hand, the second thing I can do is to multiply the workers. In warfare, we don't just try to get bigger and bigger weapons for one soldier; we also try to multiply the number of soldiers. Now, through all these other means—the media of communication—I have had a larger and larger weapon, or a bigger and bigger megaphone (whichever metaphor we want to use). And then, through Evangelism Explosion International, we are trying to multiply and to multiply exceedingly the number of soldiers or workers in the warfare of sharing the Gospel of Jesus Christ."

With the power of such conviction and vision behind it, the 1974 "venture of faith" has grown to be the third most watched Christian broadcast ministry in America and has made the Coral Ridge pastor the most listened-to Presbyterian minister in the world today. *The Coral Ridge Hour*, his one-hour telecast is available to eighty-seven percent of the nation's television households on more than six hundred broadcast stations and three cable networks reaching 35,000 cities and towns in America. Thus all of the persons attending the three worship services of Coral Ridge on a given Sunday comprise only a tiny fraction of the more than three and one-half million people who watch or hear CRM broadcasts weekly! The budget now for Coral Ridge Ministries is over $39 million.

The weekly programs are remarkable for their professional broadcast quality, combining worship services with interviews, field reports, and human-interest segments of national and international scope, offering the viewer a perspective not typically seen in the secular media's coverage of contemporary society.

The prime-time one-hour television specials, which are produced with absolute top-quality professional skill, represent the "real wave of the future." These commentaries, researched and shot in several parts of the country for authenticity and viewer interest, began in 1987 with a special entitled "Reclaiming a Nation." Also that year, Dr. Kennedy —who has narrated the entire series—appeared in "Pornography: An American Tragedy." Following during 1988 were "Obscenity: The Invasion of Privacy," "Creation Science Special: A Case for Creation," "All about Coral Ridge Ministries," and "AIDS: Anatomy of a Crisis." In 1989, it was "Abortion: A Reflection of Life," "The Seduction of Hollywood," and "The Pilgrim Legacy," done on location in Plymouth, Massachusetts. In more recent years, *The Coral Ridge Hour* has aired specials on the American Civil Liberties Union, the National Education Association, militant homosexuality, and Judge Roy Moore's battle to keep prayer and the Ten Commandments in his Alabama courtroom.

Six years after the formation of CRM (literally, Coral Ridge Ministries Media, Inc., now a free-standing organization separate from Coral Ridge Church), the daily radio program "Truths That Transform" was conceived and aired. It has also expanded rapidly since 1984; in the first year alone the number of stations scheduling the program doubled. Its messages from the pulpit at Coral Ridge are supplemented by penetrating interviews on civic and moral issues and special guest speakers. These programs are broadcast over five hundred radio outlets daily and about one hundred more weekly. Transcripts and tapes of Dr. Kennedy's messages, "Action Sheets," and selected Christian resources are sent to thousands of listeners, helping them implement biblical principles in reclaiming their communities for Christ.

In 1992, Coral Ridge Ministries launched *The Kennedy Commentary*, a 90-second daily radio feature carried on more than 300 radio outlets nationwide. This daily commentary offers listeners "bite-sized and biblical" observations from Dr. Kennedy on both Christian living and key moral and social issues.

As the Kennedy image, personality, and message began to infiltrate virtually every TV market in the United States, he became recognized as one of the leading Christian statesmen of the day—and became a much-sought-after guest on "celebrity shows." His TV appearances include *Crossfire, CBS Nightwatch, MacNeil/Lehrer Report, Donahue, The Merv Griffin Show,* and a Ted Koppel special on televangelism. (By the way, in Jim's opinion, "Paul Harvey is the greatest news analyst and commentator in the world today.")

He has been quoted in *U.S. News and World Report, Conservative Digest, The Saturday Evening Post, Christianity Today, The Washington Times, Religious Broadcasting, Christian Life, USA Today, Christian Herald, The New York Times, The Washington Post,* and a host of newspapers. Indeed, CRM has supplied him with a pretty good-sized megaphone.

It has also provided Jim with a tremendous new work load. The routine production of programs, for a pastor who oversees a church of almost 10,000 members with eighteen ministers in its various ministries, thirty-one elders, and twenty-eight deacons—to say nothing of Evangelism Explosion International and a daily office agenda matching that of any corporate CEO—has added hours spent taping both radio and television programs.

To those outside the industry, the meticulous care which

must go into an ordinary taping segment is difficult to imagine. Aside from the weekly services in the sanctuary or on-location specials, most of the "end segments" are shot on *The Coral Ridge Hour* set—now familiar to home viewers everywhere. A state-of-the-art studio complete with computerized lighting and digitized editing facilities, makes the weekly video taping a pro-forma event. It wasn't always so. Until the Broadcast Center's completion in 1994, it took two hours or more to complete a video tape segment that should have required just forty-five minutes. Retakes to correct technical bugs—insufficient light, a problematic microphone, a snagged circuit—all contributed to the delays which prompted Jim to jokingly suggest his epitaph ought to read: "Died due to technical difficulties."

Even more frustrating during the first sixteen years of producing the television program was the constant threat of noise. "We have lost thousands of takes because of outside noise," Jim says. It was often necessary to stop and retape for airplanes, motorcycles, trucks, police cars, ambulances, fire trucks, buses—anything that created excessive traffic noise. Occasionally, Jim says, "Sounds from within the sanctuary were picked up on tape, particularly if an organ or orchestra rehearsal called for too much fortissimo." One of his sermons on the subject of church and state was in such high broadcasting demand that the producer asked Jim to repeat it in church for reshooting in a more updated milieu. Not wishing to subject his congregation to repetition just to meet production requirements, Jim appeared before the cameras in his ecclesiastical robe and preached the sermon from the pulpit to an auditorium filled with empty pews.

Such are the demands of television art. Regardless of the number of retakes, home viewers always get the impression of spontaneity and enthusiasm from a man totally dedicated to his assignment. Asked if he felt all right after one difficult stint of taping that went on for three hours and forty-five minutes, he replied frankly: "It's very, very stressful and extremely exhausting. But I praise God for all of the various work that I have to do. It's hard, but I am glad that I have the opportunity to do it."

CRM has continued to grow, spilling out of its floor in the Knox Center across the street from the church into part of another floor, then into huge industrial park quarters "out west," and finally also into the modern, soundproofed studio built in the most recent church additions. CRM's international outreach grew exponentially in the late 1990s. Beyond the 158 nations CRM already reached on the Armed Forces Network, new opportunities arose for bringing the Good News of eternal life through Christ to more people in more nations. These include Holy Land Television, a Christian television station broadcasting from Bethlehem, Middle East Television, which sends its signal to fifteen Middle East nations, as well as outlets in New Zealand, Australia, and St. Petersburg, Russia, reaching a total of almost 180 nations.

The CRM printing operation has published in attractive brochures over 1,500 of the more than 3,200 sermons Kennedy has preached at Coral Ridge. These are meticulously catalogued and indexed for instant storage retrieval to meet requests for sermons by subject or title. A flood of publications on national problems such as child abuse, humanism, defense, media bias, the budget deficit, pornography, abortion, drugs, the homeless, the National Education Association, the American Civil Liberties Union have been produced. The emphasis is always put on the Christian perspective. A monthly news letter *Impact*, provides biblical instruction, news, ministry updates, and a complete listing of broadcast schedules. Frequently, petitions are made available for mobilizing Christian opinion on Supreme Court decisions, objectionable Hollywood films, abortion legislation, and the like. Books like Kennedy's *Beginning Again* for new believers are mass produced to meet the thousands of requests made each year for this guide to the Christian life.

Such volume requires CRM mailroom activity that takes

on the appearance of a United States post office, with as many as one and a half million packages going out in a year: audio and videotape cassettes and printed materials from fact sheets to books. In a single month the viewers and listeners may send in 100,000 letters. Every letter posing a question or concern is answered by CRM correspondence or pastoral resources staff.

Statistics like these explain why this outreach program is by far the largest entity among the ministries Kennedy leads—Evangelism Explosion International, Knox Seminary, Westminster Academy, and Coral Ridge Church. Its 150-plus employees far outnumber the church staff, and its $39 million budget is more than five times the figure needed to operate the church. Yet the pastor of Coral Ridge Church has never received any fraction of any revenues generated by Coral Ridge Ministries. His time and labor are free.

Most importantly, Jim Kennedy has allowed CRM to blossom into what has been termed "the Christian entrepreneur's dream." By providing clear direction, attracting quality staff, and giving people room to grow, Jim has fostered the innovation that has spawned the development of new ways of reaching people for Christ through the mass media.

Jim brings his new dream down to earth this way: "This is in keeping with CRM's mandate to utilize every communication tool available to promulgate the Gospel of Jesus Christ. First, we started with a weekly half-hour radio program in 1974. Four years later, we introduced a weekly television program and went into daily radio broadcasts

> CRM has developed into "the Christian entrepreneur's dream."

six years after that. Then, we broke in to prime-time television specials which are network-quality, sixty-minute shows. All these take the Christian message into millions of homes in this nation and around the world."

This innovative growth has continued right to the present. For example, in 1994, the state-of-the-art Broadcast Center was completed. This facility, built on the grounds of Coral Ridge Church, greatly enhanced the ministry's ability to produce top-quality video and radio broadcasts. Plus, with full fiber optic and satellite uplink capabilities, CRM could broadcast live to the nation and the world. The first live broadcast took place in November of that year.

The reach of *The Coral Ridge Hour* also has continued to expand. By 1995 Jim was reaching 59 percent of the nation's television homes. That figure grew steadily. Then in 1999, the Lord opened the doors for *The Coral Ridge Hour* to fill a prime Sunday morning time slot being vacated by a canceled network broadcast. He instructed his staff to move quickly, adding millions of potential viewers to CRM and giving the ministry the ability to reach 87 percent of the nation's homes.

CRM's global media ministry began to grow even more quickly, and the explosion in international outreach seems to have coincided with Jim's decision to follow his heart to the Holy Land. In 1997, CRM was presented with a once-in-a-lifetime opportunity: help launch a new Christian television station that would be located in Bethlehem! For Jim and Anne, it was a dream come true. They had often visited the Holy Land, but to have the opportunity to take the message of Christ back to Israel—and have that signal originating in the town in which Jesus was born—was somewhat overwhelming.

Of course, bringing the Gospel to Palestinian-controlled Bethlehem would not be easy! In fact, every possible roadblock presented itself. However, the CRM team persisted and in December 1998, the first broadcast of Holy Land TV went on the air in Bethlehem. That initial run of broadcasts lasted just a few weeks when a U.S. air attack on Iraq caused the Palestinian authority to shut down all television and radio stations. When the blackout was lifted, authorities refused to allow Holy Land TV's religious broadcasting back on the air because a militant Islamic group demanded equal time.

But God would have the final say! As CRM executives worked to re-establish the station under a commercial license, the Lord opened the door for *The Coral Ridge Hour* to broadcast on the Amos Satellite network covering 17 countries and 20 million people in the Middle East.

These same contacts gave Coral Ridge the opportunity to broadcast on the Voice of Hope radio network, covering the Middle East, China and southeast Asia, much of Europe and vast sections of the Western Hemisphere from Canada to South America.

Today, CRM broadcasts can be heard or seen on more than 600 televisions stations in the U.S. and a staggering 176 nations of the world. And it all started with a simple question that echoed in Jim Kennedy's mind, "How can I reach more people for Christ?"

Where will Coral Ridge Ministries be in 10, 20, or 30 years? Only the Lord Himself knows, but Jim is entirely optimistic, especially when he considers the explosive growth of the Church in the past century.

"According to missions experts, in 100 A.D. the Church was growing at an average rate of 100 converts per day worldwide," he says. "By 1900, that rate had grown to 943 converts per day; by 1950, 4,500 converts per day; by 1980, 20,000 converts per day; by 1995, more than 100,000 people were being converted to Christ every single day! That figure was predicted to double in less than a decade."

Kennedy says a similar pattern has unfolded here in the U.S., but the change is less noticeable due to what he calls "stealth" Christians. "In recent decades here in America, millions of nominal Christians have had a life-changing encounter with Christ, been born-again, and are now active evangelical Christians," says Kennedy. "But because they were initially classified under the broad classification of 'Christian' prior to their conversion, they have snuck under the demographer's radar." Surely, ministries like Coral Ridge have played a key role in bringing many thousands of these "stealth" converts into the kingdom.

As the work of Coral Ridge Ministries takes on the challenge of the 21st century, Jim Kennedy continues to have the same simple motivation as when he first went on the radio back in 1974. "We decided it's better to light a candle, as the Christophers say, than to curse the darkness. We're lighting a candle"—a candle that lights up millions of homes and hearts each and every week.

FINISH THE DREAM

*[Thus] was the house finished throughout
all the parts thereof, and according to
all the fashion of it.*
—1 KINGS 6:38

Ⅰn his list of Goals for 1988, Jim Kennedy wrote near the top: "To direct the completion of our new facilities." This was not a reference to some minor installation, but the beginning of a $12-million campaign labeled "Finish the Dream." There simply was not enough money in 1973 to execute all of Wagoner's original architectural plan, which called for expansive wings flanking and interconnecting with the sanctuary.

After fifteen years the new space was needed rather urgently. In the biblical conception, the Church was an army to be sent out into all the world equipped to carry out the Great Commission—this was being addressed through Evangelism Explosion and through Coral Ridge Ministries. But the Church is also a family; and in what had become a familiar pattern this church family was once again outgrowing its living quarters. It was time to take care of the needs of the family by enlarging

Jim reads new meaning into ancient symbols on the Kennedy family coat of arms.

This handsome young man in the Roaring Twenties, George Raymond Kennedy, would become the father of Jim Kennedy a few years after this picture was made.

Ermine Roberson, dressed in the high style of the flapper age, was about 18 when she posed for this portrait, never dreaming that she was to become the mother of one of America's great preachers.

Jim became accustomed to performing before large crowds at the age of 17 as drum major of the William B. Plant High School Band in Tampa. Later, he was drum major at the University of Tampa.

The distinctive Moorish architecture of the University of Tampa provided the setting for Jim's long struggle to get his academic career underway.

At 22, the nimble Arthur Murray Dance Studio instructor does the mambo with a partner.

Arthur Murray (left) and his wife honored Jim as the top dance instructor in the nation in 1953, when this picture was taken in New York City.

As a prospering and self-assured man of the world, Jim had no idea that the Lord would be calling him into His service.

Anne, 5, is on the left in this portrait with sister Jean, 6.

"This was the girl I fell in love with," Jim reminisces. "Anne looked just like this the first time I saw her in the Arthur Murray Studio."

Husband and wife. The happy occasion took place on August 25, 1956, at Anne's home church, the First Presbyterian in Lakeland.

The radiant bride poses with her bridesmaids. Flanking Anne on her left is older sister, Jean, and on her right, younger sister, Carolyn.

In his upstairs apartment at 110 1/2 South Boulevard in Tampa, Jim heard the Barnhouse radio message that changed his life forever.

The little white stone Bethel Presbyterian Church in Clearwater, Florida, was Jim's very first pastorate, as a student supply preacher at the age of 26. The church was 100 years old in 1986.

Campbell Hall accommodated most of the classes when Jim was a student at Columbia Theological Seminary.

Seminary student Jim Kennedy stands in front of the garage apartment he and Anne occupied in Decatur, Georgia, in their first three years of marriage.

The D.James Kennedy CENTER FOR CHRISTIAN STATESMANSHIP *in Washington, D.C., fulfills a long-held dream of Jim's to bring the Gospel to the epicenter of world political power.*

Jim addressed members of Congress and Christian leaders at the 1995 National Day of Prayer observance in Washington, D.C.

The Reclaiming America For Christ conference, held annually since 1994, equips believers to be effective Christian citizens.

Jim's books on apologetics, such as What if Jesus Had Never Been Born? and What if the Bible Had Never Been Written?, have helped believers more intelligently defend the faith.

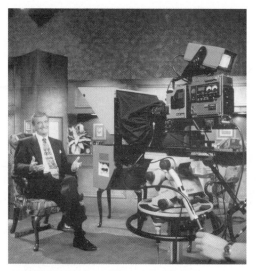

CRM's facilities for the production of top-quality television programs are on a par with professional studios.

This rendering of a mosaic is a reminder of the purpose of Knox Seminary: preparing servants of Christ for the twenty-first century.

Jim and Anne recall God's blessings at Coral Ridge Church's 35th anniversary celebration in 1994. Humorous, often touching memories were offered, including stirring testimonies of Christian commitment and evangelism.

the home according to the master plan.

With the family of almost eight thousand in full agreement, the members braced themselves. Contracts were let, parking lots on both ends of the property were promptly peeled off the surface of the ground, heavy earth-moving equipment lumbered all over the place, contractors' huts sprang up behind the church, a veritable depot of building materials was stockpiled on the site, and an army division of workmen invaded the precincts. Coral Ridge Church found itself surrounded—and at times almost overwhelmed—by the calculated chaos and turbulence of major construction. Jim cheered up his understandably disoriented parishioners by announcing that those who successfully found their way to church services for six weeks straight would be eligible to receive Explorer Scout merit badges!

The crunch this time was not really so much an overcrowding of folk as it was function. More space was needed for the expanded programs of the church. For example, with younger families pouring into Coral Ridge Church, many of whom were also seeking admission for their children to Westminster Academy, the nursery and child-care accommodations had become seriously over-taxed. Complexes designed for these purposes form the northernmost wing of new construction and open onto a spacious playground and courtyard areas.

Youth activities, too, were long overdue for a move; these had been for some time centered mostly in a nearby warehouse. A generous section of the south wing is dedicated to the youth ministry. Also, the library—after fifteen years' growth to a circulating level of more than six thousand books and tapes—was more than ready to occupy its new space, double the former dimensions, beside the chapel.

The chapel, the principal feature of the north wing and fronting on Federal Highway, was designed to handle the overflow ceremonies like weddings and funerals and to provide a place outside of the sanctuary for functions requiring a smaller auditorium. Matching the chapel on the other side of the main church building is the enormous new fellowship hall, capable of seating nearly one thousand at round tables. Movable walls make the room size and capacity adjustable. Both the chapel and the fellowship hall have their own narthexes. The exterior front of each is enhanced with an imposing tower harmonizing with the giant central tower of the church, right down to vertical windows of colored, faceted glass, spires, and crosses.

Specially planned quarters in the rear of the new construction provide for two of the busiest and biggest entities in the church: the music department and the Coral Ridge Ministries Outreach Division. The music agenda alone rivals professional conservatory offerings in quality and scope. The chancel choir has toured Europe and the United States besides performing regularly at church services and participating in classical concerts. Other choirs for different age groups—a total of twelve—keep similar schedules.

Roger McMurrin came to Coral Ridge as music director in 1971. He left a professorship at Otterbein College in Ohio in choirs, music education, and voice to take over the burgeoning program of choral performances, orchestras and ensembles, and concert planning. He directed more than three hundred singers. In two decades of service at Coral Ridge, McMurrin was responsible for the church's emergence as one of the leading centers of sacred music in the United States.

A yearly concert series brings to the area such luminaries as Van Cliburn, Jerome Hines, Roger Williams, Norma Zimmer, the Norman Luboff Chorale, the Vienna Boys Choir, George Beverly Shea, Sandi Patti, Debby Boone, and symphony orchestras from many cities. The celebrities are supplemented by the church's own orchestra, star performers such as Diane Bish in organ concerts, and a nationally recognized handbell choir and ensemble. The program's excellence is probably unsurpassed in the world of church music.

And such a program needs space. The music department

welcomed its new full-sized choir rehearsal room, with adjoining robe rooms, just outside the sanctuary choir loft, and ample instrument storage. Especially convenient is the concert series office, previously improvised but now architecturally planned for efficient distribution of tickets to the general public.

Of all Coral Ridge operations, perhaps none can more convincingly justify its entitlement to additional space than the new kid on the block, Coral Ridge Ministries. Anyone who doubts this assertion should have visited a typical taping session in the 1980s. Tapings took place in the pastor's study on the fourth floor adjoining the tower—a facility not naturally suited for such purposes. Due to the noise from Federal Highway which runs in front of the church, it was not uncommon for the sound engineer to be forced to retreat into an adjacent bathroom, close the door, place his equipment on the lavatory, and sit down to monitor the taping.

Problems of that sort have been solved by the construction of CRM's well-equipped new TV studio complex, protected by soundproofed walls and settled at the rear of the church, far from the traffic noise on Federal. This state-of-the-art facility was completed in 1994 and gave CRM the ability to broadcast live via fiber optic and satellite uplinks. The first such live broadcast took place that November, just days before a crucial Congressional election, and featured Jim's candid discussions on the key moral and spiritual issues at stake.

As new space became available, vacated areas were remodeled for optimum use. The Sunday school grew to more than seventy classrooms. Church attendance reached a peak of more than 12,000. Tight office spaces were expanded. The church family once again enjoyed room to grow for many years. But with a spiritual leader who is always looking five or ten years ahead of the flock, that may not be a safe assumption. Back in 1984, at the bottom of a statistical report dated June 10, Jim put down in his own handwriting: "Ain't seen nothing yet—best is yet to be!"

Fifteen years later, in 1999, as Coral Ridge Presbyterian Church gathered to celebrate its 40th anniversary, Jim Kennedy still had that same optimistic, growth-oriented outlook on the future. After recounting to his flock several passages from Scripture that encourage believers to consider how "much more" God can and will do, Jim looked to the next 40 years.

"As I think and pray and dream about 40 years from now, I believe, like Moses' 40 years in the wilderness, the play is just beginning. I can see a church of 35,000 members, a full-fledged Christian university in Fort Lauderdale, new permanent campuses for Westminster Academy and Knox Theological Seminary, 100 million trained in Evangelism Explosion, facilities for unwed and expectant mothers, a medical clinic for the indigent, and a nation which has been brought back to God."

Ralph Waldo Emerson characterized the institution as being "the lengthened shadow of a man." Perhaps nowhere is the remarkable coalescence of the spirits of a pastor and his church so well articulated as in a philosophy of Coral Ridge Presbyterian Church that Kennedy penned for the twenty-fifth anniversary celebration in 1985:

"The philosophy of the church begins with the realization that 'the chief end of man is to glorify God and to enjoy Him forever.' The ineffable glory of the great and majestic God whom we serve, calls forth from us the best efforts of our hearts, hands, and minds. Shoddy workmanship and half-hearted measures are not worthy to be offered to so great a God. Therefore the motto 'Excellence in all things and all things to His glory' summarizes the goal and the challenge of the church.

"Such a goal demands a striving in every area of the life of the church for excellence. Achievement in one area will not suffice. There must be a continual striving for balance and excellence in every department of church life. Too often people are offered alternatives such as: either a beautiful and uplifting worship service or sound doctrine from the pulpit; either evangelism or social concern; either a good education program or a strong outreach; either world or home missions; either an emphasis on youth or a concern for the elderly; either a friendly church or a dignified service; either beautiful music or biblical preaching. Such alternatives as these are not viable options for the church; it must ever seek to provide all of these in a well-balanced program.

"The Coral Ridge Presbyterian Church has made it a purposeful part of its planning and philosophy to seek for the best in each of these areas. From the pulpit it proclaims no doctrinal novelties nor seeks to create any new religion or fad. It endeavors to proclaim 'the faith once for all delivered to the saints,' as enunciated by Christ and the apostles; defended by Luther, Calvin, and the other Reformers; and set forth in the great creeds of Protestantism. With the reformers of the sixteenth century we hold to that faith which is *Sola Scriptura*—based solely on the Scriptures—which maintains a salvation that is *Sola Gratia*—solely by the grace of God—and *Sola Fide*—solely by faith in Christ—and in all things *Soli Deo Gloria*—solely to the glory of God."

THE
MAN
OF
LETTERS

ADVENTURES OF THE MIND

*A wise man will hear, and
will increase learning.*
—PROVERBS 1:5

Insults, to a seasoned preacher, are like mosquitoes to a farmer; they are to be expected, endured, ignored. Hadn't the Lord told one of his most maligned prophets, "be not afraid of them, nor be afraid of their words. . . . Like adamant stone, harder than flint, I have made your forehead; do not be afraid of them, or be dismayed at their looks"? But a beginner, a preacher-to-be, has not yet acquired that defensive armor of an Ezekiel. The unkind cut can carry a hurtful sting that sticks in the mind like a sand burr in the shoe.

Jim Kennedy fielded his first fiery dart while still an undergraduate student. He had no degree or credentials of any kind. He was simply preaching the Gospel in response to the clear call of God while struggling to complete his course work at the University of Tampa. In the small Bethel Presbyterian Church, across the bay in Clearwater, he was accosted by a very proper elder who disagreed with his teaching on a matter of doctrine. With the offended dignity that only the self-righteous can display to perfection, the pious gentleman took it upon himself to put the young minister-without-portfolio in his place. "Young man," he sniffed, "we Presbyterians prefer that our clergy be well educated." Then he turned and strode away with all the pomp befitting a superior person. Jim felt as if he had received a broadside from a battleship. "But you know," he says, "I feel almost indebted to that sanctimonious elder, because I made my mind up right then and there that I would get the best education I could possibly manage. I resolved that nobody would ever again be able to reject Christian doctrine because I was not properly educated to deliver it." Today, with nine college, seminary, and university degrees after his name, nobody is able to do so.

To argue that an academic degree is a written guarantee of intelligence would, of course, be foolishness. It is, rather, a certification of effort expended, a documentation of work accomplished at an acceptable—or perhaps superior—level of performance. The individual cannot say to the institution, "Turn me into a scholar," any more than the athlete can say to the coach, "Make me an All-American." The burden of getting an education rests entirely with the student's response to the opportunity for formal training the institution makes available. To borrow the college advisor's well-worn cliché: the more you put into it, the more you'll get out of it. It's a matter of exacting work from the frontal lobe.

What Jim put into the quest was nothing short of prodigious.

What Jim put into the quest for learning was nothing short of prodigious: seven full academic years plus twelve summers of intensive study, most of which were sandwiched between the heavy responsibilities of one of the most active church ministries in America. Because of the slow start at the University of Tampa (interrupted by those six years as a dance instructor), he was compelled to crowd summer work on the baccalaureate in with his seminary career, finally picking up the B.A. in 1958. The following year he received the master of divinity degree from Columbia Theological Seminary, graduating *cum laude* in the three-year program.

Seven years elapsed before Jim felt he could avail himself of a fellowship he was awarded at Columbia. In the summer of 1967 he entered the Chicago Graduate School of Theology, at that time in Winona Lake, Indiana. For about fifty years, long before other institutions followed, this school had offered summer instruction leading to the degree. It had the cream of the world's faculty scholars interested in summer teaching. Consequently, it could offer the very finest seminary instruction available and was widely recognized for its challenging theology and Greek and Hebrew studies curricula.

But Coral Ridge's pastor had no sooner involved himself in advanced course work than tragedy struck. It was discovered that Anne needed immediate cancer surgery. On the advice of the seminary president, the operation was performed at the medical center in Elkhart, Indiana, about forty miles from the campus. Back at home, the congregation at Coral Ridge Presbyterian Church held a twenty-four-hour prayer vigil for Anne, and God answered with her complete recovery and restoration to health. But it was several months before she could return to Fort Lauderdale. The long drive back and forth from campus to hospital, in addition to the deep concern for his wife, meant a very difficult semester of study for Jim. Nevertheless, at the end of the third summer, he received his Master of Theology degree with a perfect 4.0 grade average in all courses. He became the first candidate in the history of the Chicago Graduate School of Theology to be ranked *summa cum laude* in his field.

Something far more significant than the diploma came out of that three summers of mental labor: a master's thesis which later became a best-seller when published in book form. *Evangelism Explosion* has gone through four editions and has sold more than 1.5 million copies throughout the world. Considering the fact that the work is designed to be shared with others many times over, total readership would have to be several million. It would be safe to suggest that the average master's thesis is seldom read by anyone except three or four bored professors assigned to the writer's graduate committee.

It was in that same year of 1969 that Trinity Evangelical Divinity School of Deerfield, Illinois, called Jim Kennedy in his office at Coral Ridge with a gratifying announcement. Its board of directors had voted unanimously to confer upon Jim his first doctorate, in recognition of his outstanding achievement in the clergy, particularly in the areas of church growth and evangelism. He officially became "Dr. Kennedy" as a special guest at the commencement exercise when the time-honored hood was draped over his shoulders and the Doctor of Divinity degree was placed in his hand. Jim appreciated the honorary sheepskin, but he had already set his sights on "the real thing," nine more strenuous summers ahead. He intended to earn the Ph.D.

"I want to show that Christianity is a reasonable faith and that it is compatible with the highest intellectual attainments," Jim says in explaining why he determined to go for the earned in addition to the honorary doctorate. "I recognize the opposing extremes of this question. Certainly there are those who have discredited the Gospel by their refusal to avail themselves of even a minimum preparation for the ministry. On the other hand, there are perhaps even more who have acquired the learning but have become heterodox or unorthodox in their preaching; they have become heretical and have denied the faith, and have thus dishonored the Gospel in that way. I think that what we need is an intellectual preparation and training combined with a scriptural faith and a warm heart.

"One of the real advantages of an education is that it can amplify and strengthen one's influence—and that, of course, can be either for good or for evil, depending on the person. But some of the greatest minds down through the ages, like Paul, Augustine, Luther, or Calvin have been used gloriously in the Lord's work. These were very highly trained, intellectual people who applied their gifts and abilities and learning for the glory of God, and they have had a far greater impact on the world because of their years of preparation than they would have had without them."

Jim has also explained the benefit of academic credentials this way: "Many believers like to accuse Christians and Christian ministers of being uneducated ignoramuses whose views on any matter are not worthy to be considered. The indication of academic degrees obviously silences this objection and hopefully removes a stumbling block on the part of some in listening to the Gospel."

Others, particularly those in the professions devoted to analyzing public affairs, have long been aware of the important link between education and evangelism. In an interview with Dr. Kennedy, nationally syndicated columnist Cal Thomas made this observation regarding television specials produced by Coral Ridge Ministries: "Jim, I believe that your voice is critically important, not only because of your commitment to the inerrancy and the infallibility of Scripture, but also because of the intellectual perspective that you take. There are those in this town [Washington, D.C.] and the 'intellectual elite' in this country who fancy themselves as being smarter than others. But you bring an intellectual soundness and a biblical scholarship to these important issues that I think are much needed in our culture, and I'm grateful for it."

New York University offered a summers-only graduate school option, which meant that Jim could chip away at the terminal degree without giving up his pastorale or interrupting his Coral Ridge ministry. It was 1979 before he found himself at the open-air commencement in Washington Square to add doctor of philosophy to his list of academic titles. His work had been in the Department of Religion within the School of Education at NYU. Strangely enough, the challenge of his studies for the doctorate had not matched that of his earlier master's work. "It's interesting," he noted, "that the Chicago Graduate School of Theology was the only graduate school I attended that was thoroughly Christian and evangelical, and it was far and away the most exacting and demanding academic preparation I had. The hardest I ever worked was at the Chicago institution; everything there was solid instruction and really worthwhile. I did not find the secular universities measuring up to the same standards. The most intensive learning experience I ever had came at the master's level—not on the Ph.D."

Nevertheless, there are very few preachers who have survived, or even entered, the Ph.D. wars. Academe still considers the Ph.D. to be the most prestigious prize it offers, and it has set up a number of barriers to discourage the fainthearted: residency requirements, foreign language proficiency, a formidable array of graduate hours beyond the master's, a heavyweight dissertation, oral examinations covering all course work and research, and on and on. Perhaps it should also be made clear that the Ph.D. was never designed for the purpose of turning people into philosophers. Dr. Kennedy was visiting in a home when a woman, who probably had learned that he held the degree, remarked felicitously: "All of the ministers where I come from, in Switzerland, are philosophers!" She may have considered it a compliment, but Jim wanted to tell her, "They would do the people more good if they stopped preaching philosophy and started preaching the Gospel of Jesus Christ."

Translated literally from the Greek parent-words, doctor of philosophy means teacher of the love of wisdom. There could hardly be a more appropriate title for a man of letters, or a more accurate description of the pastor of Coral Ridge Church. As his reputation spread, institutions of learning—like laurel trees yielding up their leaves to fashion the victor's crown— showered four more honorary degrees upon him. In 1985 it was Doctor of Sacred Literature from Christian Bible College; in 1986 it was the Doctor of Literature from California Graduate School of

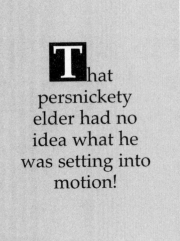

That persnickety elder had no idea what he was setting into motion!

Theology; in 1987 it was Doctor of Sacred Theology from Southwest Baptist University; and in 1992 it was Doctor of Humane Letters from Campbell University. No longer was a single line of type sufficient to contain the full record of scholarship: D. James Kennedy, A.B., M.Div., M.Th., D.D., Ph.D., D.Sac.Lit., Litt.D., D.Sac.Theol., D.Humane Let.

That persnickety elder of forty years ago had no idea of what he was setting into motion!

TURNING UP THE VOLUME(S)

*Oh that my words were now written! oh that
they were printed in a book!*
—JOB 19:23

Solomon once complained that "of making many books there is no end; and much study is a weariness of the flesh." But the backslidden monarch was totally out of fellowship with the Lord and was pretty well soured on most things when he wrote that; he was saying the same sort of thing about marriage and music and gourmet foods and entertainment and construction projects and even money. To the "Preacher" (Hebrew pen name *Koheleth*, better known to gentiles as Ecclesiastes), all was "vanity and vexation of spirit."

But most individuals fortunate enough to write a worthy book find the experience to be one of life's special rewards. There are solid reasons that propel men with a message— men like Jim Kennedy—toward authorship. With all the competition of recent communication media, such as film, radio, and television, the progenitor of all these is still around. As John Steinbeck observed, "the book has somehow kept its precious character." Strangely, one of humankind's most delicate and most vulnerable means of preserving thought—ink on paper— has also proved to be the most durable. The great movements of history and the knowledge of the ages have been passed down to the present generation, not by electronic gadgetry but in hundreds of thousands of tattered volumes written, printed, and circulated by the

There are solid reasons that propel men with a message toward authorship.

scholars of antiquity. God Himself chose this form for communicating His message to the world. He directed His first great prophet, immediately after the Exodus: "Write this for a memorial in a book. . . . And Moses wrote all the words of the Lord." From that time on, God's chosen race bore the identification, "the people of the Book."

While all the channels of public discourse exert influence on society, only the book can claim the power to effect changes in history and to restructure traditional thought. For example:

- The entire free world owes its existence to a single book, the Bible.

- One book by Karl Marx and Friedrich Engels, *The Communist Manifesto*, has been responsible for enslaving the people of nearly one-half the nations on earth under totalitarian and atheistic governments.

- *The Origin of Species*, by Charles Darwin, by convincingly arguing for the removal of the supernatural from human affairs, became the starting point for the decline of morals and spiritually-based education in most modern countries in the twentieth century.

- When Abraham Lincoln introduced Harriet Beecher Stowe, author of *Uncle Tom's Cabin*, at a political rally, he presented her as "the little woman who wrote the little book that started the big war."

- Upton Sinclair toured the meat-packing industry of Chicago and wrote of deplorable sanitation conditions in *The Jungle*. The book alone was credited with bringing about the passage of the Pure Food and Drug Act.

- In his early years as president of the Republic of China, Dr. Sun Yat-sen inclined toward Communism to the extent that he sent his future son-in-law, Chiang Kai-shek to Moscow for indoctrination. During a series of lectures to the Kuomintang (party), in which he advocated a government like Russia's, Dr. Sun was stricken with cancer. While he was recuperating he read a little paperback book that had been mailed to him anonymously; it was *A Theory of Social Control* by a New York dentist, Maurice William. The book presented a simple breakdown of the differences between Soviet Communism and American democracy as experienced by the author, who had lived under both systems. Sun Yat-sen was so impressed that when his health permitted a resumption of the lecture series, he reversed his stand, recalled Chiang from Moscow, and announced that China would hold to the Western concept of a free republic. The Chinese Reds left the party in anger, and the civil war began. Although Communism eventually prevailed, Dr. Sun kept it out of China for another twenty-five years—all because of one insignificant little book.

- A single volume, *Silent Spring* by Rachel Carson, warned against the danger of pesticides in the nation's food supply, raised society's awareness, and led to the creation of the Environmental Protection Agency.

- Regardless of whether one approves of Ralph Nader's tactics, his book, *Unsafe At Any Speed*, resulted in the adoption of new auto safety regulations, including the installation of seat belts in all cars.

Considering the potential for persuasion that may be locked up in the pages of one edition—and, in particular, its power to convince thought-leaders who influence the attitudes and actions of masses of people—it is not difficult to visualize the impact of a transforming best-seller like *Evangelism Explosion*, which has passed the 1.5 million mark. Millions of lives on every continent have been changed for eternity through the dissemination of Jim Kennedy's message about spiritual multiplication.

Evangelism Explosion was his first and his most important book. Since its publication, however, in 1970 by Tyndale House, other works have appeared on the market in a steady stream—bringing the total by 1999 to forty-four.

One of Jim's most prolific authorship years was 1973. *The God of Great Surprises* (Tyndale House) is a heartwarming review of the mysterious and marvelous ways in which God fulfills His

> *Evangelism Explosion* was his first and his most important book.

promises to those who put their trust in Him. And *This Is the Life* (Regal), a thoroughly inspirational little book, presents the best part of being a Christian—the joy of growing up in Christ and becoming conformed to His image through the power of the indwelling Holy Spirit.

A third book for 1973 was *Spiritual Renewal* (Regal). In perhaps his most personal and intimate style, Kennedy describes spiritual renewal as a continuing dialogue with God, a dialogue established and maintained through regular Bible study and prayer. The Bible, he explains, is God's way of speaking to humanity; prayer is humanity's way of speaking to God. By engaging in this daily conversation, every Christian can count on a closer walk with the Lord.

A venture into systematic theology appeared in 1974, *Truths That Transform* (revised 1996), which sets forth basic Christian doctrines along with an in-depth presentation of support from the underlying biblical sources. In scholarly yet warmly personal reasoning the author takes his reader step by step into some of the scriptural foundations of solid convictions. The pioneer Christian publishing firm so intimately related to the ministry of Dwight L. Moody, Fleming H. Revell, produced this doctrinal study, which now shares its title with the popular Coral Ridge radio program, *Truths That Transform*.

Six demanding years passed, during which Jim's deep involvement in graduate study and Coral Ridge delayed his next title, *Why I Believe*, published by Word in 1980 (revised 1996). In the introduction, Jim hints at the circumstances behind the writing of this work, which turned out to be one of his most widely read efforts, but he does not tell the rest of the story, which is of even greater reader interest.

"I was at home," Jim recalls, "when somebody called me up on the telephone and told me to tune in a local radio station where an atheist was answering questions that Christians were calling in. The guy was smart; he was chewing up his callers and spitting them out. He would say, 'Do you believe in God?' and as soon as he got an affirmative answer, he would ask, 'Why?' Then, 'Do you believe in the Bible? Why? That's a bunch of nonsense!' I didn't hear a single Christian give one reasonable answer as to why he believed anything. I tried all evening to get through to the station and was frustrated by a busy signal the whole time.

"So I decided to preach a series of sermons on 'Why

I Believe'—in God, in the Bible, in creation, in the Resurrection, in Heaven, in Hell, in the Virgin Birth, etc. I preached for four or five months on the archaeological validations of Bible truths, on scientific arguments for scriptural creation, on the cosmological and teleological evidence for the existence of God, and on the fallacies of many ethical systems and non-Christian religions. Then one day I got a call from the radio station; the program producer wanted to know whether I would be willing to debate an atheist on the air. 'Well, who is the atheist?' I asked. Sure enough, It was this same Dr. So-and-So who made a practice of devastating the beliefs of Christians.

"Believe me, I was so eager to get at this character, I accepted the invitation and was at the station at the appointed time. I had been boning up for months on every possible argument an atheist can think of, and after three solid hours in that cramped studio, that fellow did not know what had hit him. He said to the program host, 'Well, I guess I made an _____ out of myself tonight!' That was the most delightful three hours I've ever spent."

Why I Believe carries this inscription: "This book is affectionately dedicated to my mother." Ermine Roberson Kennedy, who had died shortly before the book came out, had made a profession of faith in Christ before her death.

The first book to be published by CRM was *Reconstruction* in 1982. In this issues-oriented exposition, Jim meets head-on a series of national problems which he categorizes as: liberalism in theology, relativism in ethics, humanism in education, socialism in economics, statism in political policy, corruption in government, immorality in entertainment and the arts, dishonesty in mass communication, defeatism in the rear-guard action against crime, retrenchment in international relations, and the mass murder of pre-birth humans. *Reconstruction* is strong medicine in a small package.

The year 1985 marked the publication of books that had

been in the writing stage for some time. *Chain Reaction* (Word) was a collaboration with T. M. Moore, a former vice president with Evangelism Explosion International, on changing the world through training witnesses to all nations. *The Great Deception* (CRM) is not a polemic against Russia or Red China but a penetrating exposé of Marxism and the diabolical abuse which Communists inflict on their own citizens. Finally, *Knowing The Whole Truth* (Revell) is a fascinating, statement-by-statement analysis of The Apostles' Creed, to bring that universal affirmation of Christian faith alive for those who recite it week after week.

In a somewhat different approach from the preceding books, *Messiah* (CRM 1986) reviews the specific prophecies regarding the first advent of Jesus Christ. Key predictions and their explicit fulfillment in the birth, life, death, and resurrection of the Messiah of the Jews and the Savior of the Gentiles are traced with careful attention to details of times, places, and circumstances.

In 1987 *Beginning Again* (CRM) came out in workbook format especially for the "babe in Christ." It focuses on the assurance of salvation, staying right with God, studying the Bible, practicing the art of prayer, continuing in fellowship, helping to change the world, and sharing the faith. Each chapter ends with a self-test for the reader to measure spiritual progress. The entire Gospel of John is included as the basic New Testament introduction to a growing faith.

In what is probably his hardest-hitting attack on any national evil, Kennedy's *A Nation in Shame* (CRM 1987), is grimly dedicated "to the victims of the American Holocaust." In this heavily researched investigation, he attempts to define the danger society faces concerning the human life issue and the reasons for the deep divisions of viewpoints over abortion, infanticide, and euthanasia. The ramifications of the pro-choice policy of the nation are balanced off against an alternative to "this acceptance of legalized murder." The author emphasizes that recognition of the unsavory facts about abortion is crucial to halting the erosion of American moral standards.

The final volume to appear in 1987 was entitled *Learning to Live with the People You Love* (Whitaker House—later reissued as *The Secret to a Happy Home*), a thoroughgoing documented treatise on family relationships and how they can be kept harmonious through application of Christian principles. *Your Prodigal Child*, touching on a related theme, was produced in 1988 by Thomas Nelson Publishers. Its compassionate aim of offering hope and comfort for hurting parents is supported by 235 pages of case histories, itemized instructions and suggestions, and great moral encouragement based on the specific promises of the Bible.

Jim's prolific publishing continued into the '90s. In 1991, *Turn It to Gold* tackled the tough subject of suffering, and brought comfort and fresh understanding to thousands. The fact that God sovereignly makes "all things work together for good" can, once grasped, bring peace in the face of great heartache. God, Jim wrote in this popular book, is the "great cosmic alchemist who never fails,"—who alone can turn the "lead" of our lives into gold.

Two years later Jim gave pastoral counsel on finding and doing God's will in *Delighting God: How to Live at the Center of God's Will*. As the title suggests, Jim addressed a broad range of topics, including how to be right with God, study the Bible, be pure in heart, and be successful "God's way." And he offered practical help, as well, on marriage, forgiveness, and coping with grief.

In *Foundations for Your Faith* (Revell, 1994), Jim took readers on a "quest to know and worship God better." This theology with a practical purpose used the *Westminster Confession of Faith* and *Larger* and *Shorter Catechisms*. The aim, Jim said, was not merely to learn interesting facts about God, but "to be forever transformed by God in how we think and live." To help make that a reality, *Foundations for Your Faith* became, in 1995, the "Life-Transforming Truths from a

Never-Changing God" trilogy (Revell). The three new titles, to which study guides were added, are *What is God Like?*, *How Do I Get to Know God?*, and *How Do I Live for God?*

In 1994, *Character & Destiny* (Zondervan) offered a definitive assessment of the "crisis of character" that would plague American politics and culture for the rest of the decade. As Jim concluded this work with a call for the "prodigal nation" to come home, one must wonder how different the history of the rest of the decade would have been had the nation more fully heeded his call.

That same year, Jim co-authored *What If Jesus Had Never Been Born?* (Thomas Nelson), the first of several works written with Jerry Newcombe, a producer for *The Coral Ridge Hour*. At a time when public mockery of Christians was reaching a crescendo, Jim offered a unique spin on the classic movie, *It's A Wonderful Life*, by taking a look at Jesus' impact on world history. "The book served as the launching point of a three-book series on how to address our culture's current backlash against historic Christianity," says Jim.

In 1996, Jim and Jerry continued the series with the publication of *The Gates of Hell Shall Not Prevail* (Thomas Nelson). This volume provides shocking documentation of the anti-Christian bigotry which has arisen in society and offers ways Christians can counter the bias. One reviewer called it "a theology of hope and an agenda of action."

Jim and Jerry would team up in 1998 for the third volume in their cultural apologetics series, *What If The Bible Had Never Been Written?* (Thomas Nelson). Coming to the defense of the greatest and most important book in human history, the authors set out to show how the Bible provided the foundation for what we call Western civilization. They also offer a theological defense for the reliability of the Bible and address the major challenges today to the spread of God's Word.

In the midst of this "cultural trilogy," Jim found time to produce *New Every Morning* (1996, Multnomah). Based on the sterling insights and stories Jim has shared in four decades of preaching, *New Every Morning* retells these truths in an easy-to-read daily devotional format.

Jim's next work, *Skeptics Answered* (1997, Multnomah), addressed the crucial questions that skeptics of the faith ask and Christians must answer. Chapter One, entitled "Skeptics Are Welcome," captures the essence of Jim's life-long evangelistic model. A man who is totally unashamed of the Gospel and has taken the time to research and study the tough questions of Christianity has always been ready to talk with honest seekers. "I pray this book will help you as you dialogue with skeptics or if you are a skeptic," wrote Jim. "In Christianity, honest answers exist for honest questions. Skeptics are welcome!" You can almost hear his Lord speaking, "Come, let us reason together."

An axiom of the book trade is that prolific writers are prodigious readers. GIGO (Garbage In—Garbage Out) did not originate with computers—what goes into the writer's head determines the quality of what comes out. A library of good books is the starting place of the next good book. The first thing Jim did after hearing that radio sermon by Dr. Donald Grey Barnhouse was to purchase a book. *The Greatest Story Ever Told* by Fulton Oursler and a copy of the Bible constituted his entire Christian book collection. A peek into the pastor's study today reveals approximately twelve thousand selected volumes.

The study itself is a delightfully secluded hideaway four floors above the main entrance to the church and accessible by elevator. It clings to the south side of the gigantic central tower like the eyrie of an eagle in a canyon wall. An irregular L-shaped room, blue-carpeted, it measures about thirty feet square in its largest dimension. Five narrow windows in beautifully colored faceted glass and three in clear glass admit a soft light, which is supplemented, of course, with strategically placed library lights.

Aside from a walnut desk, credenza, and chair, forty-four bookcases, each three feet wide and seven feet tall, are arranged in a number of configurations: side-by-side along the walls, individually between windows, and back-to-back in an impressive six rows of double-sided library stacks. A card catalog of thirty-six drawers records the massive collection. And—oh, yes—there is the prayer chair, an upholstered blue piece that CRM brought in to serve as a prop for television tapings, but which the pastor has used ever since for spiritual, rather than physical, support.

To the bibliophile, especially to one whose interests extend to religion, the neat rows of titles offer a veritable reading smorgasbord. There are seventy-two multi-volume series of expository works, twenty-seven sets of the great sermons of the past, eighteen sets of standard commentaries, thirteen sets of general reference books like encyclopedias. A mere glance at the shelf labels reveals the wealth of resource material available:

major prophets	philosophy
minor prophets	epistemology
New Testament	occultism
Gospels	humanism
theology	psychology
Divine attributes	logic
Christology	ethics
Jesus Christ	abortion
life / resurrection	history of philosophy
resurrection	religion
miracles	atheism
literature	creation-evolution
Americana	religion and science
biographies	Bibles
Christian biographies	Bible study
economics	Bible evidence
Communism	Bible inspiration
education	Bible prophecy
Greek	Bible dictionaries
Hebrew	Bible history

Christian Church history	Bible characters
cults	Judaism
marriage	archaeology
evangelism	Christian life
homiletics	grace
poetry	faith
trivia	predestination
knowledge	eschatology
sermons	apologetics
God	Holy Spirit

In blessed contrast to the pastor's business office, where the pace is about as frenetic as the pit of the New York Stock Exchange, no telephones derail a train of thought, no impatient foot traffic outside aborts the gestating idea, no sounds of choir, organ, and orchestra rehearsals distract a laboring imagination. Only quiet, peace, solitude, and trustworthy books—creativity's best companions.

And, of course, order. In each volume is a reference number tying it to the card catalog for quick locating and easy returning to the assigned place. In every book, opposite the flyleaf, is a simple bookplate: "From the Library of D. James Kennedy." That perfect order, it should be noted, was the work of a volunteer, Mrs. Cay Hunter, who maintained the collection ever since the study was built in 1974 until her retirement in 1997. Mrs. Hunter's patient work of cataloging each new acquisition and replacing each week the forty or fifty volumes that the pastor may have consulted for his Sunday sermons, is now being ably carried on by Anna Mae French.

In the earlier years Jim kept the books coming in by the box load at a pace that would frighten away most professional librarians. His helpers shuddered when they heard the pastor was in Grand Rapids, Michigan, which for decades has been one of the great centers of evangelical book publishing. Jim calls it "the secondhand bookstore of America" for preachers. "Places like Kregel's will have a basement containing over a hundred thousand used theological volumes of every description. I used to go through with a grocery cart and buy hundreds of books every time I went to Grand Rapids." By such individual, painstaking effort Jim has accumulated a highly selective library of valuable pastoral resources over the years.

In addition, the studious pastor stays abreast of current events by reading regularly not only the popular news magazines, but a weekly desk-tray full of periodicals with more esoteric titles, such as: *Biblical Archaeology Review, Christian History, Imprimus, The Blumenfeld Education Letter, The Trinity Review, Chronicles: A Magazine of American Culture, The Challenge, Bible-Science Newsletter, National Review, Scoreboard, Media Watch, Policy Review, The Heritage Foundation Backgrounder, Congressional Quarterly, Impact, Creation Ex Nihilo, Emerging Trends, The Freeman, CSCE Digest, Theology,* and *News and Notes*—more than forty specialized publications in all.

There may be possible differences of opinion over how accurately certain areas of the church are named—a narthex, an architrave, a transept. But there is no room for disagreement concerning the designation reserved for that lofty, isolated retreat overlooking busy Federal Highway. It is preclusively the study—an environment in which only the serious scholar can feel completely at home. A goodly measure of what you have received from the lips or the pen of the Coral Ridge pastor germinated there. It started with a prayer, it quickened into a thought, it expanded into a theme, and it flowered into a message fit to be shared with the world—fit, because in every instance it has been intended for the glory of God.

HEART BALM AND BRAIN FOOD

*And I will give you pastors according to
mine heart, which shall feed you with
knowledge and understanding.*
—JEREMIAH 3:15

Everybody knows that the purpose of preaching is to appeal to the hearts of people, to bring them to repentance, and to inculcate in them an abiding faith. But people's minds also require feeding with knowledge and understanding of all they have come to believe with their hearts. Spiritual growth, which essentially follows salvation, involves the edification or building up of the whole person—not just the emotions at the expense of the mind and will.

Jim Kennedy was astonished by his discovery as a young man of the reality of paradise. He could hardly believe the good news that eternal life was a free gift and that obtaining it was not at all a question of what he might be able to accomplish, but totally and exclusively a matter of what Christ had already done for him. He was astounded and amazed by the very existence of God's saving grace. As a child of God, he has never lost his profound wonder of the moment he first believed. The secret of his preaching is that each time he enters the pulpit he brings to his congregation that same astonishment and heartfelt gratitude to God for His goodness and for the love that led Jesus Christ all the way from an eternal paradise to a Roman cross, where He atoned for human sin.

The transmission of such sensations from an individual to a crowd requires expertise—an art the seminaries refer to as homiletics, the art of preaching with eloquence, the method by which the minister becomes a fisher of men. How he baits the hook in a very real way determines the size and quality of the catch. As the New Testament Church record makes clear, it is the Holy Spirit who adds daily to the Church such as should be saved; but the same record chronicles the Holy Spirit's use of individual personalities with their varying gifts and training and experiences. An ex-newspaperman who has been called into the ministry would be expected to employ some different techniques from a baseball player-turned-evangelist. A preacher with a strong intellectual bent will naturally weave into his powerful spiritual motivation his own unique characteristics, put together in a package we call pulpit style.

So it is not surprising that Jim Kennedy brings his own identifying particularities—"preacher traits" that give him a pulpit manner all his own.

BODY LANGUAGE

Because physical appearance and bodily movements create the very first impression that registers with the audience, perhaps this is the logical place to begin. Jim usually wears the handsome royal blue doctoral gown and red-collared hood of his alma mater, complete with black velvet trim down the front and three chevrons on each sleeve. For television end segments, however, he may wear a tailored business suit. His jet-black hair, lightly silvered over the top, always appears perfectly groomed.

As he begins to speak, each sentence seems to be delivered with premeditated emphasis and force accompanied by intensive facial expressions and visible movement of the upper body, arms, and hands. Unlike many of his colleagues today, Jim does not have the option of striding back and forth across a wide platform or tripping up and down stairs while preaching in the pulpit at Coral Ridge. His position is pretty well fixed underneath the tester and almost in the embrace of the sacred desk. Therefore, his frequent turning, lifting of the arms, or bending at the waist from his usual ramrod-straight posture, tend to be more noticeable than are more exaggerated movements by what have been called the "peripatetic preachers" ("those who walk around").

On one occasion, Jim was physically tired after a hard day but had to do a taping session in the late afternoon. When the producer stopped the operation after a minute or so and said, "Jim, you've got to bring your energy level up—it's too low," the normally sedate pastor startled the television crew by suddenly shouting and thrashing like a Norse berserker working himself into a frenzy before an impending battle. Suddenly calm again, he grabbed hold of the desk and said in mock relief, "Whew! I'm glad I'm not a charismatic!"

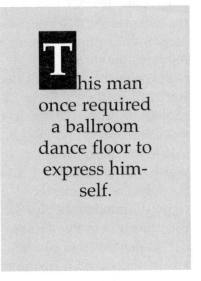

This man once required a ballroom dance floor to express himself.

For a man who once required a ballroom dance floor to express himself in physical movement, this preacher—now constrained to keep his feet planted on the spot marked "x,"—does a marvelous job of communicating with vigorous nods, with facial signals that convey to the farthest pew and to the television screen the genuineness of the words they accompany. His hands, like animated punctuation marks, add unspoken eloquence to the message.

VOICE

While the Lord has inspired many a person with a "slow tongue," like Moses, to be among His most powerful spokesmen, it would be difficult to argue that the gift of a mellifluous and commanding voice is of no advantage in preaching. Ministry effectiveness can be limited—at least as far as some listeners are concerned—by a stammering monotone or a gravelly hoarseness or a nasal whine. Of course, many servants of God have overcome such handicaps. But a resonant, rich, cultivated baritone voice can magnetize an audience to the message. Add to such eloquence learning and a desire for constant self-improvement, and you have an Apollos or his modern counterpart.

"For every summer of each year since I left seminary," Jim says matter-of-factly, "I have spent the time studying something related to the art of preaching, whether it's voice, oratorical speech, intonation, inflection, or vocabulary. What every public speaker is doing is painting pictures with words. One summer I studied just figures of speech—Spurgeon was a master at this. Another summer I studied figures limited to the five senses and how these are found in Scripture and in the writings of great preachers.

"I spent another summer doing a study of colors. Women are very good at knowing many shades and hues of color; most men can name only seven or eight. But there are literally hundreds of colors. Too much preaching is in black and white; but specific color words add to the appeal of spoken language just as color does to television. There is always something more to be studied in any of the arts. You never 'master' writing, speaking, painting, or singing; you spend your whole life at it. Unfortunately, too many preachers stop learning these things as soon as they leave seminary."

One comment a first-time listener is apt to make about Jim's preaching style is: "He certainly has a good delivery." Those who have heard him for many years believe that if he hasn't mastered the use of his wonderfully endowed and expertly disciplined vocal cords, he is very, very close to it.

ATTENTION GETTERS

The Word of God spoken with authority and sincerity is generally the best way for a minister to call to order the multitude of distractions that wander through congregational minds at the outset of any sermon. Few pronouncements can improve on "let us now hear the infallible Word of our God" and the recitation of a Scripture text followed by, "And may His name evermore be praised!"

But occasionally, a few well-chosen words may jab more deeply into a somnolent listener's mind and cause it to snap to attention for the message. One of Jim Kennedy's special talents is his marksmanship: when he fires a verbal pistol into the ear, the bullet smacks right into the bull's-eye of the brain:

- "All of us will soon be dead."

- "Today your eyes are going to look upon things which human eyes are not fit to look upon."

- "You hypocrites! You supercilious hypocrites! I know what you've been saying about me." Only later does the audience realize that he is speaking for the Roman procurator, Pontius Pilate.

- "You need a lawyer!"

- "I am about to preach the greatest sermon I have ever

preached. As a matter of fact, I am sure it will be the greatest sermon you have ever heard." His subject was humility.

- "There is a lot of talk today about sex." Guaranteed to get attention.

- "He was an animal lover, and that is why he purchased a newborn tiger cub."

- "The dread knell has struck!"

- "Do you have a problem this morning? I have a problem solver. Do you have a big problem this morning? I have a problem shrinker."

- "What's wrong with gambling?"

- "We get letters! I get letters and you get letters! We all get letters!"

- "Caterpillars do not lead very exciting lives."

- "September 1, 1983, is a day which will go down in infamy."

- "The letter was a mother's cry."

- "You have been called to a command performance!"

- "I suppose some of you think it is easy to be a minister of Jesus Christ . . . to live in a glass house and always to do the right thing. . . . Well, let me tell you, my friend, it is not!"

With openers like these, sermons from the Coral Ridge pulpit get and hold the interest of those in attendance and in television and radio audiences. A good beginning—whether it is for a thirty-minute sermon or a page-one news story, a television commercial, or a one-act play—is vitally important to the total communication and therefore to the end result that can be expected.

MEMORIZATION

Jim doesn't claim the photographic memory which has

been such a boon to the careers of many public speakers. "I had a terrible memory," he recalls. While still at the Arthur Murray studio in Tampa, after his decision to go into the ministry, he was walking through a department store when a book title on a distant wall seemed to jump out at him: *The Famous Roth Memory System.* He bought the book, went back to his office, and in two hours read it all. Calling his secretary into the office, he directed her to list one hundred common items—house, baseball, pencil, etc.—and to number them. "She thought I had lost my mind. But after reading that book, I found that I could recall the object for any of the one hundred numbers she read off to me. I was astonished; that really changed my life in many ways. For example, in seminary I had a church history test coming up the next day and had no time to review for it. I got a book which listed the significant events of Church history, picked out the three centuries the test would cover, and memorized each event and its date. I think I used 123 dates on my exam. The professor gave me an A+, but I wonder to this day if he thought I cheated."

Jim can easily commit to memory up to ten minutes of poetry or prose by going over it many times during the week before a sermon is given. He found Napoleon Bonaparte's famous speech on the deity of Christ so eloquent and convincing that he used the entire speech in a sermon. He recited about 75 percent of the total message, more than twenty minutes, from memory. He still continues his study of mnemonics (the training of memory) right down to the present time.

"The Bible says that if we will hide God's Word in our hearts and meditate upon it, He will give us good success. I believe that, and I started out in seminary to learn a chapter of Scripture a day. Right now I am committing the Gospel of John to memory, adding ten or twelve verses each night before I go to bed. The trouble is that the farther you get into the book, the longer it takes to review; and if you can't review, then you gradually lose it. But memorizing Scripture is very helpful. It's a great help, not just in preaching, but in living and learning and doing everything you have to do."

DRAMATICS

T. DeWitt Talmage, a famous American minister around the turn of the century, delivered a remarkable sermon in which he called for preachers with dramatic talent to use it for the sake of the Gospel. He was not calling for acting or pretending in the pulpit, but for injecting reality and personality into the message. "Too often," he said, "we preachers moan religion, we groan religion, we wail religion. . . . And yet the theater and drama carry away people by the millions while we groan and drone them right out of the churches." In his sermon, Talmage made reference to leading pulpiteers of the past who made outstanding use of their dramatic ability. George Whitefield, for instance, is considered by many to have been the greatest preacher who ever lived. He was so effective that the famous actor, David Garrick, once said he would give ten thousand pounds if he could only enunciate "Oh!" with the feeling that Whitefield put into it. So unusual was the preacher's dramatic prowess that the critics, instead of referring to him as "the David Garrick of the pulpit," chose to call the world's top professional actor "the George Whitefield of the platform!"

Jim Kennedy never was an actor. But in his writing and his sermon delivery he displays all the gifts and instincts of a Thespian. Those who have heard him for any period of time know that he often speaks the lines of an apostle, a Pharisee, a Judas Iscariot in startlingly realistic tones. A Christmas message, "Merry Tifton," is a modern parable that calls for the preacher to impersonate the speech of a range of characters from Dixie drawl to New Yorkese; the first half of the sermon is pure theater. And, lest we forget, it was Jesus who made the parable the dramatic art form we know today.

A Reformation Day address carried the congregation back to Martin Luther's ordeal before the Diet of Worms before an electrified crowd of five thousand in the huge cathedral that was his hall of judgment. Jim painted the timeless scene, reminiscent of the gruesome trial of the preceding century that had condemned John Hus to be burned alive at the stake, with masterful dramatic suspense as the Roman legate fired off the question: "Will you or will you not recant?"

"That question was like a spear piercing to his heart. Luther's knees weakened, his head spun, and his imagination conjured up visions of roaring flames consuming the body of Hus. Luther's friends had been right. There would be no debate; there would be no opportunity to defend his teachings. Such had never been intended. Luther pleaded for a little more time to consider.

"Dr. Eck [the Catholic legate] repeated, 'We want an answer, a direct answer without horns or hoofs. Will you or will you not recant?'

"The flag for the last lap had been raised. As Christ had once stood before Pontius Pilate, a representative of imperial Rome, so Luther stood now before representatives of another kind of Roman authority. Being part of perhaps the most critical moment in modern history, Luther made a decision to change the course of future centuries. Looking to God for strength, he said, 'My conscience is bound by the Word of God. Unless I am convicted and refuted by Holy Scripture, since it is wrong to go against conscience, I cannot and I will not recant anything.' This included a belief that both councils and popes may err.

"A huge roar went up crying, 'Burn him! Burn him!' And in the midst of that roar, the legate said, 'You cannot prove that they have erred.'

"Luther cried out, 'I will prove it if you will give me a chance to speak.'

"Over the howling and baying of the people, Eck was

heard to cry again, 'Will you or will you not recant?'"

At this point in Jim's sermon, a visitor seated near the front of the church—who happened to be one of the nation's best-known publishers of religious books—had been so caught up and carried along by the sheer drama of the words coming from the pulpit that he momentarily lost touch with his surroundings and thundered out at the top of his voice: "No!" Jim was so startled that he almost lost his place in the narrative, which he was reciting entirely from memory, but he went on with his message. Later he confessed, "It was all I could do to keep going." If the proof of successful drama is, as the experts define it, "the voluntary suspension of disbelief" on the part of the audience, then Jim's presentation had met the ultimate test.

Soren Kierkegaard, the Danish theologian and philosopher, once made the insightful observation that many people think of the church as a sort of "holy drama," where the preacher is an actor, God is the prompter, and the congregation are the critics (they pass their critique as they leave church with a "Good job, preacher," or in more detail at the dinner table where they have "roast preacher"). But the truth, according to Kierkegaard, is that the congregation are the actors, the preacher is the prompter, and God is the critic. "How are you-all doing with the sermon today?" Jim once asked, after referring to Kierkegaard's illustration. A couple of weeks later, a man stopped at the door after the service and said to him, "Nice prompting, preacher."

"But dramatizing, as a discipline, is not easy," Jim observes, "It's always hard. It's like soaring up in the air; the higher you go, the farther you can fall if everything isn't handled just right. I have prayed that the Lord would give me more of that opportunity and that He would enable me to do it."

The truth is that Jim Kennedy could have made a superb character actor in legitimate theater. The passing years have brought to his naturally handsome features a somewhat Lincolnesque imprint—a masculine visage softened by a kind heart. Deep concentration lines crease the forehead above and between heavy brows; dark hazel eyes with penetrating gaze are framed by distinct laughter wrinkles at the outside corners; teeth as white and as straight as a movie star's flash from behind mobile lips; and a determined chin gives him an air of authority and complete self-control.

But while drama may be his talent, acting is the farthest thing from Jim's mind. His heroes are not the Charlton Hestons and the Gregory Pecks of this world, but the Charles Spur - geons and the Peter Marshalls. "Really great preaching, in my opinion, is one of the most marvelous experiences in the world. It is what all of us in the ministry should aspire to."

ERUDITION

One of the telltale symptoms of a *literatus* (genuine intellectual) is a recurring monomania (single-minded compulsion) to employ the *bon mot* (an especially fitting word or expression) as long as he can be sure of avoiding any impression of pedanticism (excessive or inappropriate show of learning). To the man of letters, truly "right" words are as irresistible as French chocolates—not always easily digested, perhaps, but a delight to the tongue. As a matter of fact, it was a Frenchman, Guy de Maupassant—probably the premier short-story writer of all time—who took this as his motto: "Whatever you have to say, remember that there is one noun to name it, one adjective to describe it, one verb to give it life. Keep searching until you find that one word."

This means that, in preaching, an occasional esoteric word or phrase may be used if it is explained. And that is the precise role of the traditional "parson"; the "parson" was generally the one "person" in the community, or one of the very few, who had been fully educated. His challenge was to get his message down to where the "sheep"—people largely without any formal schooling—could feed upon it. Today, there are enormous numbers of college graduates in every congregation. At the same time, many clergymen, especially on television, have scarcely made it through high school, or perhaps attended a Bible college for a while. Consequently, the attitude among many worldlings is not that Christianity is so high they cannot attain to it, but that it is so low it is contemptible and beneath their consideration.

"I think it is good occasionally," Jim concludes, "just to take a shot over the bow to let it be known there are some things the unbeliever doesn't understand; it can make him sit up and realize that the Christian message is not beneath his level of intelligence at all. One in a sermon is usually enough; a whole service full of elite expressions would certainly be counterproductive."

One example of the use of such verbal harpoons is the exotic expression borrowed bodily from other languages. In every such case, translation and full explanation are given to clarify the appropriateness of the choice. Jim has used "awakeners" like these:

- *mirabile dictu!* (strange to say, marvelous to relate)

- *vox populi, vox dei* (the voice of the people is the voice of God)

- *"Resurgam!"* should be the motto of every Christian ("I shall rise again!")

- Ah, the *amicus Caesarae* (friend of Caesar)

- We come to the pinnacle of the *ordo salutis* (way of salvation)

- the *arrhabon* of tradition (down payment)

- *en arché ein ho Logos* (in the beginning was the Word)
- here we have the *protoevangelium* (first Gospel)
- Indeed, *avisé la fin* (consider the end)
- There are two very distinct *Weltanschauung* in the world today (manner of looking at the world or worldview)
- *El Gibbor* (the mighty God)
- *Nun-ki* (prince of the earth)
- *Isidis* (attack of the enemy)
- *Al Akrab* (scorpion)

The first five expressions above are taken from the Latin; the next three from Greek; then one example each from French, German, Hebrew, Akkadian, Coptic, and Syriac. These are rather special word selections. When they are clarified and applied to the thought at hand in the sermon, each one adds immeasurably to the flavor of the whole, like a blueberry in a muffin. And the listener is hardly aware of the time, the labor, and the intellectual resources that bring such minutiae of the world's vast learning to his passing attention.

The preparation of an exegetical sermon—one which "exegetes" or interprets Bible texts—is much easier than, say, a historical sermon in which names, dates, events, and related information must be researched and authenticated. Volumes of commentaries and concordances stand ready to assist any pastor in explaining every word and phrase of scriptural passages. But if the topic is scientific or biographical, facts must be ferreted out of any number of documents in hours of painstaking research. This is not to say, by any means, that fact-based sermons are superior to those drawn exclusively from Scripture; some of the very best preaching is exegetical. Jim estimates that approximately 75 percent of his preaching is exegetical or textual/topical. But it should be obvious that messages from the Coral Ridge pulpit on the

Christianity of C. T. Studd, Abraham Lincoln, Henry Drummond, David Livingstone, John Bunyan, George Washington, John Knox, William Wilberforce, Mary Slessor, J. S. Bach, John Milton, William Carey, and many others required a scholarly background plus hours of studious preparation.

Now, if the subject is extremely technical, the preacher may lead his audience through a veritable minefield of jaw-breakers, sharing with them such tangy treats as: *Eoanthropopus dawsoni, Hesperopithecus haroldcookii, Homoneanderthalensis, Zinjanthropus,* and *Australopithecines.* He will make direct reference to these for one purpose: to expose the absurdity of the scientist who thinks he can actually remove God from His own universe and substitute an often ludicrous theory for the creation account given in the Word of God. While Jim treats scientific knowledge with respect, he zeroes in on the pseudoscience against which Paul warned the young Timothy to be on constant guard.

In a fascinating, thirteen-week sermon series, "The Real Meaning of the Zodiac," an incredible study of astronomy, mythology, linguistics, and Bible prophecy, Kennedy's love of words and their significations presented his audiences with an etymological feast. An excerpt:

"It is very interesting that when the names of this constellation (*Naz* [hawk]) and its major star (*Seir*) are combined, we get the words *Naz-Seir.* Jesus Christ is called the *Naz-Seir-ene. Naz* means 'sent or caused to come swiftly,' and *Seir* means Prince. *Naz-Seir* means 'the sent Prince,' the One who is sent forth quickly, a Prince of all the earth who is to come into the world.

"Bible scholars were at a loss to explain by what prophet or in what sacred prophecy it was said that Christ should be called a Nazarene. They had looked in vain in the Old Testament for some reference which would indicate just what that was referring to without finding it. So though they have said that He would be a Nazarene, there is no prophecy of that in the Old Testament. Yet the prophecy that He would be the 'sent Prince' come into the world for us has been in the sky from the beginning of creation."

The emphasis has always been squarely on Jesus Christ, whether the language has been of childlike simplicity or an occasional utterance to wrinkle the pundit's brow. To this preacher, vocabulary is but another tool chest to be opened and used to make the communication of the Gospel more exciting and to bring glory to God.

HUMOR

When Ronald Reagan took over the reins of government from Jimmy Carter in 1981, the galling problems facing the nation and spreading gloom around the world didn't go away; some, like the deficit, actually worsened. But somehow, things *seemed* to be better. For eight years America felt better about itself than it had for a long time. Why? One of the basic reasons historians cannot brush aside is simply that the man had a wonderful sense of humor. He had the rare ability to laugh at the right things at the right time and in the right way and thus bring relief and renewed confidence to a specter-ridden society. A psychiatrist knows that a person who can laugh at himself and his frustrations is unlikely to become a patient. Even the Bible reminds that "a merry heart does good, like medicine." The reader has already seen, in chapter 8, a demonstration of Jim Kennedy's sparkling feel for humor. He relishes dropping in the appropriate anecdote among weighty concepts to provide welcome comic relief or to steer the prevailing mood of a situation in an unexpected direction. During a particularly heavy afternoon of dictation, for example, with an ominous foot-high stack of letters to be answered still piled high on his desk, Jim suddenly stopped speaking. His secretary, looking up from her dictation pad, was horrified to see him slipping slowly out of his tall chair and out of sight below the desk top. Before she could cope with the "emergency," she saw only his hand above the surface of the desk, clutching a white handkerchief and waving it in weary surrender. The serious-minded pastor can dispense impromptu good humor in the most unexpected situations. In response to a request from his youth minister that he make a surprise appearance before an auditorium full of the church's young people, Jim cut short a session in a television studio several miles away and hurried to keep the appointment. Remembering the young minister's emphasis on making it a "surprise experience" for the youngsters, the senior minister walked in calmly, mounted the stage, and with all the finesse of a slapstick artist hit the youth minister in the face with a cream pie.

One of the self-improvement courses Jim subjected himself to in the late 1960s was the Evelyn Wood Speed Reading Course. He wanted to enlarge his capacity for taking in more information in a shorter time. He was conscientious about his daily practice sessions, and before long he could actually skim through the entire Bible in one hour, the Gospel of John in just one minute, and original Greek at the rate of one thousand words per minute.

The exercise called for a special positioning of the body into a sort of wrestler's crouch, with one arm encircling the book and pinning it down firmly so that the pages could be flipped as rapidly as possible with the other hand, which was equipped with a rubber finger tip to insure traction.

Faithful to his daily self-discipline, Jim was in just such a stance aboard a plane, bearing down on his Bible and zipping through the pages as fast as he could turn them. Out of the corner of his eye he could see that a passenger across the aisle from him was totally transfixed at the sight of a man on a plane wrapped around a Bible and whooshing through the pages almost faster than the optic nerve could absorb. Finally, the poor fellow could stand it no longer. He came over to where Jim was pursuing his new skill and asked in disbelief, "You're not really reading that Bible, are you?" Jim, in a calculated release of roguish humor, replied without looking up: "Finger exercise."

Jim regularly delights his audiences with funny stories to ease them into his subject or to bring them back from too much theology to the everyday world. Here are some others he has smuggled into the sanctuary:

"The man of the house had plopped himself into his easy chair before television all fall, watching every football game that was on. His wife, fed up with being ignored, had had enough. She went in, stomped her foot, placed her hands on her hips, and said, 'Now I want to know, which do you love the most—me or football?' Silence. Finally, after a long period, he looked up at his wife, tried a weak smile, and said: 'I love you more than I love hockey.'"

"Peter Marshall used to tell about a church member who had always tithed, but told his pastor that he was now making a million dollars a year and simply could not afford to tithe that much. The pastor said, 'All right, let's pray about it. Lord, this man has a serious problem. Please reduce his income back to where it was so that he can tithe again.'"

"The old preacher was celebrating his fiftieth wedding anniversary with the bride of his youth. 'Did you ever at any time think about divorce?' someone asked. 'Never!' he thundered. 'Not even one time?' another persisted. 'Absolutely not. Never once did I consider such a thing! Murder, yes, several times. But never divorce!'"

"One wag, when asked what sign he was born under, said, 'The best I remember, it said Maternity Ward.' When someone asks you that, tell them: 'I have a slight problem when you ask me what sign I was born under because, you see, I was born twice.' That answer will give you a good entree into the Gospel."

"The children in Sunday school had been learning Scripture verses. The day came for the big quiz, and the question was asked: 'What is the Bible definition of a lie?' Little Johnny was on his feet, all smiles—he had the answer. 'A lie,' he said, 'is an abomination unto the Lord and a very present help in time of trouble.'"

"The Supreme Court justices, on the occasion of Sandra Day O'Connor's ascension to that high bench, took the much younger and only female member of the court out to dinner. The waiter stopped at her chair first and asked for her entree order. She gave it, and then he asked, 'What about the vegetables?' 'Oh, they'll order for themselves,' she answered."

"The public school teacher, recently warned about the illegality of prayer in the classroom, entered the building at the close of recess and found a group of students kneeling in one corner of the classroom. 'Students! Students! What are you doing?' she gasped. One uninhibited little fellow looked up and said, 'We've been shooting craps, Teacher.' 'Oh, my,' she breathed. 'I was afraid you were praying!'"

"Origen, an early church father, speculated that in Heaven we will be perfect—and therefore, since a sphere is the most perfect geometrical form, we will all be spheroid in Heaven. Some of you are already approaching—indeed, some of you have virtually arrived at—perfection!"

To those who know how to use it, humor is a welcome needle prick that can let the pressure out of a blister, release some of the pain from a boil, extract the splinter from a sore finger, and restore a smile to a downturned mouth. Jim Kennedy knows how to use it.

BALANCE

It is one thing to possess certain gifts and skills. It is quite another to put them to good and productive work. Yes, many preachers can make their parishioners feel, make them repent, make them think, make them listen, make them smile. But the consummate employment of such natural gifts and acquired skills depends upon a sense of timing and of fitness. The word fitly spoken becomes like golden apples in silver pictures. The adroit use of the pregnant pause, the blending of the simple with the abstruse, the right application of humor as a foil to scholarship are reflections of the mind of the speaker. That mind is like the console of a great organ where all of the vast resources of the instrument are kept under control to produce perfect harmony.

In reaching out to people's hearts and minds, Jim Kennedy displays his genius for maintaining balance at all times. His preaching never approaches the banal, the stuffy, the frivolous, the maudlin, or the specious for the simple reason that his self-discipline is rooted in true humility under God. The listener carries away from a Kennedy sermon an awareness of the presence of a profound and sincere reverence permeating the entire message and church service. Jim's pulpit performance, after all, is not a matter of his techniques but his priorities—Christ, salvation, eternal life, Heaven, victory, and the glory of God.

In his own words, the Coral Ridge preacher assesses his calling in terms reminiscent of a man describing his first love: "I believe in the absolute primacy of preaching. There's nothing like it. Jesus not only came preaching, but He said to us, 'Go, preach the Gospel.' That's what we are engaged in doing. God is pleased to save the world, and it is the preached Word that He has used.

Alexander White saw the great glory of preaching. He said, 'If God has called you to be a preacher, don't stoop to be a king.' The way Phillips Brooks put it was: 'Let us rejoice together that in a world filled with so many good and great things to do, God has given us the happiest and the best. He has called us to be preachers of His truth.'

"And what a joy that is. What a glorious privilege that is. Every Sunday afternoon as I take off my robe and hang it up on the back of the door, the thought now enters my mind that the day will be coming, and not too long hence, when I will hang that up for the last time. And that thought, which has recurred more and more frequently in recent years, has made me realize afresh how glorious is the privilege of preaching the Gospel of Jesus Christ:

- "To stand before this sacred desk, to open that Holy volume, to look out into the faces of men and women who soon will be standing before the great assize giving answer to their Creator;

- "To proclaim the glorious truth of everlasting life offered to us through Christ our Savior;

- "To unburden our souls of that message which God has laid upon them and to know that the eternal future of many, humanly speaking, hangs that day upon what we say;

- "To call men and women to repent of their sins and to follow the King of kings and Lord of lords;

- "To convince, as well as to woo; to arouse, to calm, to charm, to enlighten, to persuade, to convert—all in the power of the Holy Spirit.

"This is the greatest calling in all of the world, and this is what we are called to do as preachers of the Gospel. But who is sufficient for these things? Woe unto that man whoever supposes that he has arrived in the art of preaching. It is a trust that calls forth our greatest efforts of heart and mind and body and soul."

FOR A GODLY EDUCATION

*Train up a child in the way he
should go: and when he is old,
he will not depart from it.*
—PROVERBS 22:6

Even in the most casual conversation, his words seem to be chosen with deliberation, as if each is being screened mentally before it is allowed utterance. The tonal inflections of his phrases and sentences sound as if they are consciously modulated and under the control of a disciplined spirit at all times. His countenance reflects a gracious disposition, and his manners are genteel, almost courtly.

But such genuine attributes may divert the attention of those who don't know Jim Kennedy, from another quality of character beneath that amiable and cultured exterior. It is a flint-like resolve, a spirit of determination that will not brook discouragement, that cannot be dissuaded by faulty logic or inflamed emotion, and that does not compromise with the goal of excellence. A national magazine said of him: "He is as tough as they come. . . . He works quietly but with powerful effect."[5]

When such a man wants to build a place of worship and can't start it in a church building, he does it in a schoolhouse. When he envisions a worldwide Gospel outreach and doesn't know how to do it, he struggles and studies until he discovers a way. When he becomes distressed over the lack of quality Christian education in his community, he finds three hundred prospective students and starts a school of his own.

Why would the pastor of the fastest-growing church in his denomination want to get involved in all the problems of creating and nurturing a school in 1971? Like every other impetus in his life since he was twenty-four, this drive was also motivated and powered by a conviction drawn from the Word of God. He had learned from Scripture that apostasy and anarchy can dominate the life of any nation if the coming generation fails to share the beliefs and ethical values of godly parents. He noted with dismay that while the Pilgrim Fathers signed the Mayflower Compact stating that they had come to America "for the glory of God and Advancement of the Christian faith," it is unlawful today for children in the public schools to read it or to hear it read or even to pray publicly to the God of the Bible. That, he felt, was as far from godly roots as was the generation that followed the divinely protected days of Joshua—"a generation which knew not the Lord" and ushered in the blackest four-hundred-year period of desolation experienced by any ancient nation. In all that time, there was no stable government, as "every man did that which was right in his own eyes." It's all recorded in the book of Judges.

Until 1837, virtually all education in this country was private and Christian.

Few Americans realize

that for 217 years—from 1620 when the Pilgrims landed until 1837—virtually all education in this country was private and Christian. Secular public education was not even a consideration. It is a rather recent phenomenon developed in the nineteenth century. Nearly all of the first 123 colleges and universities established in America were built to the glory of God and the advancement of the Christian faith—those are the words by which Harvard, Yale, William and Mary, Columbia, Princeton, Rutgers, Dartmouth, Brown, and many others advertised themselves. All were founded by Christian denominations, and all were grounded in the Christian view of life. Under the brilliant leadership of Horace Mann, a Unitarian, secular public education was established in the 1830s, to be paid for by tax dollars, with laws making state education of children compulsory. Our educational system today is a result of Mann's philosophy. At about the same time A. A. Hodge, the famous Princeton seminarian, made a prophetic comment: "I am as sure as I am of the fact of Christ's reign that a comprehensive and centralized system of national education, separated from religion, as it is now commonly proposed, will be proved the most appalling scheme for the propagation of anti-Christian and atheistic unbelief, and of antisocial nihilistic ethics—individual, social, and political—which this sin-rent world has ever seen."

What was the result of over two hundred years of private Christian education? In the early 1800s, according to John Quincy Adams, only .004 percent of the people were illiterate—unable to read or write. After 150 extra

After 150 years of public education, America has forty million illiterates.

years of increasingly secularized public education and more than $1 trillion of tax money to finance it, the illiteracy rate by 1992 had risen to 21 percent or forty million functional illiterates in America—people who can hardly read a road sign or write a check. An estimated four million adults, eight percent of the population, do not have even these rudimentary skills. Public education took another downward turn in the twentieth century when John Dewey's "progressive education" ideology was introduced with Dewey's dedication to the Darwinian theory of evolution as its starting point. Dewey was convinced that things and events were not supernaturally caused and that humanity could have dominion over the environment only by relying on human reason. In other words, to the secularist view was added the humanist religion; as the *Humanist Manifesto* states, "No deity will save us; we must save ourselves."

It should be acknowledged that Dewey was never openly hostile or cynical toward evangelical Christianity as were many other intellectuals of his time. He clearly felt that Christians were out of step with reality and the coming trends of the future. Sadly, his tolerance of orthodox faith encouraged Americans to embrace his ideas. Although Dewey's philosophy is no longer accepted as the intellectual framework for our public school system, most of the basic presuppositions of Dewey's viewpoint still dominate it. Tens of thousands of Christian people labor diligently in the public school system, often placing their jobs on the line by teaching moral standards and upholding the existence of God, but Dewey's influence strongly outweighs their impact. America's schools are now thoroughly materialistic.

Aware of this thinking, Jim Kennedy got involved in the fight to redeem education. He planned to start a Christian school offering an education centered in God. "We cannot have a world in which God does not exist, a creation without a Creator," he says. "It is a reality which has been ripped away from its source. When students come to absorb this reality, chaos ends up in their minds. A secularist today also basically is amoral. He or she cannot take a position on morals because, without a divine revelation, you cannot have a sound foundation of morals." He points to today's parents' tragic familiarity with rape, drugs, promiscuity, suicide, alcoholism, delinquency, poor performance, assaults on teachers, even murder.

"We banished God from our schools on behalf of this glorious new system that was to have created a marvelous education and a wonderful new society. Instead, we have a moral jungle and an academic nightmare," he concludes. "I am serving on a national committee which is trying to help get prayer back into the public schools. This I would like to see happen, but I must confess that deep down, I have a sneaking suspicion that it is somewhat like putting a Band-Aid on a cancer patient or like opening up the evening session at the local bar with a word of prayer. I am not so sure how meaningful that might be. Nevertheless, we will try. But I thank God that the Christian school movement is growing faster than any other sector in education today—at one report, a Christian school was being created every six hours. That's four each day or fifteen hundred a year!"

Once Jim made the decision to provide a godly educational environment for the children of Coral Ridge Church parents and for other Christian families who could show serious intent, Westminster Academy was set up, not as an independent school, but as an institution deliberately placed under the spiritual oversight of the church elders. A school board was composed of parents of school-age children from the church. A curriculum was planned, guidelines and policies were set, available buildings were outfitted as temporary classrooms, a faculty was hired, advertisements were released—and the school opened for classes from early kindergarten through the twelfth grade.

The founder was meticulous about every detail of getting the school started right, including the preparation of a logo or crest to identify Westminster Academy on its official letterhead and publications and memorabilia. Jim had ordered artwork featuring the lion, which was to be the school mascot. He had discovered about 150 appearances of that majestic creature in the Bible, which is used symbolically, of course, to represent Jesus Christ, "the Lion of the tribe of Judah," particularly in connection with his triumphant Second Coming as the all-conquering King of kings. He was not satisfied with the model drawn by a professional artist, so he researched a few books, bought a drawing pad, and set himself to creating a school crest. He drew a pair of lions rampant, facing each other and separated by the sword of the Spirit topped by the helmet of salvation, and overlaid with the shield of faith—all familiar figures from Ephesians 6. He then dissected the shield into four fields, placing W and A in the upper and both halves of the open Bible in the lower. In nearly microscopic size on the Old Testament side are the actual Hebrew characters with which Genesis 1:1 begins, and on the New Testament side appear the Greek words for "In the beginning was the Word. . . ." Finally, faithful to heraldry traditions, Jim penciled in significant Latin slogans such as: *In Omnibus Ipse Primatum Tenens* (that in all things He may have the preeminence); *Deus and Patria* (God and Country); *Excellentia in Academica* (academic excellence); and *Soli Deo Gloria* (solely to the glory of God).

Such scholarly concern for the symbol was prophetic of the quality of supervision that would bring fame to the school itself as an educational institution. Within five years, Westminster Academy would become the first Christian school in Florida to be accredited by the Southern Association of Colleges and Schools and to win recognition by the Florida Council of Independent Schools. Even before the birth of Westminster Academy, inquiries had been made into the possibility of obtaining an educational radio frequency for Christian broadcasting. Many delays and roadblocks had to be overcome before Station WAFG (Westminster Academy for God) became Broward County's first noncommercial channel. The twenty-four-hour FM circularly polarized system has effective radiated power of three thousand watts. The especially engineered facilities installed in fourth-floor quarters went on the air full time in 1974 and now reach daily into South Florida. As its name, Westminster Academy for God, implies, the station is designed to aid the growth of the Christian community and serves the community at large through public affairs programming, educational programming, and a relevant application of the Word of God to the community's needs and aspirations.

Almost from its beginning, the school has been under the direction of Dr. Kenneth Wackes, a former missionary to New Guinea, who has seen the program expand from its first graduating class of eight students in 1973 to ninety-nine in 1998. Year by year, classroom space, laboratories, gymnasium facilities, new offices, computerized installations, a new athletic field and swimming pool have kept pace with an enrollment now right at thirteen hundred students, served by ninety instructional staff. An unusual qualification of every person employed at Westminster Academy is a full, unashamed confession of Jesus Christ as Lord and Savior and a commitment to putting God at the center of every educational activity.

The headmaster and the pastor share with equal fervor and conviction the concept of the school as a ministry. "I have benefited from and enjoyed greatly," Dr. Wackes says, "the degree of freedom that he has given to me to head the ministry at Westminster Academy without interference. I enjoy brainstorming with Jim because he is always excited about and open to new approaches and new ideas if it appears that they are the result of careful investigation and good research. I've also found him to have a pastor's heart and have benefited greatly from the times that I have been able to share personal concerns with him and then to have him pray with me."

This mutual trust plays an important role in the joint effort to achieve the highest educational goals. "On several occasions," Dr. Wackes adds, "when I have mentioned to him that he has not attended a school board meeting in sixteen years [Jim is an ex-officio member], he replied that there was no need for him to attend because he trusted my leadership entirely. Obviously, that not only gives me great encouragement, but is also a motivating factor to do all things well and never to bring embarrassment to the church or to Dr. Kennedy through a lack of effort or poor planning on my part. He has my highest respect as a leader, a thinker, an expositor of Scripture, a fellow minister, and one who has wisdom from above."

Is the emphasis on Christian lifestyle compatible with academic achievement? A roster of the nearly 1,700 graduates of past years reads like a Who's Who of professional leaders. It includes doctors, missionaries, engineers, lawyers, college professors, ministers, and successful businessmen. A whopping 93.4 percent of Westminster Academy's students go on to college.

This Christian school can also compete in sports. Students who are qualified to play football, basketball, volleyball, soccer, baseball, softball, tennis, golf, and to participate in cross-country, water polo, swimming, or track find themselves in competition with Class 2A schools from all parts of Florida. In 1999, the Westminster boy's baseball team and the girl's fast-pitch softball teams won their respective state titles.

Each year, the Florida Coaches' Association, which represents all secondary schools in the state, both public and private, selects the most outstanding school athletic program. In one stretch of eight years, that distinctive honor went to Westminster Academy seven times. "Excellence in all things" is obviously more than just a catchy Coral Ridge slogan.

By creating an environment which frankly exalts the spiritual, the academic, personal discipline and all-out patriotism, Jim feels that "the rotting corpse of secular humanism, together with all of its adjacent evils and misery," can be replaced by a new and vital Christian education that will awaken the American vision of a godly republic. "Christ must rule," he says, "over every thought, every action, every plan, every area of life. It is this vision of Christian education that we must pursue with all our hearts, minds, and souls. Such a view taught to our children shall create, by God's grace, such a Christian civilization as has never been seen in the history of the world."

In 1989, the pastor received the go-ahead from the Session of the church to open Knox Theological Seminary. This signaled the fulfillment of another dream of Jim Kennedy, who early in his ministry at Coral Ridge, was offered a professorship in Greek at Belhaven College. "My goal is that Knox Seminary will combine quality academics with a passionate commitment to the sovereignty of God, the inerrancy of His Word, the Great Commission, and the Cultural Mandate. Knox graduates will stand for truth without compromise and have a zeal for evangelism."

In its first decade, Knox has already made its mark. The seminary has a distinguished faculty, including Dr. R. C. Sproul, to provide training in classic Reformed theology. Departments include: Church History, Missions and Evangelism, New Testament, Old Testament, Practical Theology, Spiritual Life, and Systematic Theology and Apologetics. Degree programs offered by Knox include: Master of Divinity, Master of Evangelism, Master of Biblical and Theological Studies, Doctor of Ministry and Graduate Certificate in Biblical Studies. Graduates are now serving in ministry from Alabama to Idaho, and as far away as South Korea.

As Knox carries the banner of the Gospel into the 21st century, it is clear that God has exciting plans in store. The seminary, located in the Knox Center, rests literally in the shadow of Coral Ridge Church, and has already outgrown these facilities. Space is needed for the library's 40,000 volumes and a recent enrollment of 255 students overwhelmed the classrooms. These factors give even more impetus for the construction of Knox's new campus on recently acquired land in Fort Lauderdale. Knox is also moving ahead with a distance-learning program that utilizes the latest Internet technologies. These efforts will enable Knox to dramatically increase its ability to train and equip the next generation of Christian leaders.

"Knox is already offering the very finest in theological training," says Jim. "And as we follow the model of the great Scottish reformer, John Knox, I pray that our students and graduates will take to heart his now famous prayer, 'Lord give me Scotland or I die!' This passion, combined with sound theological training, will bring a new Reformation to our world."

CAPTAIN AND TEAM

But now are they many members,
yet but one body.
—I CORINTHIANS 12:20

The true intellectual is somewhat at risk; human beings are social by nature with a built-in gregariousness, or "flock instinct." That rare individual whose appetite for knowledge is coupled with the ability to digest it almost as rapidly as he can consume it, may be lured up the slopes of Mount Parnassus until he finds himself quite alone. He relishes the higher elevation—even requires it—but he does not necessarily wish to leave the rest of the flock still grazing at the foot of the mountain (perhaps a few have ventured part of the way up). The studious man does not seek solitude; he seeks learning. But in the very process, the ancient Greeks believed, the solitary muse finds such a man and imperceptibly nudges him apart from the group, as the Angel of the Lord drew Moses away from the rest.

In plain words, Jim Kennedy possesses a powerful intellect—an uncommon characteristic. However acquired, it is the sort of commodity that distinguishes an individual from fellow sojourners. Now, if an intellectual man is self-centered, he will undoubtedly exult in such a distinction to his own glory, as did the sixteenth-century poet who wrote:

> My mind to me a kingdom is,
>> Therein such present joys I find,
> That it excels all other bliss
>> That earth affords, or grows by kind.

But when the life is Christ-centered, as the life of Jim Kennedy has been since his new birth in the early 1950s, then that bright mind is but one of the important dimensions often forgotten in the statement, "Thou shalt love the Lord thy God with all thy heart, and with all thy soul, and with all thy strength, and with all thy mind." Every thought is brought into obedience to Christ. That has been the testimony of great minds since the days of the brilliant apostle Paul.

> **In plain words, Jim Kennedy possesses a powerful intellect.**

Nevertheless, the "setting apart" is observable; certainly Paul's personality was unlike those of any of his fellow Christians. His colleague, Peter, was frankly puzzled at times, confessing that there were "some things hard to be understood" in Paul's epistles. But he greatly revered Paul's wisdom and what his knowledge—and his zeal—meant to the spreading of the Gospel. If you are familiar with the lives of both men, you will have no great difficulty determining which of the two could be most accurately described as a "people person." Peter gets the nod.

Jim, by his own admission, is shy—in spite of his world-wide reputation as an evangelist, his almost constant position in the spotlight, his schedule of daily and weekly radio and television appearances. He is not, like so many of his cohorts in public life, an extrovert. He has never had to seek publicity because from the early days of his preaching career it has been thrust upon him. His personal relationships, which could be measured only in astronomical numbers, are somehow never mechanical, perfunctory, or artificial. They are genuine, direct, and—most of all—personal.

For example, a student at Broward Community College had been studying the theory of evolution. Confused and disturbed, she wrote out a list of the questions that bothered her most, mailed them to the pastor at Coral Ridge Church, and asked if he would check each with a yes or a no answer. Jim read her letter, called the campus to get her telephone number, and talked with her for two full hours until all of her doubts were laid to rest—all that in the middle of a busy day. The coed was so touched by that personal attention to her needs that she moved her membership to Coral Ridge. "I couldn't believe that a man who has as much on his mind as Dr. Kennedy has could be so concerned about somebody he never heard of—especially me," she said. "He must really care about people."

When many in leadership roles have discovered that "it's lonely at the top," they have used their somewhat insulated position to protect themselves from exposure to personal contacts, limiting them to as few as possible and those of their own choosing. Jim has not spared himself in this way, as one of his fellow ministers reports: "I remember that, after preaching three or four times on a Sunday and then conducting the new members' class after the evening service, he was willing to stay until midnight to talk and pray with an individual about his relationship to Christ." Another recalls seeing him "at the end of a fourteen-hour day, changing a woman's tire in the parking lot in the rain."

But what of the day-by-day, year-in and year-out contacts in the workplace and in the home, where personal relationships are tested to the utmost? Those who have been close to Jim Kennedy for a long time can offer a candid and realistic view of a personality that appears to be extremely complex and, at the same time, remarkably simple.

The key to understanding how the pastor relates to his staff members is to take stock, first, of the kind of workday put in by "the boss" himself. There is no predictable pattern to the wide variety of items that may crop up on his calendar, but a quick glance at his daily schedule book provides evidence that the fourteen-hour work load is not exceptional; it is typical. As for the appointments themselves, one day's agenda might read like this:

8:00 A.M.	Speak to Church Music Explosion Breakfast
9:00 A.M.	Meet with local pastors to discuss issues related to lawsuit asking Federal Court to examine First Amendment rights concerning the licensing of a church's ministry
10:00 A.M.	Book publishing representative here to discuss manuscript
10:30 A.M.	Call E.E. to fix clinic planning discussion date
10:45 A.M.	Hear from Christian activist who is attempting to halt removal of crosses on military graves in Hawaii
11:00 A.M.	Confer with lighting consultants on portions of new church construction. View furniture samples for chapel
11:50 A.M.	President of Covenant College to drop by for a few minutes
12:15 P.M.	Luncheon with executive producer, CRM
2:00 P.M.	Staff meeting (lasts until about 4 P.M.)
3:00 P.M.	Leave staff meeting early to do TV end segment taping for "Spiritual State of the Union" message to be aired soon (taping session—

three hours)

7:00 P.M. Do invocation for TLC Women's Pregnancy
Council dinner at Boca Raton Club

Portions of the mornings are supposed to be set aside for sermon preparation. Wednesday afternoons are marked for dictation and office correspondence, but they seldom work out that way. Thursday afternoons are set aside for Coral Ridge Ministries taping sessions and Thursday evenings for Evangelism Explosion classes and team visits to homes. Evening meetings with other groups, such as the Session, require the pastor's presence at the church about four nights of every week. Irregularly scheduled speaking engagements may take him to any part of the United States. Bedtime? Typically around 11:00 P.M. Some brilliant talent and administrative experience are to be found in employees at Coral Ridge Presbyterian Church. There are educators who could command university deanships, former business executives who could draw salaries in six figures, creative communication experts who could locate anywhere in the media market. They *could* because, in many cases, they *did* before leaving successful careers to become part of Jim Kennedy's team on modest wages. A corporation maxim is that one of the measures of a leader is the longevity of those who work with him—how many years they choose to stay at their jobs. Nine members of the church staff have been with the same pastor at Coral Ridge for an aggregate service record of 197 years.

The pattern of employer-employee relations could not be clearer. First, Jim sets an inspiring example for those who work with him. Secondly, he is fond of quoting Andrew Carnegie's administrative philosophy: surround yourself with people who know more about their jobs than you do; then give them the freedom to function under your authority. Virtually every employee confirms that principle to be the key to their boss's success in management, each expressing it in a different way:

Mrs. Mary Anne Bunker, executive secretary (thirty-five years): "It boggles my mind to think of all the Lord has done and is doing through His faithful servant from the tiny beginning of Coral Ridge Presbyterian Church to the present time. Because he is totally committed to Christ, he inspires others to live for Christ and to strive to be more like Him. What greater joy and reward could there be than working for a man who is changing the world for Christ! I thank God for the privilege of serving His servant in this exciting place."

Mrs. Ruth Rohm, personal secretary (thirty-three years): "I feel that I have been working in the shadow of a great man—although not evidenced in the day-to-day working relationship. This became apparent as Dr. Kennedy's ministry from a humble beginning in 1959 began to unfold into the worldwide ministry it is today. He has remained modest in the midst of being held in such high esteem by so many in this land and around the world."

Dr. Synesio Lyra, minister of pastoral care (twelve years): "Dr. Kennedy gives his 'decision makers' all the room needed to do their tasks, but at the same time expects full accountability and productivity. His integrity is beyond measure, and he demands the same from all of those on his staff."

Mrs. Ruth Cotts, former librarian (twenty-seven years): "The genius of his relationship with his workers is the way he makes known exactly what he expects from them and then leaves them alone to do the job. He is always compassionate, expecting the best, and intolerant of shoddy work. Dr. Kennedy is the clearest-thinking man I have ever met. In all issues, ideas, or problems concerning life in the church, he goes to the heart of the matter with an answer based on Scripture."

Mr. Dan Scalf, former executive vice president of CRM: "This man either inspires or devastates; that depends on the worker. You know if he is satisfied with you because you know the kind of person he is. He doesn't have to do a lot of complimenting and soothing; quality performance is the test."

Rev. William A. Swets, pastor emeritus, now deceased: "Jim has been a wonderfully gracious 'boss.' I do not remember even one occasion when he became angry with me or belittled me. He has treated me as a fellow minister committed to Jesus Christ and to the ministry of the Gospel and has allowed me to do my work accountable to God."

Dr. Andrew H. Boswell, Jr., minister of adult ministries (nineteen years): "Jim Kennedy knows what he wants. He seeks to get men on his executive staff to do what he thinks ought to be done. He relies on his Session to find the right man, though examined and approved by Jim. Once on the job, you are expected to do the job. He gives you plenty of opportunity to fulfill your ministry. If you don't make it, it's not his fault. He is confident that you will get the work done; he expects it."

Rev. Robert A. Koren, pastor emeritus (minister of visitation for twenty-two years) "He always presents something new and challenging. Never without something to read, he is articulate and conversant with the Bible, with world personalities, and with world and local needs. He demands the setting of goals, leaving the implementation largely to each staff member. His enthusiasm and determination to serve with his whole being to God's glory is what challenges me to try to do likewise, now and in the years ahead."

Rev. Dick Bond, vice president, Youth Evangelism Explosion: "He has a presence and a charisma which make him larger than life and yet a real knack for being down-to-earth—almost as if to say, 'What's all the fuss?' Relatively few people experience having to be 'on' virtually all of the time—under the careful and sometimes critical scrutiny of watchful eyes—being called on to speak, chair, preach, teach, manage, emcee, film, deliberate, moderate, officiate, etc. I have watched this man be pulled in a hundred different directions in one day and yet not lose an ounce of enthusiasm or composure. I am challenged and encouraged in my job by Jim's example to me."

Dr. Kenneth Wackes, headmaster, Westminster Academy (over twenty-eight years): "When he hires you, he puts his whole confidence in you. On the other hand, if you don't do a good job, you won't be here long. The people who don't stay are people who are looking for a lot of direction in their jobs. They won't find it here."

Dr. Ron Kilpatrick, librarian, Knox seminary; former minister of Christian education (fifteen years): "Jim makes time to sit down with me and discuss specific needs or problems. He has a perceptive mind and clear suggestions on ways to improve our program. He has a pastor's heart and a bold vision followed through with action to fulfill Christ's Great Commission by the end of the century."

Mrs. Carol Wilson, former concert series director (seventeen years): "It has been wonderful working with Dr. Kennedy and knowing his total support in the ministry of the concert series. He has appreciated the fact that the concert series has shown a real outreach; and working with churches all across the United States has taught me that such pastoral support is not to be taken for granted. He makes me feel that the concert series is our mission together."

Mr. Mike Jennings, former director of deaf ministries: "I have always been impressed with how a 'hearing man' could catch the vision for deaf ministry. Dr. Kennedy has always been extremely supportive of a ministry that most simply ignore. It is a blessing to work for a man with such a broad vision for the church."

Other members of the staff offer similar responses.

The captain of this able squad, Jim Kennedy, underscores teamwork: "I really, truly believe that this is a team effort. I have tried to gather good people around me and allow them to do their jobs without breathing over their shoulders. Yet, at the same time, I can have a pretty good idea of who is doing a good job and who isn't. I do want people who are as committed to ministering for Christ as I am and who don't need someone pushing them all the time to do so. We have many such good people here. "I have tried to select the kinds of qualified people who would give Coral Ridge Church a balanced ministry. Charles Spurgeon, who has been a great inspiration to me, called for an 'all-round ministry,' one which reaches out to all people in every way. That's where this team concept comes in. We have many, many experts who know vastly more about their fields than I do. There was a

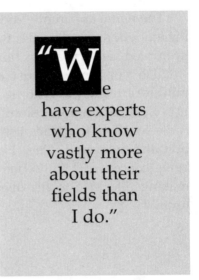

"We have experts who know vastly more about their fields than I do."

time, of course, when I had to try to do everything here myself—I was the janitor, I ran the old mimeograph machine, I led the first choir rehearsal, and so forth. But now we have a very fine team who are responsible for the excellence of our programs. It's by no means a one-man show."

But leadership, by its nature, is pretty much a one-man show. Jim has filled that role with ability, with dedication, and with humility.

Humility—perhaps that's the real secret. Ability and dedication can be found here and there, but genuine humility is probably the most rare of all human traits. One of Jim's employees remembers an incident (which Jim has forgotten) during his own student days at a Christian Bible college in one of the northern states.

He and his friend were seated in the college auditorium waiting for a convocation to begin, when in walked the Kennedys, who took seats directly behind the students.

When the young future employee turned around and, without fanfare, began giving his testimony to the guest couple, his friend tugged at his sleeve and whispered, "Dr. Kennedy!"

The name apparently didn't ring a bell, and the witnessing student pressed harder with his message. "Coral Ridge!" prompted his companion, but again the clue fell on deaf ears.

"Do you know Christ as your Savior?" the student-minister fired at the visitors. "Have you been born again?"

"Evangelism Explosion!" was the final desperate but futile warning. Jim graciously listened to the entire presentation and answered, "Yes, I am a Christian. Thank you for being concerned." At no point did he disarm the student by making reference to his own record in evangelism. That's humility.

STRICTLY PERSONAL

For what man knoweth the things of a man,
save the spirit of man which is in him?
—I CORINTHIANS 2:11

I n a sermon entitled "Communication in the Home," the pastor of Coral Ridge Church notes that virtually all writers in the field agree that the most important factor in developing a happy home is communication. He points out, in fact, that any interpersonal relationship depends on the correct use of the power that has been given to humanity alone—the power to speak.

At the same time, he observed, "I am convinced that communication is more involved with the ear than with the tongue—the awesome power of the listening ear. The mother who stops the cooking when her five-year-old child comes running into the kitchen with some exciting news about finding a four-leaf clover is a real listener. Such communication is the key to a happy home life.

"But first of all, there has to be a communication with Christ. Then the relationships within the home can be expected to be loving, joyful, open, and honest because He motivates us to share [same Bible word as communicate] in the right spirit."

Family relationships in the Kennedy household are about as inconspicuously normal as under any other average roof in America. Sharing the home with her parents is their only child, Jennifer, who was adopted as an infant in 1962. Jim describes her as having been born with "the gift of joy." Now an attractive young professional woman, Jennifer looks back on her days as a P. K. ["pastor's kid"] with the fondest of memories and deep appreciation for her "tremendous opportunities" growing up in the home of parents in the very vortex of the most vital Christian experience. She remembers her father, first, as "somebody who bought the neatest toys and put them together for me and played with me"; then as a friend who stayed beside her through all the growing years; and especially as a godly counselor who along with her mother led her to a saving knowledge of Jesus Christ.

As a tiny girl of three, Anne recalls, Jennifer exhibited a remarkable understanding of the Bible stories she was being taught. Miserable with chicken pox, she asked her mother wistfully, "Why did Adam and Eve have to sin?" Following a spell of naughtiness at age four, Anne said to the little girl, "If you've acted like this today, what will you be like when you're a teenager?" Jennifer thought for a moment, then replied, "Sufficient unto the day is the evil thereof." Anne felt as if she were witnessing the fulfillment of Psalm 8:2: "Out of the mouths of babes. . . ." In a minor confrontation with Daddy at age ten Jennifer insisted on addressing him as "Jim." He tolerated the whim for a week or so, then decided he should deal with the situation head on. "Sweetie," he said, "I would like to have a little talk with you." "OK, Jim," she said accommodatingly as she sat down beside him. Here's how he handled it: "Dear, everybody in the whole world can call me 'Jim.' There is only one person in all the world who can call me 'Daddy'—that's you. So from now on, I'm

'Daddy' to you. OK?" Jennifer was won over by his logic.

A graduate of Westminster Academy and Auburn University, Jennifer pursues an active career in nursing education in Fort Lauderdale hospitals.

The house the Kennedys have occupied since October of 1971 is just half a mile from the church on a quiet, dead-end street of neat, middle-class residences. The white stucco and red brick dwelling, on its 75x100-foot waterfront lot, is typically Floridian, right down to royal palm and ficus trees in the yard and miniature swimming pool and boat dock in the rear. Neighboring homes along the canal sport boats designed to motor or sail all 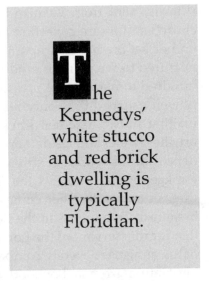 the way down the Intracoastal Waterway under an obstacle course of drawbridges, down to Port Everglades and the open sea. The Kennedys have not been avid boaters over the years; a little gray rowboat tied up at the landing has only one oar. Jim confesses that he probably went out on the water just once, paddling in a circle for less than an hour. High tides in the fall have been known to cover the boat dock entirely, but otherwise the setting is placid and scenic, with the tower of Coral Ridge Presbyterian Church clearly visible to the southwest. After dark, the church lights come on behind the colored glass mosaics in the tower, giving it the appearance of a giant Christmas tree in the sky.

Inside their home, Anne's role in the partnership becomes clear. She has served as Jim's typist, pianist, soloist, first Sunday school teacher, first Evangelism Explosion trainee and trainer, traveling companion to more than thirty countries, bookkeeper, hostess—and, here, homemaker. As immaculate as a picture in *Better Homes & Gardens*, the modestly furnished interior is tastefully decorated, pleasant, and comfortable. Anne's most cherished possessions are the Cable-Nelson console piano her mother, a music teacher, sacrificially sent from Lakeland during the early days of the church and a rare collection of Swarovski crystal. Also high on her list are her hydroponic tomato plants, which she has nurtured to the point of producing an incredible total of four hundred tomatoes! The pressure of daily schedules has pretty well usurped time once reserved for favorite hobbies like making music together. Jim's oil painting and water-color brushes were laid aside some twenty years ago, but evidences of his work are still around. Both find tennis handy for keeping fit. Anne is the early riser; she usually walks three or four miles, then comes back home in time to fix Jim's breakfast. Two thorns in the flesh, not one, have been a burden for this servant of the Lord to carry throughout the years of his ministry. Severely compacted cervical vertebrae, possibly dating from a boyhood football injury received in a head-on tackle, have generated almost incessant daily pain which Jim has had to learn to live with. Recent surgical fusion of the most troublesome neck bones may have been of some benefit, but it did little to alleviate the sometimes excruciating pain and headaches he experiences even in the pulpit. While the congregation is never aware of it, Jim is forced to have with him at all times a supply of aspirin-based painkillers.

Equally plaguing is the asthma, which had also made life more difficult for his father and his grandfather. He has a medicated pocket atomizer close at hand for the attacks that come without warning and have been critical enough to send him to a hospital. Fortunately, such emergencies have been infrequent. Because he never complains about these physical difficulties, most people have no idea of the discomforts he endures. "I start the morning," he says, "with 'This is the day the Lord hath made; I will rejoice and be glad in it.' I begin the day by consecrating myself to the Lord and by asking God to cleanse me, to fill me with His Spirit, to strengthen me, to guide me, and to use me for His glory. In going through the Bible on the subject of peace, one thing that struck me is that peace is not something passive; the Bible, over and over again, tells us that peace is something we are to seek and to pursue—very active words. We are to pursue peace the way a hunter pursues game or a person pursues a goal. I think it's possible to live a life in the midst of many responsibilities and to do it without becoming overly anxious and frustrated. It's really a great thing."

Is there anything that brings fear to this man's heart? Yes, there is—one thing. "I tremble at the thought that I ever, ever might do anything that would bring reproach on the ministry and on the Gospel of Jesus Christ. That really is a tremendous concern that influences and shades and colors everything I do. I pray that God will never let me fall into any situation that would discredit Christ or the ministry." In a day when scandal-mongering televangelists are regularly staked out by a scandal-hungry press, thus bringing the whole Church under suspicion, such a concern is understandable. Jim received a call from *The Washington Post* during the height of the Bakker/Swaggart scandals. A woman reporter was on the phone."We would like to do a story on your ministry," she said. "May we come for an interview?"

"Of course," Jim replied.

"Will you allow us to look at your financial records?"

"Certainly. Look as much as you like."

"You will let us see the books?"

"Why not? They're open to anybody. We have nothing to hide. Come spend as much time with them as you want to."

"Thank you." End of conversation. No request for appointment, no interview, no inspection, no story. Squeaky-clean is not considered newsworthy.

What is the real news? Well, like everything else at Coral

Ridge, the story is all wrapped up in the character of the man himself. Consider the house—built by the church in 1970 for $70 thousand to serve as a manse. After moving into it from the $19,300 home they had built for themselves in 1959, the Kennedys were offered an arrangement with the church whereby they could purchase the manse in installments to provide a home for their retirement years. Unlike the spacious estates of some "prosperity preachers," as pictured in aerial shots published by the media, an air view of the Kennedy home would require an arrow to point it out from all the other houses in the neighborhood.

Nor is there a Rolls-Royce or a Jaguar in the garage. Jim drove first a Ford, then a Pontiac, for nineteen years. He has purchased and driven five cars during his life. In 1984 in celebration of his twenty-five years with the church, he was presented with a sport-model Mercury Cougar, which was replaced with a 1989 model. He now drives a Pontiac. Anne, who drove what parishioners describe as a "tiny" Pontiac and later a Ford for twenty-seven of the approximately thirty years at Coral Ridge, now owns a more recent two-door car. Her husband has a travel allowance for his ministry-related trips, but no expense account.

All of the operations at the church are audited by Capin Crouse LLP, a CPA firm with an established reputation and a recognized expertise in serving not-for-profit organizations. Membership in the Evangelical Council for Financial Accountability means additional professional certification of all bookkeeping procedures at Coral Ridge.

The preacher's salary, fixed by the Session at $4,800 back in 1959, has moved upward steadily. "But I honestly don't know what my salary was last year," Jim admits, "and I probably couldn't come within $2,000 of what it is now." (It is a surprisingly modest figure, plus house and car provisions and book and study allowances.)

Over the years, Jim has refused a total of twelve raises. When asked why, the pastor replied simply, "Because I don't want to make more money. I do not want to make a high salary, purely for the sake of my testimony. Why is it that some of these other fellows have been so highly criticized? Because of making a great deal of money. As CEO of all these ministries that receive about $60 million a year, I could demand a ton of money. But I have always felt that a minister should not be in it for the purpose of making money. Peter said we are not to minister for gain, and I have always felt that way about it. It's an important point."

Because he feels so strongly, Jim has never accepted any revenue from the television and radio ministries. He receives no royalties on any of his publications

> "**I** do not want a high salary, purely for the sake of my testimony."

that are offered over the air, even though he could legitimately do so. Royalty income is restricted to copies sold in bookstores around the country, as with any other author. As for speaking engagements, whenever people ask him what he charges to come and address a particular group, he tells them that's their problem. The speaking honorarium for many prominent pastors is a well-publicized charge, fixed anywhere from $5,000 to $15,000 per engagement. Jim has only once quoted a fee for the hundreds of speaking requests. That one exception was a strategy used to deal with an overly persistent man who was determined to book Jim if it meant setting a date three or four years in the future. Finally, in near desperation, Jim left instructions: "Tell him my fee is $5,000." That was a sure cure for the fellow's importunity.

The most astounding monetary testimony has to do with tithing. Challenged by the example of a Christian college president who was returning a larger percentage of his salary to the Lord each year, Jim began the same experiment. In his own words: "I started increasing the portion of my church salary that I was giving back—to 30 percent, then 50 percent. God was still providing my needs, so I increased it to 75 percent, to 90 percent, to 100 percent, and He was still providing my needs. When I gave away 100 percent of my salary, I had more money left than I'd ever had before. So I decided to tithe the second time around—that is, to go to 110 percent— and the next year I had more money left than I had had the previous year. I eventually got what I was giving away up between 100-150 percent of my salary, and still the Lord was providing for my needs for five or six straight years. So, we decided to up our giving to 200 percent. God simply gives me what I need in other ways."

This enabled Jim in 1998 to reach the long-sought goal of giving back to the church 100 percent of all of the salary he had earned at the church since he arrived in 1959. He did this to demonstrate the truthfulnesss of the promise of Malachi 3:10, where God says: "Bring ye all the tithes into the storehouse, that there may be meat in mine house, and prove me now herewith, saith the LORD of hosts, if I will not open you the windows of heaven, and pour you out a blessing, that there shall not be room enough to receive it." God has clearly stood behind this promise

"So much for secular mathematics," says Jim. "God has His own higher mathematics, and you can't outgive Him."

It would be difficult to find a more refreshing approach to the whole subject of ministers and their money in the late twentieth century. You are not likely to find it reported in the mass media because it does not fit the stereotype already embedded in the mind of the average "objective" journalist. The cynical, crass view of Church leaders that many worldlings have today is best illustrated in an experience related by Ben Haden, founder of Changed Lives. Aboard a plane between Philadelphia and Atlantic City, he found himself seated next to a garrulous gambler who told of winning and losing several fortunes in the casinos. When the man ran out of what he considered worthwhile information, he asked Ben, "What's your racket?" "I'm a preacher of the Gospel," Ben replied. "Preaching!" came the excited response. "I hear that's where the money is these days. If I knew something past John 3:16, I'd like to try that game myself."

Unfortunately, that may pretty well represent the world's understanding, or its desire to understand, God's ministers today. But those who have known Jim Kennedy personally through the years appear to agree unanimously that it is a great privilege to know a real one.

PART FIVE

THE MAN AND HIS COUNTRY

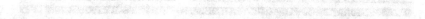

THE CULTURAL MANDATE

Render therefore unto Caesar the things
which are Caesar's; and unto God the
things that are God's.
—MATTHEW 22:21

One of the puzzling discoveries that a study of some of God's outstanding servants may bring to light is the seeming inconsistency in how He calls out and anoints certain persons to perform His will. The man upon whom the Lord has already laid an enormous burden of responsibilities, it often appears, is the very one He will turn to when a new and more difficult assignment has to be filled.

Moses, for example, was originally given one clear-cut task: take this miraculously endowed rod which is a reminder that My power rests upon you, and lead My people out of bondage in Egypt and into the Promised Land. Added to that mission later on was the considerable job of writing out the God-revealed constitution for a theocratic society and explaining it to the children of Israel. Moses found himself in the unwanted role of chief law enforcement officer, a disciplinarian of 2.5 million ex-slaves. Next, he was recruited by the Lord as a wilderness guide for a hazardous thirty-eight-year trek around the Sinai Peninsula, with whose geography he had become familiar during his earlier studies as Pharaoh's heir. As if he didn't have enough to do, he began to preside as a counselor or magistrate over civil disputes. The Bible tells us that he judged matters both great and small and—thanks to the extreme litigiousness of his people—that he held forth daily "from morning unto even."

On top of this staggering load, he was also Dr. Moses, repeatedly called upon to heal cases of snakebite, leprosy, and other self-induced plagues suffered by a rebellious generation. And would you believe that God appointed him to serve as curator of national archives? That made it his duty to undertake the recording of all history up to his time—five huge volumes, all written by the hand of Moses himself. How much time do you suppose that left him for his most pressing mandate, that of "prophesying" or preaching to a spiritually needy people? Sermon preparation takes time, you know.

This sort of piling-on of assignments could be found in the lives of many other faithful men of God, like Samuel (an administrator or judge, also accountable for performing the full range of priestly functions, then founder and president of the first theological seminary, commander-in-chief of Israel's armed forces every time the Philistines attacked, mentor to King Saul for almost forty years (not an easy job for any professional consultant), and—just to keep Samuel from getting bored—the Holy Spirit used him as scribe and historian. Abundant evidence in and out of Scripture convincingly supports the axiom that "God uses only busy people." It is as true today as it was thirty-five hundred years ago.

A glance backward just two or three decades would reveal a busy Jim Kennedy. Specifically, the dozen years from 1962 through 1974 were whirlwind years for Coral Ridge Presbyterian Church. Located on Commercial Boulevard at the time, it was already becoming the fastest-growing church in the denomination. Virtually every major program of the ministry was exploding into existence. The physical facilities were expanded every year until the move to "the big church" on Federal Highway.

Not much imagination is required to picture Jim forging through his seven-day weeks (he didn't take Monday sabbaths until years later). These years witnessed the conception and birth of Evangelism Explosion, of Westminster Academy, of Radio Station WAFG, and later television and radio hookups around the world, of a continuing outreach through book publishing, of fostering daughter churches in Tamarac and Coral Springs, and of new target areas like the Gangway (youth program) and the Greenhouse (an extremely fruitful outreach conducted entirely by laymen for young singles, street people, and other types not generally attracted to church services). These burgeoning programs and projects prospered with unprecedented growth and vitality.

But in precisely that same time frame the Lord began to inculcate a new awareness in Jim: although his ministry was flourishing, his nation was bleeding. America was hurting with an anguish it had not experienced since the Civil War. Inside the church there seemed to be no limit on healthy growth and spiritual blessing and rewarding fellowship. But outside, the very fabric of national life was being tested and pulled to the point of ripping apart at the seams.

America was hurting with an anguish not experienced since the Civil War.

Do you remember these traumas of the years 1962 through 1974?

- Cuban missile crisis (1962)
- school prayer, Bible reading now unlawful (1963)
- President John F. Kennedy assassinated (1963)
- Vietnam War heating up (1964)
- draft-card burning, campus revolts spreading (1965)
- sexual revolution in full swing (1966)
- mind-altering drugs a new national menace (1967)
- Dr. Martin Luther King, Jr., Robert Kennedy assassinated (1968)
- terrorism, crime rates shattered (1969)
- cold war with Russia intensifies (1970)
- Communism infiltrates Central America (1972)
- abortion legalized in *Roe v. Wade* (1973)
- Watergate scandal brings down a president (1974)

Such tragic national developments laid a new burden on Jim. No matter how occupied he was as an ambassador for Christ, he was compelled by the Holy Spirit to involve himself more actively in the shaping and disposition of vital public issues.

But are not preachers sent out from the seminary with just one clear command ringing in their ears: "Go ye therefore into all the world and preach the Gospel to every living creature"? Assuredly, that Great Commission given by Jesus to His disciples just before He ascended into Heaven constitutes the marching order of every dedicated follower of God. The primary purpose is to win souls for God's glory. But is that all Christians do? Do they just produce more Christians who will produce more Christians ad infinitum?

Jim Kennedy tackled this question head on in the early

years of his ministry. In his instinctively practical approach to theological matters, he perceived that there was vastly more to the Gospel than making heavenly reservations for people who otherwise were on their way to Hell. As eternally imperative and important as that is, there had to be more. "I finally realized that the answer lay in the Cultural Mandate," he says. "That is the real purpose of evangelization. It is the reason we were created in the first place."

Perhaps you have never heard of the Cultural Mandate. It's right there in the opening chapter of the Bible, in Genesis 1, where so many other exciting things are happening that many believers read right past it. It is God's very first command, just as the Great Commission was His final command. As such, it obviously demands our close attention. "Be fruitful," God says in Genesis 1:28, "and multiply; fill the earth and subdue it; have dominion over the fish of the sea, over the birds of the air, and over every living thing that moves on the earth." That's the Cultural Mandate, also known among theologians as the Dominion Covenant. God's people are to exercise lordship over the world in which they live, as accountable stewards to the Lord God who made them and it. They are to apply the teachings of God and His Word to the totality of life.

"People do not acknowledge the fact that the ultimate purpose of creation was to glorify God. Human beings set out to glorify themselves and fell into sin. The Great Commission was given to reconcile this world to God through Christ in order that glory may be given to God in accordance with His original purpose," Jim explains.

"There is a popular idea that, as Christians, we shouldn't try to do anything for the world. This notion is typified by the phrase, 'You don't polish the brass on the *Titanic*,' implying that the world is going to pot anyway, so stand clear and let it sink. The trouble with that is that if we don't polish the brass on our *Titanic*—which has been afloat for a couple of thousand years now—if we don't sweep the decks or clean the portholes, we will soon be living in a titanic, filthy mess. If we don't do anything about trying to clean up our schools, our government, our courts, our laws, our magazines, our movies, our television programs, we will find ourselves on a Titanic that has become so foul that it is unfit for us or our children to live on."

The Cultural Mandate says to the Christian, "Get involved. Don't just curse the darkness—light a candle." The pietistic notion that the Church and its members were not sent to clean up the pond but only to fish in it suggests a withdrawal from corrupt societies; this guarantees that they will become more corrupt. If the free institutions of a democratic republic are abandoned to the amoral judgment of unbelievers, how are Christians to qualify for Jesus' description of them as "the salt of the earth"?

Where freedom of religion is a fundamental principle of the government, as in America, Jim's position is that every Christian should be a dedicated patriot, alert to every danger that would hamper the perpetuation of the Gospel. It is hardly realistic to expect that the Church can remain independent and in good health if the nation's health and well-being are long neglected. The individual follower of Christ is challenged by the Cultural Mandate not to take his light and shut himself up in the closet when homosexuals, prostitutes, pimps, and criminals are coming out of the closet and parading down Main Street.

While Jim may not have taken his cue directly from the man whose radio sermon in 1954 led him to Christ, it is interesting to reflect on what Dr. Donald Grey Barnhouse wrote many years ago in *Eternity* magazine: "First, let me say that I reserve the right to write on any subject in the world that affects the lives of human beings, and that, naturally, covers practically every question under the sun. The field of politics is no exception, and it will become increasingly the province of the minister of the Gospel to speak out on political matters as we are forced to fight for even the most elementary of our liberties."[6]

Here is Jim's update: "A reporter from *Newsweek* called me and said he had heard and read that I had been speaking about religion and government and related matters, and he wanted to know why that was. I said, 'Well, for the last year everybody in America has been talking about religion and government. Why shouldn't I be talking about them?' I have seen talk show host after talk show host express astonishment whenever a guest minister has commented on these topics. What they usually say is, 'But don't you believe in the separation of church and state?'

"What they mean by that question is, 'Be quiet! We don't want to hear what God has to say about government or about morality in legislation. We don't want to hear about these things. We want to go our own way. We want to build a wall of separation and hide God behind it. We want to keep America's children from knowing about Him.'

"As a result of this kind of mentality, the Christian faith has been isolated more and more into a tiny private sector of life, removed from the whole public spectrum. I think Christians in this decade have to wake up to the fact that they have been deluded and deceived and outmaneuvered. We have to assert the truth of what our Constitution and, especially, our First Amendment mean. I am not in favor of the state controlling the Church, nor am I in favor of the Church controlling the state. But I am in favor of the influence of Jesus Christ being felt throughout this land in every sphere of its activity—in politics, in business, in education, in legislation, in court proceedings, in technology, in financing, in medicine, in research, in every level of government.

"I am in favor of the law of God being proclaimed. I am in favor of Christians becoming informed, becoming active, voting, serving their country, bringing their convictions to bear upon every part of American life. This is what Jesus meant by 'rendering unto Caesar.' He meant that you are to let your light shine in this dark world as long as you are in it,

280

while fulfilling every obligation as a responsible member of society.

"I believe that unless we act as salt, this nation is going to continue to decay until there is nothing left but a rotting corpse. We have voices on all sides doing their dead-level best to force the salt back into the salt shaker! I, for one, am determined I will not let that happen to me. I want you to know there are voices that want to silence me. But I have determined that I will not be silenced, and I will continue to speak out."

And that he has done. Under the subheading of "Quiet Courage," in an article published by the *Conservative Digest*, the point was made that

> Dr. Kennedy has kept clear of sensationalism in tackling public issues, but he is not afraid to venture into controversy. For example, in 1986 when People for the American Way announced it would be intervening in congressional elections to be sure that candidates were not inappropriately mixing religion and politics, Kennedy joined with Governor William Janklow (Rep., South Dakota) and educator Father Vincent Miceli and Rabbi Seymour Siegel to form the American Election Commission. The A. E. C. announced it would monitor People for the American Way to be sure it was not in any way inhibiting a free expression of religion. In their opening news conference at the National Press Club the four performed so well that People for the American Way backed off and was not heard from in a significant way during the rest of the 1986 election. Kennedy's performance at the press conference was nothing short of brilliant. A liberal activist who attended the press conference was heard to say, "I would sure hate to have to face him."

James Kennedy makes credible the connection between personal faith and governmental action. In a time filled with scandals and shocks which have sent the legions of the religious right running for cover, that movement is fortunate to have in the Reverend D. James Kennedy a steady hand, a voice of orthodoxy, poised and intellectually prepared to emerge as the national leader of the religious right.[7]

While he speaks out on the issues, all the way from his pulpit to nationally televised public forums, he goes beyond talk. He has participated in the pre-Iceland and pre-Geneva briefings for Christian leaders with the president of the United States. He testified before the Senate Subcommittee on Religious Liberty regarding the erosion of religious freedom in America. When he served as an expert witness in the Alabama school prayer trial, his testimony prompted the court to order further investigation of the issue, and that precipitated the Mobile textbook case ruling, which found that secular humanism is a religion that therefore should not be taught in the public schools. He testified before the House Ways and Means Subcommittee hearings on taxation of television ministries and was asked to submit his views on child exploitation to the Attorney General's Commission on Pornography.

While he speaks out on the issues, he goes beyond talk.

The outer perimeter of his involvement extends as far as the eye can see. Some of the organizations that carry the name of D. James Kennedy on their board of reference or advisory board include the following:

Christian Solidarity International
Conservative Caucus, Inc.
Council for National Policy

New Hope International
Evangelism Resources
Door of Hope International
Haggai Institute for Advanced Leadership
Faith America Foundation
Florida Right to Life, Inc.
International Literature Foundation
International School of Theology
Save our Schools
Teen Challenge of Florida
Christian Educators Association International
The Maldon Institute
A Woman's Pregnancy Center
Institute of Contemporary Christianity
National Christian Association
Plymouth Rock Foundation
Concerned Christians for More Responsible
    Citizenship
National Alliance of Christian Voters Research &
    Education Foundation
Family Entertainment America
National Christian Heritage Foundation
Council for Biblical Manhood & Womanhood
Institute for Religious Research
National Forum on the New Age Movement
International Bible Reading Association
Saraspatak Reformed Academy in Hungary
Child Evangelism Fellowship
Shepherd Care Ministries, Inc.
Council for American Private Education
South American Crusades, Inc.
Evangelism Explosion International
Religious Freedom Defense Fund
U.S. Congressional Advisory Board
National Council on Bible Curriculum in Public Schools
National Memorial for the Unborn

Project for International Religious Liberty
International Day of Prayer for the Persecuted Church
National Day of Prayer
National Abstinence Clearinghouse
Liberty Counsel
Millennium Council
Committee to Restore American Values
Creation Resource Foundation

Such concerns and activities have brought numerous awards Jim's way: Man of the Year Award of Women for Constitutional Government (1988); International Clergyman of the Year by Civitan International (1986); High Frontier Award for outstanding contribution to the defense of the nation in the field of religious support (1986); Clergyman of the Year by Religious Heritage of America (1984); the George Washington Honor Medal Award by Freedoms Foundation of Valley Forge (1971, 1976, 1980); the Philip Award by the National Association of United Methodist Evangelists (1988); the National John Calvin Award by the *Christian Observer* (1989); the Ellen Hardin Walworth Medal for Patriotism by the Daughters of the American Revolution (1998); and Global Peace Prize by the Global Peace Initiative (1999).

Adding to the Coral Ridge pastor's list of recognitions are his personal listings in the *Dictionary of International Biography, Personalities of America, International Register of Profiles, International Directory of Distinguished Leadership, Community Leaders and Noteworthy Americans, International Who's Who of Intellectuals, Men of Achievement, Book of Honor, Who's Who in Religion, Notable Americans, Who's Who in Florida, Personalities of the South, International Who's Who in Community Service, Who's Who in the World,* and *2,000 Outstanding Intellectuals of the 20th Century.*

Jim Kennedy has also served alongside a small group of Christian leaders in an ad-hoc committee that interviews presidential candidates during each election cycle. With each candidate who has appeared before the committee (and there have been more than twenty), he is sure to ask the bottom-line questions of faith. You can almost hear him now, "With all due respect to your great accomplishments in business and politics, if you died tonight. . . ."

Concerned about the enormous decision-making responsibility that rests upon the President, Jim formed a President's Council in 1985 to offer direct assistance. "Much of the information that goes to the White House and to the Capitol," he says, "is supplied to our magistrates by organizations fundamentally opposed to Christian morality. The result is that our leaders are making decisions based on flawed, biased information expertly prepared by anti-Christian lobbyists. The decision-making process, obviously, is thus badly skewed in one direction. I decided to do something about that."

Members of the President's Council, recruited from Christian supporters throughout the nation, received a *Washington Newsletter*, and quarterly white papers on public issues that were sent to the President and other key policy-makers. In the 1990s the work of the President's Council was continued through two outreaches founded by Kennedy—the CENTER FOR CHRISTIAN STATESMANSHIP in Washington, D.C., and the CENTER FOR RECLAIMING AMERICA. Together, these ministries have helped fulfill Jim Kennedy's desire to apply his faith convictions to the culture in which he lives.

To him, this marriage of faith and culture must take place. After all, as he is quick to point out, even the word "culture" is derived from the same root as "cult," which carries with it the general sense of "religion." Thus, culture arises out of religion and "no culture can thrive it if is severed from the religious vision that gave it birth."

A final word: if you would like to engage Jim Kennedy to speak, but want to limit subject matter or commentary in advance—don't ask. Or if you're planning a nice, neutral invocation or benediction that carefully avoids the name of Jesus Christ so that no one will be offended—don't bother. The same First Amendment that provides for freedom of religion, he may remind you, also grants freedom of speech as a constitutional right of every citizen. Jim sums up his convictions about the Cultural Mandate this way: "We must deal with what Christ has to say, what the Bible has to say, about issues that are affecting our society today, such as the teaching of evolution, secular humanism, Communism, AIDS, pornography, strategic defense, abortion, the media. It is incumbent upon us as ministers to help enlighten Christians as to what their responsibilities are.

"The idea that our government is somehow exempt from the control of God is probably the most dangerous issue our nation has ever faced, and is the prelude to tyranny." Thomas Jefferson could not have agreed more.

Why this passion for public issues? Why this compelling call to fulfill the Cultural Mandate? Perhaps because, at his heart, Jim Kennedy can be best described by one word: statesman. In an era when so few have maintained the personal integrity necessary for such a role, Jim has carefully guarded his faith and his family. At a time in history when so few even attempt to apply the Scriptures to their lives, he has diligently mined answers for his culture from the depths of God's Word. Most importantly, the Lord in His providence has seen fit to give Jim Kennedy a media megaphone that literally reaches across this nation and around the world.

In the chapters that follow, Jim Kennedy, the Statesman, faces these issues.

REVERSING GOD'S ORDER

"The kings of the earth set themselves . . .
against the Lord . . . He who sits
in the heavens shall laugh."
—PSALM 2:2, 4

The theory of human evolution is one of the most delightfully alluring systems of thought ever conceived by the human mind; it has an especially glamorous appeal to the young.

Sounds like heresy? It's nevertheless true. If the study of Darwin's conclusions were not thoroughly fascinating, how else could it have captivated generations of high school and college students and their professors? Why else would it enjoy almost complete, unquestioned acceptance in the mass media today? It is very obviously just about the most fun thing to be found anywhere in the literature of science. What other area of scientific speculation do the unlearned attempt to defend with such zeal? Let's face it: few pursuits can provide the ready pleasure and diversion that imagination offers, and here is a package of "scientific knowledge" that has allowed the fancies of scientists and lay persons alike to trot under a loose rein. Here, as nowhere else, is an exciting new world of "hopeful monsters," "missing links," "hominids," "ape-men," and all the rest.

Attesting to the sweeping popularity of Darwinism since its appearance slightly over one hundred years ago is the litter of "isms" it has spawned:

materialism (matter is eternal)
uniformitarianism (processes have never changed)
secularism (all religion should be rejected)
humanism (man alone is the measure of all things)
determinism (all facts are based on natural laws)
behaviorism (man only reacts to his environment)
existentialism (there are no rational choices)
modernism (contemporary standards are our guide)
liberalism (we are free from all authority)
Communism (the state decides for the individual)
fascism (dictatorship creates nationalism)
nihilism (laws and institutions are eliminated)
atheism (there is no God)

Not all of the above were helped by Darwinism; some existed centuries before the theory was formulated. But evolution has provided the rationale for the widespread popularity of these "isms" in the twentieth century. The late Dr. Robert G. Lee observed that "the best thing about 'isms' is that most of them become 'wasms.'" Ideas predicated on falsehood have a way of losing their grip on societies—but they can always be brought back for an encore, especially when prevailing attitudes have been carefully preconditioned.

But while they last, the attraction may be overpowering. The prominent Anglican, Charles Kingsley, was a contemporary of Darwin; he was so charmed by the theory of evolution that he set aside his faith and taught the atheistic doctrine in his parish. His most famous contribution to

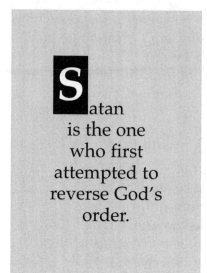

English literature is *The Water Babies,* an enchantingly beautiful book based on the same subject. No other preachment of science has so bewitched sociologists, poets, philosophers, writers, political activists, or dictators as has this one. Nor has any other purely hypothetical notion played such a conspicuous, yet hidden, role in public affairs. Where does the charisma, the allure, come from? It is from no other source than the grand master of deception himself, that beautiful angel of light once known as Lucifer. All of the "isms" listed above might as well be dumped into the same hopper because shaken down together they come out as Satanism. He is the one who first attempted to reverse God's order. It didn't work for him, but he has been able to resell the idea to humankind ever since. Isaiah paints the picture for us:

How art thou fallen from heaven,
O Lucifer, son of the morning!
How art thou cut down to the ground,
Which didst weaken the nations!
For thou hast said in thine heart:
I will exalt my throne above the stars of God:
I will sit also up on the mount of the congregation,
in the sides of the north:
I will ascend above the heights of the clouds;
I will be like the most High.
Yet thou shalt be brought down to hell,
To the sides of the Pit. (Isaiah 14:12-15)

Jim Kennedy has no problem recognizing evolution as one of Satan's deadliest tools. But along with the Good News of the Gospel, he preaches good news about evolution:

"Indeed, we are engaged in a life struggle. I might point out to you that every single anti-Christian system that dominates our world today rests its case on evolution. The two massive non-Christian movements today are: in the East, Communism; and in the West, secular humanism. Both of these atheistic systems rest upon the single pillar of evolution.

"Yet, evolution has not established itself as an irrefutable fact, as its adherents would like people to believe; but rather, it is crumbling on every side. The fortress is cracking; the walls are giving way; the citadel is coming down; there are fissures everywhere! The whole of evolution is in absolute chaos today, and the public does not know it."

For example, does the general public realize that science as we know it today was created by Bible-believing Christians who supported the scriptural account of creation? Their names are recorded in every public library, along with the branch of science which they founded: Joseph Lister, antiseptic surgery; Louis Pasteur, bacteriology; Isaac Newton, calculus; Johannes Kepler, celestial mechanics; Robert Boyle, chemistry; Georges Cuvier, comparative anatomy; Charles Babbage, computer science; Lord Rayleigh, dimensional analysis; John Ambrose Fleming, electronics; James Clark Maxwell, electrodynamics; Michael Faraday, electromagnetics; Lord Kelvin, energetics; Jean-Henri Fabre, entomology of living insects; George Stokes, fluid mechanics; Sir John William Herschel, galactic astronomy; Gregor Mendel, genetics; Louis Agassiz, glacial geology; Blaise Pascal, hydrostatics; William Ramsay, isotopic chemistry; John Ray, natural history; Georg Bernhard Riemann, non-Euclidian geometry; Matthew Maury, oceanography; David Brewster, optical mineralogy; the list goes on. Since Christians invented science, the evolutionist argument that "creationists are unscientific" would appear to be—well, unscientific.

"In the beginning," Jim points out, "science was looked upon as the handmaiden of theology. The study of creation was to lead men to the adoration of the Creator. Yet we know that in the last century, especially with the advent of the theory of evolution, science has fallen to a large extent into hands which are inimical to the Christian faith and has, instead, been forged into a weapon which has perhaps been the most deadly ever pitted against Christianity.

"Young people, including young Christians, have been led to believe that evolution has been proved, that it has overthrown the doctrine of scriptural creation and is believed by all intelligent scientists. Therefore, young people often feel that the Bible must obviously not be true. That is because they do not understand the nature of science. Science is always tentative. It never arrives at all truth or the final truth. It is always seeking to know more. It presents one hypothesis and then replaces it with another. God's creation is not changing, but man's knowledge of that creation and all that it contains is increasing and therefore changing.

"All one has to do is simply trace the various hypotheses that have been put forth by science over the last fifty or one hundred years. In any science book written fifty years ago, we would find that probably at least half of its conclusions are completely discarded today.

"For example, at the beginning of this century evolutionists said that the entire human endocrine system, including the pituitary, the thyroid, and all of the other glands of the endocrine system were totally without present function. They were judged to be only vestigial remains of some previous ancestry. Today we know that they run the entire chemical process of the body.

"The atomic age also destroyed an old scientific belief that the atom was indivisible. In fact, the word atom comes from the Greek word *atomos*—which is from *tomos*, meaning "cut," with a privative "a" added—making the meaning "that which can not be cut." Any schoolchild today knows that this never was true."

The Good News—about the collapse of Darwin's theory—is summarized under these headings in Jim Kennedy's research:

THE ORIGIN OF THE UNIVERSE

Because almost all of the leading evolutionists are atheistic, and because atheists reject God, they must necessarily postulate that matter is eternal, that it has always been around. If you get rid of an eternal God, you are left with the inevitability of eternal matter. Matter has to be eternal because, if there could be no God to create, no universe would ever have appeared. Even a "big bang" of exploding galaxies would constitute a beginning, and the evolutionist cannot tolerate a beginning.

The big bang theory was replaced with an "oscillating universe" explanation. There was still an explosion all right, and the universe kept expanding outward for many billions of years. But finally, the gravitational pull began to act on the galaxies and they began to recede, collapsing in upon themselves until they all came together in a composite mass the size of a basketball—or even smaller. Then it exploded all over again, and we have lived in an oscillating universe ever since. This is science? Jim doesn't think so:

"There is not a single scientific fact or piece of evidence or bit of data that confirms such a theory. It is based simply on the faith of evolutionists. Evolution is a religion, and it is founded on faith. I have statements from more than two hundred evolutionists acknowledging that their beliefs are based on faith rather than on evidence. What the evidence does reveal shocked many astronomers a few years ago when Dr. Allan Sandage and Dr. James Gunn, using Mount Palomar's two-hundred-inch telescope, concluded a fifteen-year study of the red shift of galaxies. They announced that although they had always held to a belief in an oscillating or closed universe, the 'premier fact' is that it is an open, expanding universe which will never close in upon itself. That is, there was a beginning!

"Isaac Asimov, probably the most prolific science and science fiction writer of all time, reacted to the discovery this way: 'I don't have the evidence to prove that God doesn't exist, but I so strongly suspect He doesn't that I don't want to waste my time. I have a hunch we'll find the matter.'

"Mr. Asimov was convinced," Jim continues, "that the original matter which began the universe will be found. Does that not cause great relief in the evolutionary community? We thought we were going to have to rest on scientific facts— but the 'hunch' has come to the rescue again! Although 99 percent of the matter necessary to cause the galaxies to collapse in upon themselves is missing (the same as the 'missing link' in the fossil record) 'it will be found.' Meanwhile, millions of children will continue to be taught, along with the hunches, that evolution is an indisputable fact."

HOW LIFE BEGAN

Spontaneous generation—that was the evolutionary byword for almost a century. It meant that life just popped into existence somehow. The trouble with that hypothesis is that it may be testable. When Pasteur came along, he did indeed test the theory of spontaneous generation and disproved it. But the faithful remained undaunted. They just argued that, even though life is not arising now, it must have arisen some time in the past because here we are. The dim, forgotten past is not testable; that way, you see, the claim could not be disproved.

What is evolution? Jim answers the question this way: "In the words of one of the most respected scientists in the world, Dr. Paul LeMoine, an editor of *Encyclopedie Francaise*: 'Evolution is a fairy tale for adults.' I am sure that, to the average American who has been indoctrinated and brainwashed with evolution for so many decades, such a statement as that is positively stunning."

"The fairy tale continues," Jim writes. "In 1936 Alexander Oparin, a Russian biochemist, devised a story in which he postulated that life arose in a primordial soup of organic chemicals. Once upon a time, molecules and atoms got together and formed biopolymers; they formed macromolecules which in turn created amino acids, which bound themselves together in chains and produced proteins. These proteins got together by the hundreds of thousands, and at last they created a living cell.

"However, the scientists realized that one thing was absolutely necessary. There must be no free oxygen in the atmosphere because oxygen destroys these rudimentary biopolymers, these amino acids, that are trying to bind themselves together. What did the pseudoscientists do? Well, in a fairy tale you add anything you want. They created a new atmosphere which is made up of methane, hydrogen, ammonia, and water vapor—no free oxygen. And so, Oparin said, that's the way it was, once upon a time. That theory was repeated in virtually every biology text and primer for the last fifty years. Tens of millions of school children all over the world have been taught that life began in the primordial sea in a nonoxidized atmosphere.

"But along came real science with its testability. Evolutionists Harry Clemmey and Nick Badham published an article entitled 'Oxygen in the Precambrian Atmosphere,' in the March 1982 issue of *Geology*, a prestigious scientific magazine. In it they said, 'Although biologists concerned with the origin of life often quote an early atmosphere consisting of reduced gases, this stems as much from ignorance of recent advances as from active opposition to them.'"

Supporting Jim's research is a statement in *New Scientist* by Dr. John Gribbin of England that the scientific folklore every child has been taught concerning the origin of life must now be completely abandoned and rewritten. Life simply did not arise in a methane, ammonia atmosphere or by any other testable natural means. It's an idea that might be believed, but not proved.

THE LAWS OF MATHEMATICAL PROBABILITY

From the beginning, evolution has been on the losing side of probability mathematics. Sir Fred Hoyle of Cambridge University, originator of the "steady state theory " of cosmogony, figured that even if the universe were twenty-billion-years-old, life would never have arisen by chance in *twenty billion times thirty trillion years*. Pretty impressive odds. His statement was: "The notion that not only biopolymers but the operation programme of a living cell could be arrived at by chance in a primordial organic soup here on earth is evidently *nonsense of a high order*."

Hoyle, who was an atheist all his life, further concluded that the only way life could have come to pass is through application of a superior order of intelligence which, he said, "you may call God." That's coming around to it the hard way.

"No less a figure than Francis Crick, codiscoverer of DNA," Jim points out, "examined the possibilities of this incredibly complex molecule coming into existence by chance. When convinced that it was not possible under the laws of probability, what did he do—leap into the arms of God? No, he leaped into the arms of 'directed panspermia.' That is a new fairy tale you ought to be aware of.

"'Directed panspermia' comes right out of Star Trek or Star Wars. It means that some highly advanced beings on some other planet sent missiles out into the universe that had sperm cells in them—and they planted us here on this earth! Naturally, there does not happen to be the first suspicion of scientific evidence to support such a theory. But it is part of the faith and religion of some evolutionists. It does not solve the problem, because even a child would ask: Where did those advanced beings come from? It simply lengthens the shadow, removing it from the area of testability and science, and its logic is called 'an infinite regress.'"

Neither by fact nor by chance has the evolution hypothesis proved convincing. But the atheist who attempts to remove God from His own universe is obliged to fill the vacuum with something else. The fanciful mathematics of "Nobody plus nothing equals everything" provided former President Reagan with one of his favorite jokes. He said that he would like to invite an atheist to a voluptuous, seven-course gourmet dinner, and then, as he finishes the feast and exclaims about what a wonderful meal it was, ask the atheist, "Do you believe there is a cook?"

THE PLENTIFUL FOSSIL RECORD

Darwin recognized that he faced a problem. If evolution has taken place, the fossil record in the rocks should reveal it. He lamented: "Geological research . . . does not yield the infinitely many fine gradations between past and present species required." He explained it away by reasoning that just not enough fossils had yet been collected; when scientists got all the fossils lined up, the intermediary species would show up and all the missing links would be there.

More than 100 years have gone by, and these intermediates still have not come to light. Is it because there have been simply too few fossils? Hardly. In our museums today, more than 100 million fossils have been categorized. In one rock formation in Africa alone, there are 800 billion vertebrate animals in fossil form. No longer can it be claimed that the record is too sparse to reflect the transitional forms. "The missing links are still missing," Jim says. "Could it be because they were never there in the first place?"

Darwin faced another problem. Not only was he vulnerable in the fossil record, he also noted, "If it could be demonstrated that any complex organ existed which could not possibly have been formed by numerous, successive, slight modifications, my theory would absolutely break down."

Enter the field of microbiology and what Jim calls "a scientific discovery which rivals those of Newton, Copernicus, Einstein, Pasteur, and, yes, Darwin. Perhaps most astonishing of all is the fact that so few Americans are even vaguely familiar with this discovery."

What is this discovery? "Irreducible complexity," the discovery that at the basis of life, at the molecular level, life is comprised of machines. "These molecular 'machines'—a trillion of them in each human cell—are astonishingly complex," says Jim. "Remove any one of them, and the machine ceases to work."

The impact on evolutionary theory is profound. Dr. Michael Behe, a biochemist at Lehigh University, in his book *Darwin's Black Box*, says this discovery strikes a blow right at the base of the tree which holds up evolution. In Behe's words, "The result of these cumulative efforts to investigate the cell . . . is a loud, clear, piercing cry of 'design!'" And design inevitably leads to a Creator. Evolution has met its match—it offers no explanation for the irreducibly complex human cell.

With these discoveries in mind, Jim says, "The evolutionists must accept more on faith than Christians do, and yet they claim to have none. But what they have placed their faith in is more than untested propositions. I believe that evolution is the 'big lie.' I believe it is the most destructive, pernicious lie that has ever come down the pike. I believe it has done and is doing more harm to the world than any other intellectual theory that I know of. I think it is quite possible that the theory of evolution may result in the death of every person in this world. I can say that, and put it in as startling a form as I possibly can. It has already resulted in the deaths of more people than have been killed in all of the wars in the history of humankind."

That might sound extreme if it were not for the demonstrated fact that evolution has had its impact on not just a few physical sciences but the social sciences as well. What was the foundation upholding Hitler's Third Reich? It was Darwin's theory of evolution! Jim documents this claim by quoting from *Evolution and Ethics*, written by the foremost advocate of evolution in twentieth-century England, Sir Arthur Keith: "We see Hitler devoutly convinced that evolution produces the only real basis for a national policy. . . . Germany has reverted to the tribal past, and is demonstrating to the world, in their naked ferocity, the methods of evolution."[8]

He is referring, of course, to all that talk about a superior "Aryan," race which Hitler borrowed right out of Friedrich Nietzsche's *Man and Superman*. Nietzsche, who gave the world his "God is dead" philosophy, convinced the Führer that his people were several rungs up the evolutionary ladder, above all others in the species—a super race, no less, who had become that way by virtue of Darwin's law of "the survival of the fittest." Armed with such impressive "facts," it was not difficult for Hitler to order the slaughter of six million Jews and an equal number of Christians. (It is not widely known that Hitler had six million professing Christians killed in addition to the Jews who died in the Holocaust. He said of himself that he was a "total pagan," and he vowed to exterminate both Christianity and Judaism.) He apparently thought that Nazism would survive as Germany's—and the world's—way of life, just as other racists and murderers convince themselves that their system will prevail.

The only answer to the evolutionists, Jim concludes, is the Christian answer.

The only answer to the evolutionists, Jim concludes, is the Christian answer. "Our commitment," he warns, "must be to stand against the evolutionary tide of our society and proclaim clearly our rational faith in the Creator-God of Christianity. We must study and 'have an answer for every man who asks us for a reason' for our faith. Our goal must be to educate those around us that the evolutionary theory is a lie.

"As we do this, we must also proclaim the Good News of God's salvation, which is found in Jesus Christ, and pray for the Holy Spirit to grant to those who accept the evolutionary world view, repentance. The root of humanity's problem is not only intellectual confusion about creation, but a heart of rebellion toward God. The message of Christ is vastly superior in hope and comfort, not to mention the fact that it is scientifically vastly superior to the collapsing evidence for evolution."

Concludes Jim, "As these discoveries begin to permeate society, as inevitably they will, there is going to be a revolution in thinking, and evolution will come to be thought of as merely a small cult of the Twentieth Century—a sect. Perhaps God has a sense of humor. As evolutionists set out to prove that there was no God and that life is the result of merely naturalistic causes, perhaps God looked down on one of those three trillion cells in the human body, each inhabited by tens of thousands of irreducibly complex machines, and He smiled and said, "Hah, wait until they get a look at this."

As the Psalmist said, when men mock God, "He who sits in the heavens shall laugh."

THE MOST EVIL EMPIRE

The fool hath said in his heart,
There is no God.
—PSALM 14:1

"Though I am not a prophet nor the son of a prophet, I believe that there is every possibility that by the year 2000 Communism will be a thing of the past."

Those are the words of Jim Kennedy in 1984 at the height of the Cold War with the Soviet Union. In the early 1980s there were few signs that Communism was crumbling. To the contrary. Reports of Soviet military might and conquests had caused the United States to launch a decade-long effort to catch up to the Soviet machine.

Still, Jim Kennedy had vision of a better future for the world. "This specter, as Marx and Engels described it, which has haunted Europe and now haunts the whole world, will have been exorcised from this planet once and for all . . . the claws and teeth of the Communist bear will be extracted, and that hulk, that carcass, will be swept by the arm of God onto the garbage heap of history, and hundreds of millions of people will rejoice." Several years would pass before even a hint that Jim's words would come true. Then, quite suddenly, in 1989 Romania's dictator was ousted, the fire of revolution quickly spread to the other Eastern bloc nations, and miraculously, the impenetrable Iron Curtain came crumbling down. Next, the Soviet Union itself, what Jim would call "the greatest experiment in socialism in the history of the world," would fragment into several independent states. Soviet Communism had truly been swept "onto the garbage heap of history."

But what was a preacher doing in 1984 making such bold pronouncements about global-political events that are obviously beyond the scope of the traditional Sunday sermon? Why would such matters of world public affairs concern Jim and his flock? An exceptional aspect of the Kennedy personality is his ability to ferret out the precise starting point for every major decision or innovation in his ministry. As though the time, the place, the person, the event were all burned into some remote brain cell like a permanent brand on a steer's hide, he remembers exactly what originally ignited his interest.

A woman who was a member of the congregation in the early days of the church happened to hand the pastor a copy of one of the best-selling books of the late 1950s—*Witness* by Whittaker Chambers. It had nothing to do, of course, with Christian witnessing but was a shocking exposé of how Communism had infiltrated White House policy-making at the highest level.

Now, Jim had always understood that Communism was bad business. His very first vote, cast in 1952, had been determined by concern over that system's sinister influence on America. When his mother asked him whom he intended to vote for in the presidential election, Jim replied, "It seems to me that just about the biggest problem America faces is Communism, and I think General Eisenhower can handle that better than Adlai Stevenson." He still did not claim to know a whole lot about the subject; even his seminary years from 1956-1959 forced an insulation from current events, like Paul's three years in Arabia while he equipped himself for the Lord's work.

Jim became so disturbed by what he read that when he returned the book to the woman, he told her he intended to preach a sermon on Communism. When she gratuitously expressed her opinion that the preacher might not possess enough knowledge of that complex topic for a sermon, she was not allowing for the intense research and study that was becoming a trademark of his preaching. A few weeks later Jim delivered his first public affairs sermon, and the concerned woman confessed her awe at its depth. The title of the sermon: "The Danger of the Communist Threat."

Thus, in somewhat the same manner that the great German philosopher Immanuel Kant recalled: "I was awakened from my dogmatic slumbers by the writings of David Hume, "Jim can point to his reading of *Witness* as the dawning of his serious interest in matters of state. He has never softened his denunciation of Communism as "the evil empire." As a matter of fact, he states that former President Reagan should have labeled it 'the most evil empire.'"

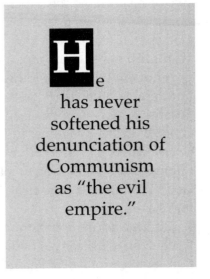

He has never softened his denunciation of Communism as "the evil empire."

But as Jim has always emphasized, the label does not apply only to the former Soviet Union or China. It identifies, rather, any political system that bases itself on atheism. This is the most evil power, "the most dangerous and deceptive ideology that has ever stalked humankind."

But wasn't that the very same complaint we heard

leveled against evolution? Is only one of the two the real villain? No—they are in one sense the same thing. Communism is the manifest, practical application of the theory of evolution to a plan of government. It is well known that Karl Marx, a contemporary of Charles Darwin, went to London to ask the naturalist if he would write the introduction to his new work, *Das Kapital.* Marx observed that Darwin had provided a scientific foundation for his own theory of dialectical materialism. By removing God from the natural sphere (in his own mind), Darwin had paved the way for Marxism, which depends on the elimination of God from the social, economic, and political spheres. Evolution has supplied the needed rationale for Communism along with virtually every harmful "ism" of the twentieth century.

Thus, with atheism as its base—no matter how impressive or respectable the superstructure can be made to look—Communism has to be recognized as unadulterated evil. God-hatred is a principal plank in the party platform. Vladimir Lenin set the moral tone for Russia's revolutionary government when he told his people that "the idea of God is unutterable vileness . . . of the most dangerous kind." Because Jesus, who personifies the love of God, said "He that is not with me is against me," there could never be a more clear-cut set of alternatives. Which Jew will the world follow—Karl Marx, denier of God, or Jesus Christ, Son of God? With all the rhetorical embellishments stripped away, that's square one.

To transform a nation into a Communist state, Marx listed specific objectives to be accomplished through infiltration, subversion, propaganda, diplomacy, war, revolution, genocide, or whatever method might advance the cause. For more than three decades Jim Kennedy has sounded the alarm that some of these steps have already been allowed to become realities and others have been given serious consideration in American life and government.

Coral Ridge audiences have been reminded on more than

one occasion of Winston Churchill's famous definitions: "Capitalism is the unequal distribution of wealth; socialism is the equal distribution of poverty; and Communism is socialism with a gun in your back." While Communism is no laughing matter, Jim enjoys passing along the peasant humor which circulated this story:

An agriculture commissar, visiting one of the collective farms, said to the farmer, "Comrade, how are things going?" Recalling the postcard he had received from Siberia from the last farmer who had complained, the peasant replied, "No complaints."

"How is the potato crop this year?" asked the commissar.

"Wonderful," was the response.

"Oh, really?" said the astonished official.

"Oh yes, it is wonderful indeed. If you were to take all of the potatoes of our crop this year and pile them up in one place, they would reach all the way up to the very feet of God!"

The smile left the commissar's face rather suddenly, and he said, "Comrade, I would remind you that this is an atheistic state. There is no God."

"That's all right, Commissar," said the peasant. "There are no potatoes either."

Few have understood as clearly as Jim just how grave a threat Communism posed to our world. Look at the original purposes of the shapers of Communism:

- Lenin: "First, we will take Eastern Europe. Then we will take the masses of Asia; then we will surround America, the last bastion of capitalism. We will not have to fight. It will fall into our hands like overripe fruit. . . . Promises are like piecrusts; they are made to be broken. . . . There must be no relationship between diplomacy and action."

- Manuilsky: "War to the hilt between Communism and capitalism is inevitable. To win we shall need the element of

surprise. So we shall begin by launching the most spectacular peace movement on record. There will be electrifying
overtures and unheard-of concessions. The capitalist countries, stupid and decadent, will rejoice to cooperate in their
own destruction. They will leap at another chance to be
friends. As soon as their guard is down, we shall smash
them with our clenched fist."

- Stalin: "The USSR is the base of the world revolutionary
  movement."

- Krushchev: "We will bury you. Your grandchildren shall
  most certainly live under Communism!"

- *Pravda*, after Brezhnev's visit to America in 1973:
  "Peaceful coexistence does not at all mean an end to the
  struggle between the two world social systems. The
  struggle between the proletariat and the bourgeoisie,
  between world socialism and imperialism, will go on
  until the final victory of Communism on a world scale."

Jim saw right through many of the failed strategies that
were being employed to cope with communism in the '70s
and early '80s. Détente, for example, called upon the free
world to accept Communist rule over 42 percent of the
people on earth and to coexist in peace, to settle for a world
that is half-slave and half-free. Americans, however, have
always tended to believe, with Abraham Lincoln, that no
nation can remain half-free and half-slave—and that this
principle applies to the entire world.

"Détente," Jim stresses, "meant appeasement. Détente
meant surrender. Détente meant failure for the free world.
No two political systems as opposed to each other as the
United States, with its constitutional republic, and Russia,
with its Communistic dictatorship, can hope to coexist without severe tensions. These tensions are real and cannot be
ignored. One system claims that there is no God, that there is

no soul, and that evil resides in private property. The other system recognizes God as sovereign over all things, the human soul as distinguishing humans from animals, and evil as resting not in property but in the heart, as Jesus taught. How can such opposites peacefully coexist?"

At one time American fringe groups went so far as to chant a panic-cry of "better Red than dead." For any holding to such a desperate view, Jim had an even more frightening message: "This vision of a 'better Red than dead' option failed to comprehend the ruthless nature of the Communist movement. Those committed to it would gladly kill a quarter of the population of the United States—or more—in order to gain control. They would use every device of torture and mass murder they know (and after 140 million homicides worldwide, they are quite knowledgeable) to discourage what they perceive to be resistance."

For those who were taught to believe that MAD ("mutual assured destruction" in the event of atomic warfare) made the world a safe place, they were still left with no possible way of resolution for the Cold War. "Mankind would be forced to live under this Damoclean sword of nuclear annihilation indefinitely," says Jim.

Even the well intentioned deterrent of wearing the general label of "anti-Communism" was not sufficient, Jim says, because it is a negative philosophy. Since it was a defensive attempt to counter each Communist move with a similar opposing move, it fails to offer people an ideal or hope any greater than those proclaimed by Communists.

What, then, set off the unprecedented events which began to rock the Eastern European Communist Bloc nations and eventually shattered the Soviet stranglehold on much of Europe and Asia? "It was a moment of faith," says Jim. "A pastor of a small church in Romania stood up to the totalitarian tyrants. Soon, church members and townspeople joined together and a fire of revolution—a fire of faith—was lit. This fire spread across the land. That is how the Soviet

Union and its allies came to a disastrous end, crashing in flames and burning in utter disaster and bankruptcy."

This is not to say the battle against the "most evil empire" is over. Far from it. Atheistic Communism is still alive and well in China, North Korea and elsewhere. Also, fundamentalist Muslim leaders have gained power in nations throughout the Middle East, leading to a new wave of persecution against Christians. Meanwhile, anti-Christian sentiment is rising in countries like India where Christians represent a persecuted minority of the population.

"The fact is, the 20th Century has seen more martyrs for Christ than in any other century. More than 100 million Christians have been martyred, and the persecution continues to today," says Jim. Long concerned with the plight of his persecuted brothers and sisters in Christ, in 1997 Jim traveled to Washington, D.C., to participate in a roundtable discussion with 100 leaders to address the issue of worldwide religious persecution. While the meeting focused on the plight of Christians and attracted many notable Christian leaders, its organizer was a Jewish man, Michael Horowitz, of the Hudson Institute.

"When I was asked by Mr. Horowitz to be a part of this effort to end persecution of my Christian brothers and sisters, I told him with alacrity I could not live with my conscience if I did not do something to help," says Jim. Thanks in large part to that historic meeting, a change has begun. In 1998, Congress passed the International Religious Freedom Act which established a U.S. commission charged with mon-

> "The 20th Century has seen more martyrs for Christ than in any other century."

itoring violations of religious freedom and recommending policy options to the Administration. "The U.S. government's influence brought an end to the persecutions of Jews in the former Soviet Union. It could bring an end to the persecution of Christians in most of the nations of the world, as well."

Jim also points out that Americans need not look beyond our own shores to see the impacts of atheism. "Communism may have died in Russia, but it's twin sister, socialism, is still alive in the United States. We use other names for it, such as the 'welfare state,' but it still is based on a state-centered, man-centered philosophy that sees God as a threat." As a result, anti-Christian bigotry finds expression in America, evident by the rush to pass so-called "hate crimes" legislation that could stifle the rights of people of faith. How should Christians respond to the "most evil empire" here at home? "We need to stand up and say, 'Enough of this! Look at what atheism has produced in other parts of the world. We don't want it here! We want the religious freedom that our Founders gave us.'"

Once again, the best weapon against any idea (Communism, atheism or anti-Christian socialism) is a better idea (faith in God and active participation in the issues of our day). The Cultural Mandate given to the Church in God's Word clearly points the way. In Jim's words: "When a land is filled with Christian institutions proclaiming the message of Christ—and when it is effectively meeting the social needs of the poor, creating beautiful and meaningful Christian art, training intellectual leaders in every field from theology to mathematics, creating a grass roots political organization which is striving for just and fair government, and educating the masses through the public media—the groundwork has then been laid for the realization of a Christian republic.

"This goal will be reached when Christian institutions are effectively touching the lives of the vast majority of people and a 'Christian consensus' is achieved. Then the government will be filled with Christians or with those who intellectually reflect many Christian ideals. The society still would not be perfect, but it would be repentant of its sins and would try to please God in all that it did. It would provide religious liberty for all and the protection of an individual's rights by establishing and maintaining a just and righteous rule.

"This is a positive alternative to atheistic governments; not domination by tyranny but domination by the living and loving rule of Christ. Economically, such a state would reflect a compassionate and free economy that would allow growth and would solve many of the problems of the poor by creating new jobs and new industries. The love of Christ would motivate people to use their wealth to advance God's kingdom.

"There will be those who will accuse us," Jim admits, "of trying to Christianize America. Are we trying to Christianize America? Yes, we are! We are trying to Christianize not only America, but every country in the world! This is exactly what Christ commanded us to do in the Great Commission. We think that would be the greatest blessing the world could ever see!"

THE NEW IMMORALITY

This wisdom descendeth not from above, but is earthly, sensual, devilish.
—JAMES 3:15

O f all the anti-Christian "isms" which have drawn renewed vitality from the Darwinian assumption that man is nothing more than a complicated animal, unaccountable to a loving Creator who never existed anyway, none is sadder than the tidal wave of late-twentieth-century sensualism.

Feeding the flesh whatever it craves is being called a "right" or a "preference" by millions among the most enlightened and sophisticated populations. Unstinted physical gratification—food, sex, steroids, alcohol, a play ethic in the place of a work ethic, mind-altering drugs—appears to be as much in vogue as the latest clothing fashion. To support such "lifestyles," unfortunately, it is apparently necessary to lower many of the traditional barriers that have served to restrain human pride, aggression, lust, violence, and lawlessness. "Sin is in" is the flippant slogan spreading from tabloid mentality to saturate the media.

"Sin is in" is the tabloid mentality that saturates the media.

Society, particularly in America, gives the somewhat boorish impression that the fulfillment of carnal desire is something new, a worthy conversation topic, so popularized that once-common terms have all but disappeared from the vocabulary. How long has it been, for example, since you have heard words like these in ordinary conversation, especially in their original, positive connotations?

sobriety	honor
true-hearted	gallantry
wholesome	chastity
purity	thoughtful
gentlemanly	restraint
well-behaved	demure
decorum	polite
mannerly	self-denial
modest	innocence
proper	well-bred
abstinence	ladylike
genteel	virtuous
virgin	chivalry
teetotaler	upright

What you will more likely hear mentioned on talk shows today is a discussion of whether oral sex is likely to transmit venereal disease as readily as sodomy does; how to use laxatives to increase your ability to gorge on favorite foods; whether homosexuals have a right to adopt a baby; the street value of cocaine as compared with crack; what turns a good father into a wife and child abuser; how to teach ninth graders the proper use of the condom; how many beers you can absorb without becoming a DWI case; how a woman can build massive muscles like a man; why more of America's workmen hope to retire before the age of fifty to enjoy a life of leisure; all about children having children; how drug dealing corrupts public officials while it enriches the street criminal; and on and on *ad nauseam*.

There is one "old-fashioned" word that has not changed, the Word of God. Nor has its unremitting censure of "the sins done in the body" taken on a different meaning. From the Genesis record of our first parents feeding on that which was an abomination in God's sight, to the closing curse in Revelation 22:11—"he who is filthy, let him be filthy still" (which means through eternity)—the message is unaltered. From a grieving Jeremiah, who complained that the people of his day "were not at all ashamed, neither could they blush," to an outraged Paul, who breaks off his report on the state of pagan morals with, "it is a shame even to speak of those things which are done of them in secret"—Scripture maintains a consistent and terrible condemnation of all such "abominations of the flesh."

Today even the most liberal theologians, who would prefer to believe in innate human nobility, are beginning to reconsider the biblical doctrine of total depravity or original sin. It is getting more difficult for any person who is familiar with God's Word to go on ignoring its teaching on personal and social morality. Perhaps its warning on this subject was best summed up by Ruth Bell Graham, who said: "If America keeps going in the way it is going now with its ungodliness and wicked sin, and if God doesn't bring down the rod of punishment and chastisement upon this nation, He will have to apologize to Sodom and Gomorrah at the Judgment."

What are we to think about these things? What direction are such trends taking us? How, exactly, does immorality cause ruin in a society? And what do we need to do? Certainly, if any issue is of lasting concern to preachers, it is immorality. Let us take our questions to Jim Kennedy, who has spent the major portion of his time and energy fighting immorality—preaching against it, praying about it, opposing it in public forums, promoting legislation against it, and encouraging the victory over it through application of the Gospel to every area of individual and national life.

Q. Dr. Kennedy, what led to this upsurge of immorality?

"What has happened in our own country and around the world in this century amounts to a revolution—a tremendous sexual revolution. First, pornography, then adultery and incest and homosexuality and bestiality. There is every kind of perversion, giving rise to an absolute epidemic of venereal diseases—more than twenty transmissible venereal diseases are now raging in the United States.

"All this is one of the predictable results of the theory of evolution. Evolution gets rid of God, and therefore it gets rid of purpose. Without God there is no purpose in the universe. There is probably no term more anathema to an evolutionist than 'teleology,' which means that things have a purpose. Though the eye may seem to have a purpose, to an evolutionist it has no purpose; it is just there by chance. If there is no real purpose, there is no meaning; if there is no meaning, then obviously anything goes! There are no moral absolutes.

"Aldous Huxley, leading atheist and evolutionist and author of *Brave New World*, said this: 'I had motives for not wanting the world to have meaning; consequently I assumed that it had none, and was able without any difficulty to find satisfying reasons for this assumption. . . . For myself, as no doubt for most of my contemporaries, the philosophy of meaninglessness was essentially an instrument of liberation. The liberation we desired was simultaneously liberation from a certain political and economic system [capitalism] and liberation from a certain system of morality. We objected to the morality because it interfered with our sexual freedom.'

"In the name of 'healthful liberation' from repression, we have seen an enormous rise in sexual promiscuity—premarital, extramarital, and abnormal sexual relationships—with a focusing of the attention of the country's media and various institutions upon sex. We have been told that with this sexual liberty there would be a corresponding decline in mental illness, in psychoses, and in neuroses of various kinds. Quite the contrary is true. During the time when the American population doubled, the number of patients in mental hospitals increased by more than twelve times! Studies indicate that the alarming suicide rate increase, especially on college campuses, is tied to the new 'freedom.' The obvious results of the humanist push for licentiousness—moving out of liberty into license—cover the social landscape like so many corpses."

Q. Where does such "liberation" lead?

"Just study the rise and fall of the nations of history. The old kingdom of Egypt, the middle kingdom of the same country, the kingdom of Israel, then of Judah, Assyria, Babylonia, the Medo-Persian empire, Greece, Rome—all these went through two phases. During their ascendancies, they adhered to moral strictness, to sexual continence, to codes that frowned on any kind of premarital or extramarital sexual activity.

"But when they reached the pinnacles of success, these great civilizations allowed laxity and moral looseness to set in. As all manner of promiscuity, homosexuality, and 'kinky' sex began to take place, those nations precipitously declined and were destroyed. These are the indisputable facts of history."

Q. What happens to the Church in the process?

"In order for immorality to overwhelm a civil society, at some point the Church must have abdicated its role as 'salt' in society. But it doesn't happen overnight. In fact, to most, it is an imperceptible process in which this New Immorality breeds a New Tolerance, which in turn silences the Church and allows the foundations to continue to crumble."

Q. Explain what you mean by "New Tolerance"?

"I remember at one of our Reclaiming America For Christ Conferences, we invited Vice President Dan Quayle to speak. The newspapers stated, 'Dan Quayle Urges Family Values; Protesters Preach Tolerance.' I thought, wait a minute! Who is being intolerant? It certainly wasn't us—we were holding an orderly meeting. It was the protesters outside who were intolerant. They were the ones vehemently objecting to the fact that we were encouraging faith in God, strong families, and abstinence before marriage. Those protesters simply couldn't tolerate our beliefs.

"I shared this story with my church and made a statement I have oft-repeated in the subsequent years: 'Tolerance is the last virtue of a completely immoral society.' When immorality gains a stranglehold over a society, all virtue is cast aside and everything is tolerated. Everything, that is, except any person who dares to oppose the New Tolerance! The United Nations even went so far in its Declaration of Principles of Tolerance to state that tolerance involves the rejection of dogmatism and absolutism. It's interesting that they can be so dogmatic about rejecting dogmatism! Thus, in America today, tolerance is the only virtue, and the only sin of a sin-soaked society is the failure to be tolerant."

Q. What are the repercussions of the "New Tolerance"?

"The repercussions are dramatic. Since New Tolerance says all truth is relative, and all truth is equal, the Christian who holds to absolute truth is labeled 'intolerant' and Christian views become unacceptable 'hate' speech. We have seen this in the push for legislation against so-called 'hate crimes,' which are really crimes against intolerant thoughts and beliefs. These 'hate crime' laws could then be used to silence the Church right in the midst of the key cultural battles of our day. It's already happening in Canada, where if I were to go on television and read Romans 1, I could go to prison. Unless the Church takes a stand, we will see Christians labeled as 'hate criminals,' our views censored, and attacks on our faith move quickly from ridicule and mockery to outright censorship and persecution."

Q. What is behind this "New Immorality" rebellion?

"The absolute despair of modern humanity is what is behind the rebellion, the sex perversion, the violence, the drug dependency, the suicide rate, the music with its twin message of hate and hedonism. The young have been advised to throw out God, the Bible, Christ, and all absolute standards. They have been told thousands of times that they are nothing more than evolved animals on a meaningless planet and that the events of history and of their lives are controlled by chance and fate. They have been encouraged to take the view of a world without God to its logical conclusion. The only code to live by is survival: exploit those about you or be exploited; personal pleasure is the only value; instant gratification is the only reward. This is the tragedy of despair.

"As we weep for the curse which the evolutionists and the secular humanists have placed on our generation, we must look to Christ. As long as Christ is proclaimed and His light used to dispel the darkness, there is hope. He can remove the penalty of unbelief. He can bring conversion, revival, and reformation. His grace is greater than unbelief, and the symphony of His love can transform the discordant music of this world.

"Only Jesus Christ has the power to say: 'I took your sin, your immorality, all the way to My cross. You take My righteousness—all the way to Paradise.'"

Q. What are we to do as a nation?

"What is needful is that we repent of our part, because this is a revolution in which every person has been affected. All of us are involved. We need to realize just how much our thinking has been influenced. We tolerate behaviors today that just twenty years ago we would hardly have allowed to be mentioned. We have been morally anesthetized.

"We need to get rid of the Freudian concept that man is practically a sexual apparatus with legs, running around looking for copulation to fulfill his *raison d'être*. This is not man as he was meant to be—body, soul, and mind; this is man in a state of addiction. We need to have a view of total man. We need to have an understanding of total love and to realize that love is not to be equated with sex. Though it is a very important, God-given, and beautiful part of love, it is not love itself.

"You and I have to involve ourselves in the governmental process enough to bring about the needed legislation to deal with this massive social problem. 'But you can't legislate morality!' is the argument you will run into here. The truth is, you cannot legislate anything but morality. We have laws against rape, incest, bestiality, and adultery because these are immoral, hurtful, and antisocial practices that tear the very heart out of the family structure on which representative government is based.

"The real question is: whose morality is going to be legislated? The murderer's, the thief's, the drug pusher's, the sex offender's? Or is it going to be the morality of the law-abiding citizen? Is it going to be the morality of the secular humanist, preaching human evolution from lower animal ancestors, or the morality of God as expressed in the Judeo-Christian tradition? In other words, we need first of all to make sure that we are in Christ; then we must make our voices heard. Make a call; write a letter; stand up; express your mind. Remember that you are backed up by the Cultural Mandate commissioning you to carry your part of the battle for righteousness. By the grace of God we can return this nation to what it was in the beginning."

Q. What about homosexuality?

"It is the consensus of all psychologists and psychiatrists who have worked with these people that if there is one thing a 'gay' person is not, it is gay. That is an ill-chosen term, and again it is the lie of the deceiver. Counselors find homosexual men and women (the word is not from *homo*, man, but from *homos*, same)—persons attracted to those of the same sex—to be the most miserable of human beings. Trapped, they feel inescapably condemned by society as they desperately reach out for some fulfillment. Deep down, they usually hate themselves, all the while trying vainly to justify their lives as being right and normal.

"Most medical authorities today regard homosexuality as essentially an acquired behavior, the result of psychological rather than physical disturbances. People are not 'born this way' although such factors as body build, temperament, or energy level may exert a predisposing influence on the establishment of homosexual behavior patterns. Regardless, it is not only a sickness but a sin.

"I received a letter from a person who signed it as 'a homosexual Christian.' The letter was a rather pitiful attempt to justify homosexuality on the basis of Scripture. That is somewhat like trying to justify adultery on the foundation of the Sermon on the Mount. It is interesting that I later received a pamphlet from a 'homosexual church'; I discovered that the individual's letter had been simply one long, extended quotation from the pamphlet—the same argument expressed in identical words. The apostle Paul, when he wrote on this specific topic, warned, 'Be not deceived.'

"Unfortunately, the Bible comes down hard on *arsenocoites*, which is often translated as 'those that abuse themselves with mankind,' but which literally is 'male intercourse' in the original language. The Bible in this instance says nothing about condemning the attitude or lust; it is the act itself which is condemned, along with those who do it. Scripture does not provide one loophole regarding the homosexual act.

Q. Then is there no hope for the homosexual?

"Praise God, there is hope for every sinner. Paul clearly says to the Corinthians, 'And such were some of you' (adulterers, fornicators, murderers, homosexuals) and then adds: 'But you were washed, but you were sanctified, but you were justified in the name of the Lord Jesus, and by the Spirit of our God' (1 Corinthians 6:11). It is through the blood of Jesus Christ that these people may be cleansed from their sin and released from the shackles that bind them. I know numbers of homosexuals who have been transformed by the Gospel of Christ and have come to lead normal and healthy lives."

Q. Is AIDS a punishment from God for sin?

"We face in AIDS an epidemic that has claimed more than 400,000 lives in America and an estimated 5 million have died from AIDS worldwide so far. There have been 688,200 AIDS cases reported to the CDC in America. Is this a modern-day plague from God? The question alone is offensive to the ears of the average person today. It is not inconsistent with the biblical view of God for Him to send plagues on societies as punishment for their refusal to follow His moral decrees. All will die of something—if not AIDS, then some other illness, accident, or crime. We are under the curse of God for sin, and part of that curse is physical death.

"In this broad view it can be seen that AIDS, just like all other illnesses, has been created by God and released into our world as a general punishment for sin to bring about death. This affects all mankind, both the just and the unjust, since both can become ill and die. AIDS is being spread largely by people who disregard God's ethical commands against sexual promiscuity and drug abuse. Two of the key pillars of the 'new morality' begun in the 1960s were 'free sex' and abundant drug use. AIDS is a stop sign from God.

"It is important that we recognize the fact that just having AIDS is not a sin. A person who has it is not necessarily any worse a sinner than the person who does not have it. Many people who have committed fornication do not have AIDS, and God does not point to the infected individual as one who bears greater sin. There are many innocent victims of this terrible disease—babies are born with it—and there will be many more. When we speak of the disease being a plague, we do not mean that it is sent upon individuals for individual sins. Rather, it has been released into the world to make us aware of our sinfulness and of our need for God."

Q. What should Christians do about AIDS?

"As Christians we must weep over the anguish of those who suffer with AIDS and minister to them with the love of Christ, who did not withhold His compassion or healing from the despised lepers of His day. Yet, we must demand that our government treat the disease as a disease and protect us from those who would be irresponsible and who would spread the virus to others.

"AIDS can have a positive effect if our nation will understand it as a warning from a holy God. I hope America will heed this warning and turn from all sexual sins."

Q. What is the status of pornography?

"For more than thirty years now there has been an open sewer in our society. Its vile flow has not been stemmed, despite many hundreds of court cases and attempts by legislatures to come up with laws acceptable to federal judges. Transliterated from the Greek, *pornography* means the "writing of the harlot." Of course the term today embraces all kinds of drawings, photographs, texts, motion pictures, television, radio, telephone voice messages, computer software, and—currently—videotapes designed for private consumption. Books, magazines, newspapers and now the Internet—

all have shared in the dissemination of pornography origi-nating in the hearts and minds of sometimes talented but morally depraved persons who are insensitive to any respon-sibility for the pollution they are contributing to society.

"The explanation for the existence of the smut industry is simple: looser moral codes, generally called 'permissive-ness,' have allowed crime-connected enterprises to take in revenues estimated at $8-12 billion per year. It is a shame the American public would think of supporting such a system, which has been a blight on the lives of a whole generation of our children from the day they were born until now."

Q. Didn't the Supreme Court settle this issue?

"It tried. In one decade pornography lawsuits taken to the Supreme Court constituted five percent of the total case-load of the high court as the justices wrestled with questions of definitions and First Amendment rights of free expression. As the number of cases mushroomed, the august body com-plained, 'This was not intended to be a high court of obscen-ity.' And Justice Potter Stewart wearily admitted, regarding the question of what is and what is not pornographic: 'I don't know how to define it, but I know it when I see it.'

"In one five-to-four split decision after another, the court ended up declaring that obscenity is that which appeals to the prurient (lustful) interest, that which has no redeeming social value, and that which does not conform to the local community's contemporary standards. In this way, it was able to return the whole can of worms to the states in which the pornography cases originated.

"There has been some tightening of local controls. A very dedicated layman in our church, after hearing a sermon I preached on the subject—in which I concluded with the assertion, 'You can change the world'—decided to do some-thing about pornographic bookstores here in Fort Lauderdale. He actually quit his job and mortgaged his home to raise the money to form an organization which he called

Alliance for Responsible Growth. He enlisted the coopera-
tion of the mayor, the sheriff, and many other influential
people in the community.

"After this group researched what was happening in
other cities, it brought pressure on the city council to pass an
ordinance outlawing all pornographic bookstores. It required
five or six years to fight all the court battles the pornographers brought, but the last shop was closed down. The same
thing has been done in Cincinnati and in Jacksonville on a
wider scale. During the first five years that Cincinnati was a
'clean city,' the incidence of rape dropped by an amazing 83
percent! This shows that citizens acting in concert can clean
up their cities.

"It also exposes the cynical and heartless fallacy of the
argument that sexual sin has become sophisticated and is, at
worst, a 'victimless crime.' In an historic telecast, just before
he was electrocuted at the Florida state penitentiary, Ted
Bundy described in great detail how pornographic pictures,
mostly in magazines and on film, drove him into a full-time
career of raping and murdering. Approximately one
hundred families across the United States lost their beautiful
daughters to the lustful rampage. Ask them what 'victimless
crime' means. Ask the thousands of women who, from childhood, have experienced the absolute horror and loathsome-
ness of incest, often resulting in the birth of an illegitimate
child sharing the same father with his or her mother.

"The victims are all around us, and none are more tragic
than children, many of them abandoned and homeless, who
have been drawn into the clutches of the pornographers.
Pedophiles have developed a complex, computerized network through which traffic can be carried on in this most
lurid and reprehensible of all illegal activities.

"Perhaps you doubt whether any civilized nation could
go so far as to legalize 'kiddie-porn.' In Holland, one of the
nations exporting huge volumes of child pornography to the
United States, there is no law against producing pornogra-

phy involving children—no law protecting children. The Dutch supreme court has refused to extradite a British subject who has been shipping child porn to England from Rotterdam. Why? Simply because he had not violated any Dutch law."

Q. What is the greatest danger in all this?

"The greatest danger with all sensual sins is desensitization. Until the present generation, divorce was considered to be a stigma by the community because it was understood that community life is built on the foundation of stable families.

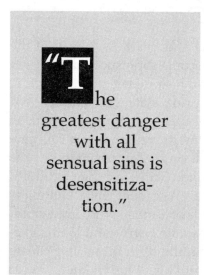

"The greatest danger with all sensual sins is desensitization."

Today, with half of all marriages ending in divorce, people tend to be unconcerned about the effect of such a trend, not only upon the quality of life in the local community, but upon the national social fabric.

"A few years ago homosexuals were abhorred as 'sex deviants'; now they live together openly as 'married couples.' The word incest was almost unmentioned outside of courts of law, but in San Diego there exists a Childhood Sensuality Circle that contends that incest is a healthy practice. Bestiality was a subject considered too repulsive for any conversation; today it is discussed on talk shows and cartooned in pornographic magazines. Adult pornography was tolerated long enough for the purveyors of child pornography to establish a legal defense against those who would abolish it. Even in the 1960s the idea of 'kiddie-porn' was considered to be not only detestable, but criminal.

"What all this proves is, you can't play games with Satan

because he will always take you farther than you originally meant to go. His power over the flesh is especially formidable, and each compromise with purity gives him a yet stronger grip. He delights in our debates about whether a diet of obscene material affects behavior or whether it is, after all, perfectly harmless—because he knows the answer. It would take logic of an incredible kind to argue that education is a total waste of money because it has no effect on the future lives and careers of students. By the same logic, you would have to say that preaching, which puts ideas into people's minds, produces no results in the conduct of individuals. By this logic, advertisers aren't really persuading the public to buy their goods and services although they pour billions into the effort year after year.

"It is as true today as it ever was that 'as a man thinketh in his heart, so is he.' Feed the flesh what it demands and it will grow more and more dominant; neglect to feed the spirit and it will grow weaker and weaker to resist the flesh. The Bible tells us that there is continual warfare between the two. The victory will be determined by which one you nourish. While it is true that the devil cannot rob a Christian of salvation, he can certainly use sensual sin to take away the Christian's peace and joy in the Lord and to render his witness in the world totally ineffective.

"America must decide if its cultural ethic on sex will be based on secular humanism or on Christianity. If the nation decides to follow the secular path, the continued evil exploitation of women and children can be expected to increase."

A
NATION
IN
SHAME

*Yea, they sacrificed their sons and their
daughters . . . and shed innocent
blood . . . and the land was
polluted with blood.*
—PSALM 106:37-38

For Jim Kennedy, no issue facing the American
people shares the opprobrium of what he labels "the
American holocaust"—the premeditated destruction of the
lives of more than 38 million unborn babies since 1973, the
year of the *Roe v. Wade* decision legalizing abortion. He has
fought any legislation that devalues life and the medical
acceptance of infanticide and euthanasia with his personal
participation, sermons, books, media interviews, two stun-
ningly produced hour-long specials for prime-time television, "Abortion: A Reflection of Life," and "Who Lives? Who
Dies? Who Cares?"

"On one hand," he observes, "we hear statements made
that 'abortion is a woman's choice,' and on the other hand we
hear claims that 'abortion is murder.' We listen to news commentators as they speak of laws that will allow people 'the

right to die with dignity.' We watch as courts sanction the right of parents to decide to refuse treatment for their child, allowing the infant to die. Such an act is said to be 'necessary and merciful' because the child is handicapped. As we are bombarded by these stories, we realize that some basic and important element is eroding within our society."

What Jim is fundamentally concerned with is life—the right to life (the very first unalienable right listed in our Declaration of Independence), the quality of life (the gift that Jesus promises "more abundantly"), and life everlasting (the whole purpose of Jesus' Gospel of salvation). One of the most startling statements in all of God's Word is "all those who hate Me love death." The proverb warns both individuals and nations that to turn away from God and His wisdom and His expressed will is to become a lover of death. For those who have studied Scripture carefully, it is clear that, because of deliberate and stubborn rebellion, our nation is fast becoming infatuated with death.

It is clear that our nation is fast becoming infatuated with death.

Consider the current terminology in American dialogue: abort—to stop life; infanticide—infant murder; euthanasia—"beautiful death."

More important than liberty, precious as it is, is life. Of more value than the pursuit of happiness or economic success or even religious freedom, is life. A citizen deprived of life has obviously been deprived of every other conceivable right. The Founding Fathers placed the right of life ahead of all others because they held such truths to be self-evident. How has America been able to turn itself, in one generation, away from its life-honoring heritage to accept passively the slaying of more unborn children since 1973 than the total number of casualties suffered in all of the country's wars since 1776?

The focal question in all abortion debates seems to be: Whose concern is it? Jim believes it is primarily God's concern; He gives life and He takes life. There are more than one hundred texts in the Bible dealing with the unborn and the Creator's interest in them. Secondly, the child, if able to express itself, would certainly have something to say about its desire to survive and to enjoy life. Even society at large has a stake in the death of millions of its future citizens. A familiar illustration points to Ludwig van Beethoven, who—given today's technology—would undoubtedly have been aborted because of such "predictable" threats as siblings already handicapped, syphilis in his parentage, etc.

Most often ignored, perhaps, are the deep concerns of the grandparents-to-be, aging couples whose very hearts are usually woven into the future by the sight of children's children. That prospect is one of the most gladdening promises of the Word of Life recorded in virtually every one of its sixty-six books. And what of the father's rights? Isn't he as involved in the adventure and excitement of newly created life as the mother? Yet the prevailing philosophy of legal and medical authorities tends to isolate the mother from all others and to unload the entire problem on her because she is the one carrying the child. Of course, she is entitled to sympathy and help and support, especially if she has been betrayed and abandoned to cope with such enormous fears as illegitimacy, possible physical handicap, financial problems, and other social pressures sometimes far beyond her ability even to understand. But is killing a better way? Can murder be considered "coping"?

The abortion "solution" has been one gigantic "cop-out," a semantic hoax, a clever subterfuge. The trick has been to get rid of the old-fashioned idea that an unborn baby is a real baby. How many times have you heard an abortionist speak of the occupant of the womb as a "baby"? In an almost amusing application of doublespeak, they invariably refer to the unborn child as the "fetus." *Fetus* is a perfectly good Latin word which simply means "an unborn baby," but today it is used to signify some inhuman clump of tissue. Jim has made note of the irony: "Martin Luther knew how important it was that the Latin Scriptures be translated into the vernacular so people would understand them. And the abortionists know how important it is to translate the English words into Latin so that young women won't know what is going on."

The object of such language manipulation, it is easy to see, is to change the facts, to assert that the fetus is not a human life or, if that cannot be defended semantically, that it is a sort of human being without "personhood." "This dredges up some very interesting reminiscences from history," Jim says. "It reminds me of 1857 and the *Dred Scott* decision argument (*Dred Scott v. Sandford*), in which the Supreme Court indicated that the black man (slave) was not a person. It also reminds me of Nazi Germany, where it was maintained that the Jew was not a person. The Nazis knew that before they could enslave or exterminate human beings, the first thing they had to do was to depersonalize and dehumanize them. They had to be semantically destroyed before they could be physically destroyed. That is exactly what is being done to the unborn children of our society today."

In an ominous development, the same depersonalizing tactic was used to support infanticide in the Baby Doe case— he was "not a person" and therefore could be killed. The same argument was used to support the destruction of the mentally deficient or the handicapped—"not fully persons." Before Hitler killed a single Jew or Christian, he had already murdered 275,000 handicapped people. It is significant that abortion had been prevalent in Germany for twenty years before the public would stand for the elimination of 275,000 of their own citizenry because of undesirable handicaps.

God said to the prophet Jeremiah, "Before I formed you in the womb I knew you; before you were born I sanctified you" (Jeremiah. 1:5). In considering this text, Jim asks the question: "Is the Lord referring to a blob of tissue that He knew or to a person? God does not sanctify an appendix or a tumor—but a person."

To illustrate the absurdity of the pro-abortion premise that unwanted babies should be killed (they prefer the euphemism "unwanted pregnancies should be terminated"), Jim suggests another irrationality: "Every wife has the right to be wanted by her husband. We would all agree with that. If some young woman should come into my office and tell me that she is not wanted by her husband and her heart is broken, imagine if I would say to her, 'My dear, I think that is the saddest thing I have ever heard. It breaks my heart to hear that your husband, that mean old wretch, doesn't want a lovely thing like you. There is only one thing to do.' Then I open my desk drawer, pull out a gun, and *bang, she is dead!* That solves the problem! 'Bring in the next counselee. . . .'

"In the case of a baby, it is not only irrational; it is also a lie. There are 1.3 million abortions performed every year in this country. There are two million couples looking, often unsuccessfully, for babies to adopt. Many adoption agencies have had to close for lack of infants. Couples have had to wait five or ten years to adopt a child. One reason is that they are all in the incinerator—the victims of abortion!"

Without challenging the often-heard claim that the woman has a right over her own body (although suicide is not a right recognized by the law), Kennedy clarifies that the baby in her womb is in no way a part of her body. From the instant of formation of the embryo, it has its own blood stream; not one drop of the mother's blood ever enters the fetus, or vice versa. The baby's body has separate and unique genetic information and biological material. It produces its own nest, the placenta. It is the baby that produces its own umbilical cord and its own sex (*half of the time it is a different sex from the mother*). It will have a different blood type from that in the mother's body—"incompatible blood," the doctor calls it. That miraculous "thing" inside of the woman is another person. The ovum fertilized by male sperm is not a part of her body at any stage of development. Her right over her own body is limited by another person's right over his or her own body. Inconvenient, perhaps, but that's the way God made it.

The awe-inspiring key to life is conception. When the female egg is fertilized by male sperm, the first evidence of conception to become visible will be the presence of blood in the ovum. No blood, no life. One of the most ancient of all biblical teachings is that "the life is in the blood." For a very simple illustration of the truth that life begins, not along the way somewhere in the second trimester, but at the very instant of conception, consider this scenario:

A Japanese woman has an ovum which has been fertilized by her husband (a Japanese male) surgically removed from her uterus. The fertilized cell or embryo is placed in a glass dish under the strictest of clinical procedures and is kept alive *in vitro*—in the glass dish outside of the mother's womb—until it can be safely implanted in the uterus of another woman, where it continues to grow. When full term is reached, that woman delivers a normal baby.

The question: if that surrogate mother who carries the developing child for nine months is a black woman, will the child be born with Negroid features? Or if she is a Caucasian person, will the child have the skin color and other distinguishing traits of a white boy or girl? Neither, of course. It will be full-blooded Japanese with all the customary characteristics of Japanese babies. The sole determinant in the whole complicated process was conception; that's when a new Japanese person was created.

Much of the fight for legalized abortion has been waged with unfair logic—the so-called "hard cases." Truly heartbreaking situations are used to put pro-life advocates on the defensive: a pregnant woman in a deep coma whose chances for recovery, according to an abortionist, would be enhanced by terminating the pregnancy; the young incest victim; the woman who carries a rapist's child. Such exceptional cases are the ones that make the headlines. The truth is that fewer than 1 percent of all abortions are performed to save the mother's life. Fewer than 2 percent of all abortions are done because of rape or incest. The real problem lies with the 97 percent—repeat, 97 percent—of abortions on demand, simple killing-for-convenience.

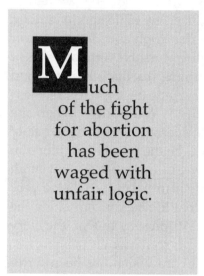

Much of the fight for abortion has been waged with unfair logic.

The heinous nature of this "killing for convenience" becomes evident when one considers what actually happens in an abortion. "Of course, the media will never let you see an abortion," says Jim. "They will show us all sorts of human suffering, but no babies that have been aborted." In one type of abortion, says Jim, "so-called 'doctors' reach in the mother's womb with forceps and rip off a leg; then they rip off another leg; then they rip off an arm, and the baby may still be alive, fighting to avoid the forceps! Finally, they crush the baby's head and extract it. Another procedure injects a saline solution in the womb that literally burns the baby alive."

In the mid '90s, the horror of abortion finally broke through the national media blackout as pro-life conservatives shined the light on one of the horrendous abortion procedures—the partial-birth abortion. In this procedure, babies in the third trimester of development (some just days or hours from birth) are partially delivered before the abortionist begins performing the abortion. Says Jim, "The government says it's all right to pull a baby three-fourths of the way out of its mother's womb, stick a pair of scissors in the back of its neck, and kill it. This is a total abomination." Faced with such a graphic display of the brutality of abortion, the tide of public opinion slowly began to shift. Congress passed bills banning the partial-birth abortion procedure. Each time, those bills were stopped by President Clinton's veto pen.

"The time has come," Jim warns, "for those who value human life to become active and fight this gross moral evil of our time. There is not a rational argument that can be presented for the flood of abortions that has launched this nation into a sea of blood. God condemns those who shed innocent blood. We are going to bring down on this nation the very wrath of God. I am certain that eventually this hideous blot on the escutcheon of humankind will be wiped away. Just as slavery went the way of other evils and just as Nazism passed away, so also will this butchery of the innocent pass away. However, it will leave a scar on the historical character of our nation. It will shock our children and our children's children that we allowed such a slaughter to occur. We must do all we can to help those members of our society who are the most helpless and silent sufferers of all—the unborn children."

Infanticide, the twin horror to abortion, refers to the taking of an infant's life outside of the womb. Many Americans do not realize that medical sources estimate that nearly five thousand handicapped infants are allowed to die each year through denial of routine lifesaving care. In much the same way, euthanasia, or "mercy killing," rose ten times in five years in the 1980s, and pro-euthanasia groups trebled in number. The idea that such killing is "merciful" grows directly out of accepting the evolutionary view of humanity, which sees human beings simply as mammals of no more significance than any other animals. If they shoot horses with broken legs or gas chickens diseased with salmonella, what's the big deal about "terminating life support" for the handicapped, the mentally incompetent, the terminally ill?

The question once more is, Who is in charge of life? A life may be filled with hardship, suffering, pain, and disappointment. Yet out of the most difficult circumstances and struggles, God forms characters that will leave the deepest and most profound impact on history. Modern humanists want to remove suffering from life; God uses suffering to deepen our faith and understanding of life.

How can we answer the "freedom to choose" advocates in a democratic government? That right is not handed over to citizens in matters of infanticide and euthanasia—or even in suicide. It is not ethically within the power of the family or the individual to take human life; government reserves that right to the state, an authority backed up by Scripture. To grant life-and-death authority to the family over its members would lay the groundwork for undermining Western civilization; the government would be unable to stop its citizens from committing murder. The battle here is between barbarism and civilization.

Modern advances in technology that enable doctors to keep persons "alive" long past their normal dates with death are often cited as the reason for infanticide and euthanasia—that these life support systems force us to give people the "right to die with dignity." Again, the hard cases are always brought to the forefront of the argument because they would open the door to wholesale acceptance of "mercy killing." But people have been quick to find reasons for mass murder ever since Pharaoh ordered the death of all the male children in Egypt and Herod slaughtered the innocents in Bethlehem. With or without technology, we must understand that there is a time to live and a time to die. We may want technology to grant us eternal life, but this would be a false hope and a misuse of technology. Our hope of eternal bliss rests in Jesus Christ alone—not in any life-prolonging medicine or machinery.

Jim Kennedy's purpose is to rip the mask of intellectual and moral sophistication away from those who promote euthanasia and infanticide as social cure-alls. He responds to the problem of all such "mercy killing":

"Christians must become active and fight this evil. We must first become informed about the issues and recognize that the instances of infanticide and euthanasia are increasing in the United States every year. Then we must speak out in our communities about the barbaric acts that are being allowed to take place.

"We must realize that 'mercy killing' is not merciful at all, but is merely a gaunt refusal to face the role of suffering and struggle as potentially positive factors in our lives and in the lives of others. The Christian community needs to be able and available to provide pro-life counseling to people who might be considering abortion or these other forms of taking life. True Christian charity and compassion can go a long way toward preventing such cases.

"We need to be alert to distorted facts and irresponsible use of catchwords like 'the right to choose.' The new social planners are more systematic than the Nazis were in the use of effective public relations techniques, but the end result will be the same—compulsory murder of handicapped children, the insane, the severely ill, and the aged.

"We must understand the complex nature of modern technology and the new questions it raises. We cannot 'cop out' to the easy answer of legalized euthanasia, but must struggle to find ethical and personal solutions to the hard cases that arise. It is the duty of Christians to be leaders in the defense of the right to life.

"It is also important that informed Christians contact their government leaders. Our lawmakers need to be educated so they can take a godly stand against legalized murder. The rights of the unborn need to be reinstituted into our law through a constitutional amendment.

"Finally, we must understand that our true battle is with

the principalities and powers of darkness and not with any human group or organization. It is Satan, whom Jesus called a murderer from the beginning, who is behind this new thrust to kill the unborn, the handicapped, and the aged. If the Christian Church can be mobilized into an effective spiritual assault team to fight the forces which would have us accept these abominations, we can have every confidence that God will grant us a victory."

RECLAIMING AMERICA

Blessed is the nation whose God is the
Lord: and the people whom he hath chosen
for his own inheritance.
—PSALM 33:12

The dictionary defines a patriot as "a person who loves, supports, and defends his country and its interests." More than the average person you find in a service uniform, more than the typical politician you see in public office, more than most professional speech-makers you hear on national holidays—Jim Kennedy is a patriot. The only institution he loves, supports, and defends with greater devotion than the government of the United States is the Church of Jesus Christ. These priorities make him a genuine patriot.

"There are those who gnash their teeth today," he observes, "at the very mention of the fact that America was founded as a Christian nation. However, history cannot be easily dismissed, even though it is often ignored in our schools and in many of our modern revisionist history books. For those who will take the time to read, the principles, the institutions, and the foundations of the life of this country were indeed, in every way, Christian in nature."

One of the things Jim enjoys most is documenting the claim concerning the Christian origins of America with a barrage of irrefutable chunks of evidence taken right out of the historical documents. For example:

The Mayflower Compact: "In the name of God, Amen . . . having undertaken for the glory of God and advancement of the Christian faith . . . a voyage to plant the first colony in the northern parts of Virginia. . . ."

Governor William Bradford, Plymouth Colony: ". . . a great hope and inward zeal they had of laying some good foundation, or at least to make some way thereunto, for the propagating and advancing of the Gospel of the kingdom of Christ in those remote parts of the world."

New England Confederation: "We all came into these parts of America for one and the same end and aim, namely, to advance the kingdom of our Lord Jesus Christ and to enjoy the purity and liberty of the Gospel of peace."

John Quincy Adams: "The highest glory of the American Revolution was this: it connected in one indissoluble bond, the principles of civil government with the principles of Christianity."

Daniel Webster: "Finally, let us not forget the religious character of our nation . . . that is the happiest society which partakes in the highest degree of the mild and peaceful spirit of Christianity."

George Washington: "Religion and morality are the central pillars of civil society."

Samuel Adams: ". . . the rights of the colonists as Christians

. . . may be best understood by reading—and carefully studying the institutes of the great Lawgiver and head of the Christian Church, which are to be found clearly written and promulgated in the New Testament."

Noah Webster: ". . . the religion which has introduced civil liberty is the religion of Christ and His apostles . . . and to this we owe our free institutions of government."

Robert C. Winthrop: "It may do for other countries, and other governments, to talk about the State supporting Religion. Here, under our own free institutions, it is Religion which must support the State."

Jedidiah Morse: "To the kindly influence of Christianity we owe that degree of civil freedom and political and social happiness which mankind now enjoys. In proportion as the genuine effects of Christianity are diminished in any nation, either through unbelief, or the corruption of its doctrines, or the neglect of its institutions; in the same proportion will the people of that nation recede from the blessings of genuine freedom."

U. S. Supreme Court: "Our laws and our institutions must necessarily be based upon and embody the teachings of the Redeemer of mankind. . . . It is impossible that it should be otherwise; and in this sense and to this extent our civilization and our institutions are emphatically Christian. . . . These, and many other matters which might be noticed, add a volume of unofficial declarations to the mass of organic utterance that this is a Christian nation." (*The Church of the Holy Trinity v. United States*, 1892)

Newsweek, December 1982: "New historians are now discovering that the Bible, perhaps even more than the Constitution, is our founding document."

U. S. District Judge Frank McGarr, 1986: "The truth is that America's origins are Christian and that our Founding Fathers intended and achieved full religious freedom for all within the context of a Christian nation in the First Amendment as it was adopted rather than as we have rewritten it."

To pronounce the words "First Amendment" in the presence of Coral Ridge's patriot preacher is to touch the protoneuron, the most sensitive nerve, in his theology of morality in government. "Of all the tenets of our constitutional system, the First Amendment is probably the most misunderstood and the most misquoted. Ask the average person on the street what the Constitution says about religion or the Church, and you will be told: 'Oh, it says they are to be restricted.' Ask what the First Amendment says, and the vast majority will reply that it says there should be a separation between church and state.

"Usually, they'll even quote you what they think is the language of the First Amendment: there is to be a 'wall of separation' between church and state. That is not what it says, but a passing phrase in Thomas Jefferson's letter to the Danbury Baptists in 1792 suggested that there should be 'a wall of separation between church and state.' That innocent phrase has become, in the minds of a majority of Americans who seldom take a glance at the history of their free institutions, a substitute or a replacement for the First Amendment that actually spells out the role of the Church in a democratic republic."

Well, just what does the First Amendment guarantee in the way of freedoms? Besides naming specifically (1) freedom of speech, (2) freedom of the press, (3) freedom of assembly, and (4) the right to petition the government concerning grievances, it says this: "Congress shall make no law respecting an establishment of religion, or prohibiting the free exercise thereof."

Armed with the literal wording of the mandate, Jim asks this question: "Is the subject the Church? Ministers? Religious people? No, none of these. The subject is Congress. It tells us that *Congress* shall make no law respecting an establishment of religion and that *Congress* shall make no law forbidding the free exercise of religion. The entire Bill of Rights (the first ten amendments) was written for one purpose: to restrain the power of the newly created federal government and to protect the freedoms of the people. That is why people like George Washington and Patrick Henry demanded a Bill of Rights so that this new leviathan of government that was being created would not consume the people's rights.

"The First Amendment—and this has to be understood clearly today—limits Congress. It says nothing about what the Church may or may not do. It only limits what Congress may do; it is a one-way street. It does not erect a wall between church and state; a wall limits people on either side of the wall equally. But this was written specifically to limit the powers of government so that the people would have full protection of their rights to free and unrestricted worship. We have seen in our day a 180 degree turnabout from what the First Amendment says, with liberals and secular humanists proclaiming that somehow the First Amendment's purpose is to protect the government from the influence of religion! This is to argue that only the ungodly are unbiased and fit to rule. Atheists, agnostics, and amoralists—only those who have nothing to do with religion—are the ones to be entrusted with public office at all levels. You see the complete reversal from our historical roots: a government founded largely by Christians (those few who were not were Deists) is best run in our time by those who reject Christ and who hate God! The restrictions that were intended to be put on the government have been taken off and have been put on the Church instead."

What, then, is the relationship between the state and the

church? In the Middle Ages, Roman Catholicism taught that the state was under the Church. In the eleventh and twelfth centuries, the papacy achieved dominance over all of the states of Europe. Today, at the other extreme, some would put the Church under the state—as in Communist lands.

"I believe," Jim says, "there should be a separation of the church and the state as the reformers taught. This, however, should not be a separation of God from the state, which is increasing in our country today. The Bible very clearly states that the nation that forgets God 'shall be turned into Hell.'

"The Founding Fathers of this country did not intend to establish a government separated from God. When the Constitution was being formed, Benjamin Franklin declared that it was not possible to build a political state without the help of God. Therefore he moved that each session of Congress responsible for drawing up the Constitution should be opened with prayer. How utterly foolish, then, are the current efforts of those who would do away with prayer before the opening sessions of the House of Representatives and the Senate. Nothing could be ultimately more damaging to our country.

> "The Founding Fathers did not intend a government separated from God."

"While the Church (Christ's Church) and the state must be separate, the Church must be ready to be a prophetic voice to the state and to remind it of its responsibility to God in administering justice. The Church is obligated to submit to the civil laws of the state as it honors the divine appointment of the government. However, this submission ends when the state directs the Church to act contrary to God's laws or seeks to control the free government of the Church. Even if the Church is persecuted, it must not surrender its ultimate loyalty to Christ.

"This view of the state is based on the perspective of humankind as fallen and sinful. I believe that the founders of America, who had a clear understanding of the biblical teachings, knew that man was a fallen creature and basically evil. Since their time, humanists and non-theistic concepts have endeavored to establish the belief that people are basically good. But our founders had a purpose in giving us a limited government, stating that all power not specified in the Constitution is reserved for the state and local authorities—that is, for the people.

"Why did they distribute the power like that? Because they had no doubt that man, being intrinsically sinful, will misuse power if given the opportunity, they divided the federal government into three equal parts—to avoid the collection of power into too few hands. Thus the executive, legislative, and judicial branches of government effectively prevent the takeover of power by any individual or group bent on the tyrannical control of this country. It's a wonderful system."

And it is wonderful as long as Christians do their part and obey the Cultural Mandate so that God might be glorified in His own world. However, something happened a hundred or so years ago: pietism. It began as a good idea, but like many good ideas, it degenerated. The pietists called for a warm pious center in Christianity—a personal relationship with Christ, a personal devotional life. Of course these are essential. But the descendants of the movement's founders began to change its teachings. They began to maintain that this warm personal relationship with Jesus was the totality of Christian life and that there was nothing else. Jim points out the results:

"Accordingly, Christians began to retreat from politics as being dirty business; they retreated from government as being corrupt; they retreated from science as being godless; they retreated from the media as being dishonest and irresponsible; they retreated from the arts and literature and music as being sensual. They left these spheres to unbelievers who were happy to fill the vacuum. There was, as Francis Schaeffer has so aptly described it, the emergence of a post-Christian culture which we now have in this country. Christians have been told that it is not their place to try to influence public policy on the basis of their private morality. They have been taught that to do so would be unspiritual as well as unconstitutional. Consequently, the secular humanists, with their principles devoid of faith and purpose, have been allowed to gain the offensive while the Church has cowered on the defensive. Martin Luther's admonition was that Christians belong wherever the battle is the hottest; but, sadly, Christians have been running from the conflict, retreating from their responsibility to be the salt of the earth." That is how Jim Kennedy diagnoses America's state of health at the end of the twentieth century.

The cure? Return to the Cultural Mandate given by God, he says. Involve Christian young people in influencing the minds of other young people. Flood the media with them. Encourage them to go into politics and government and the court system. Help them work their way into executive positions in business and industry and advertising. Return Christian teachers to the classrooms to teach the truth about science and economics and history. Invade the college campuses with educated and dedicated Christian professors. Get Christian practitioners into medicine, Christian talent into the arts, Christian performers into entertainment.

"While others retreat," *Conservative Digest* reports, "James Kennedy is advancing. While some face troubles at the hands of swarms of investigators from numerous agencies, Kennedy's reputation and trust remain intact. While there is talk about evangelical Christians abandoning public policy in favor of a return to Pietism and withdrawal from the responsibility to make the world a better place, Kennedy is preaching the opposite. At the same time, while some who call themselves Christians eagerly look for a political savior, the message of D. James Kennedy continues to be what it has been for the past quarter of a century: "Christians have a duty to govern—a civil as well as a religious responsibility—which includes the translation of Christian principles into daily life."[9]

In other words, personal involvement and Christian action make up the prescription for healing America's sickness. Jim has been able to speak with four presidents of the United States and with many congressional, state, and local politicians during his ministry, and he has pressed the same message upon them all. Included among the other men in high office to whom he has communicated the principles of the Cultural Mandate was Menachem Begin, head of the State of Israel. "I have great respect for the Jews, Mr. Begin," Jim told him. "I worship One every morning." He then presented the Gospel of Christ.

Personal involvement and Christian action are the prescription for healing America's sickness.

Jim has also become personally involved in the Cultural Mandate through carefully-crafted sermons with titles like: "Reclaiming America," "Christianity and Politics," "The Exalting of a Nation," "Government: A Fearful Master," "God and Country," "What Price Liberty?" and "Patriotism: One Nation under God." He has made it his custom to deliver a special sermon at the beginning of each year entitled "The Spiritual State of the Nation." Timed to coincide with the President's "State of the Union" address, Dr. Kennedy uses the platform of his national television "pulpit" to address key issues facing the nation from a spiritual vantage point. These messages, among his most popular and insightful, chronicle the great cultural trends that have confronted our nation in recent years, as well as their spiritual impact. In addition, Coral Ridge Ministries has produced hour-long specials on current national problems and has many more in the planning stage.

In a campaign to get out the vote in the 1988 presidential election, hundreds of thousands of elaborately printed "Election 88: A Christian Perspective" brochures were distributed nationwide. The brochures informed citizens precisely where each candidate stood on such issues as abortion, abortion funding, budget deficit, birth control and parental consent, capital punishment, education, Equal Rights Amendment, the candidates' faith and practice, freedom fighters around the world, homosexual rights, national defense, occult practices, political philosophy, school prayer, Supreme Court appointments, and tax increases.

In 1989 Jim was host to a dramatic Roots of America tour which took participants to England for sightseeing and lectures at the places where the Pilgrim Fathers received their inspiration. The tour proceeded to Holland, to the actual debarkation site of the colonists, then to Plymouth Rock and throughout historic places in New England where the nation was born. The care and planning for a production of that sort, as compared with the ordinary church tour, should be obvious. The motivation in such efforts is not to entertain but to instill a deeper patriotism based on America's historical heritage.

As the decade of the '90s dawned, it became clear to Dr. Kennedy that a new chapter in America's history was about to be written, and Christians would play a key role. Thanks to the efforts of Coral Ridge Ministries and others, Christians were finally awakening to their duty to reform society. Now it was time to mobilize the troops. As part of this new awakening, in 1994 Coral Ridge Ministries held its first "Reclaiming America For Christ" conference. Hundreds of Christians from across the country came to Fort Lauderdale to gain the practical tools they needed to take back their communities for Christ. Now an annual highlight of the Coral Ridge Ministries calendar, Reclaiming America For Christ conferences have featured a "Who's Who" of Christian leaders, including: Dr. Bill Bright, Vice President Dan Quayle, Gary Bauer, Chuck Colson, House Majority Leader Dick Armey, Beverly LaHaye, and many others.

Most importantly, thousands of attendees returned home and put in practice what they learned. Reports began to come in from across the country of citizens speaking out at school board meetings, running for local elected office, and organizing their own grass-roots coalitions. One attendee, John Hostetler of Indiana, heard the call of the Lord to run for Congress confirmed while listening to Dr. Kennedy expound on the Christian's duty to be both salt and light in society. Later that year, Rep. Hostetler was elected to represent the 8th Congressional District of Indiana.

Rep. Hostetler's victory was part of a sweeping political "revolution" that saw a dramatic shift in power in Washington, D.C., with ramifications that were felt in every state of the union. Most analysts focused on the fact that Republicans gained control of both Houses of Congress for the first time in a generation. But Jim discerned a more significant spiritual trend that could shape American culture for decades to come. "The sleeping giant of evangelical Christians has at long last shaken itself awake," he would announce from the Coral Ridge pulpit just days after the November 1994 elections in a message entitled, "The Christians Are Coming." What had awakened this sleeping giant? "The stench of a culture rotting all around us," he said.

Citing exit poll results, Kennedy remarked that in 1988, just 18 percent of voters were "evangelical Christians." By 1992 the evangelical vote had jumped to 24 percent, and in the 1994 elections, 33 percent. Dr. Kennedy immediately sent an open letter to senators, representatives and governors to discuss the implications of this dramatic shift in voter demographics. In the letter he predicted that this trend would continue throughout the decade, making evangelicals "the largest single voting block in the country." He also issued a warning that unless social issues were "brought from the back burner to the front burner," the Republican party would soon suffer the same fate that had befallen Democrats—a prediction that would be fulfilled later in the decade.

As Christians took a more prominent role in government, Jim saw a need to bring a strong Christian witness to our nation's capitol to sustain and support this new move. "The future of our nation depends in large part on the character of our leaders," he would say. So in 1995, Coral Ridge Ministries announced a new outreach in Washington, D.C.— The D. James Kennedy CENTER FOR CHRISTIAN STATESMANSHIP. The CENTER would bring a fresh breeze of evangelism to Capitol Hill, disciple members of Congress and their more than 18,000 staff members, and equip this new generation of Christian leaders to fulfill the cultural mandate. Reaching Washington, D.C., with the Gospel had been a lifelong dream of Jim Kennedy. He had often noted that more evangelistic efforts take place in foreign nations than in his nation's own capital—the epicenter of world political power. Just as the Apostle Paul longed to preach the Gospel to those in Rome (Romans 1:15), so Jim Kennedy longed to reach his "Rome." Now, the time was right, and quickly the CENTER FOR CHRISTIAN STATESMANSHIP began taking the Gospel to leaders in Congress. Today, the CENTER is a leading voice for evangelism and statesmanship in our nation's capital.

Still, there was more work to be done to reclaim our nation. By the mid '90s it became evident that this new "army" of Christian citizen-activists needed training and equipping to reclaim their communities for Christ. Once again, Jim Kennedy stepped forward to help fill the void, founding the CENTER FOR RECLAIMING AMERICA in 1996 as an outreach of Coral Ridge Ministries. Based in Fort Lauderdale, the CENTER is a national "clearinghouse" for grassroots citizen activists. Want to know how to write to your congressman? Contact the CENTER. Ready to run for school board? The CENTER's field staff can guide you through the process. In essence, the CENTER places in the hands of Christians the tools of government which are available to all citizens interested in effective social and political action, such as:

Voting: This is the backbone of the citizen's ability to place into public office men and women who will represent a Christian view in government. Christ's order that we "render unto Caesar the things that are Caesar's" included the vote.

Petition: When those who represent us hold ideas that we believe to be of danger to the welfare of the country, we have a right to petition our leaders, asking them to reconsider their actions. A petition should be written by a lawyer and made into a legal document. The people who sign the petition should be informed of the effect it had on their leader's decisions.

Personal appeals: If your leaders receive from you a well thought-out letter, a telegram, or a phone call for which you paid money, they will know that you are a concerned citizen who will recall how they vote on given issues. This is the democratic process.

Education: Once we come to what we believe is the proper biblical perspective on an issue, we need to express this to the public at large through printed material, presentations before civic groups, and open debates. Education leads people to a rational understanding of the truth; mere propaganda only wants acceptance of a viewpoint without proper consideration of the facts. Inform yourself thoroughly.

Boycott: When we see a clear connection between a social or political evil and a private economic interest, we should refuse to do business with the organization involved and should encourage our friends to do the same.

Positive social action: By giving time, money, and energy to help meet the needs of unfortunate people in our community and society, we can do a great deal to change the world. Such a program can open doors to those who want to know more about the Christian world-and-life view.

Political campaigns: Most successful politicians are those who are able to organize effective grass roots organizations to spread their message on a one-to-one basis. If you find a candidate you believe in, give his office a call and ask what you can do to help him get elected. They will always have something you can do for the cause.

The CENTER FOR RECLAIMING AMERICA also has given Christians a national voice in the key cultural issues of the day. For example, in 1998 the CENTER'S National Director, Janet Folger, developed a fresh perspective on the entire issue of homosexuality. For years, homosexual activists had been working to label Christians as "homophobic" and "hate mongers," and with the media's help, these labels began to stick. So Folger shared with other Christian leaders a plan to place the most powerful cultural force of all—the Gospel—right into the center of the debate. Dr. Kennedy wholeheartedly endorsed this idea, which became the highly successful "Truth In Love" media campaign. "It's not about hate, it's about hope," he said, as newspaper ads (and later, television spots) gained national notoriety and the hope of the Gospel took center stage.

Another important aspect of Kennedy's strategy for reclaiming America for Christ involves the courts. Over the past several decades, Jim has watched an unelected tribunal called the U.S. Supreme Court take unto itself vast powers. He says the Court has used this new power to stray from the Constitution on key issues of religious freedom, undermine our culture, and unleash a barrage of legal attacks on the rights of Christians. "What has happened to cause the corruption of our culture, the rash of school shootings, the purging of God from public places? There is no simple answer, but I believe most of the blame must be laid right on the marble steps of the U.S. Supreme Court. Through its decisions, the Court has created an anti-God worldview which has resulted in a hellish milieu of ungodliness and immorality."

The courts have had a dangerous ally in the culture war—the American Civil Liberties Union. "I prefer to call them the 'Anti-Christian Liberties Union,'" says Jim. "The ACLU has been behind every major attack on religious liberties in the past 50 years—including the *Everson v. Board of Education* case that established the false doctrine of separation of church and state in our jurisprudence."

Activist judges and anti-liberty groups like the ACLU have stifled the rights of Christians. In fact, in recent years the attacks on the legal rights of Christians have become so pronounced that Jim decided to team up with some of the leading voices in evangelical Christianity (including James Dobson, Marlin Maddoux, Larry Burkett, Bill Bright, and Don Wildmon) in co-founding the Alliance Defense Fund. The goal of ADF is simple: identify the crucial faith and family court cases and then offer funding and legal support to fight and win these battles. Founded in 1994, the ADF has had a major impact, taking part in virtually every major legal case concerning religious liberty, family values, and the sanctity of life. In its first five years, ADF helped win more than 80 individual religious liberty cases—including six of seven cases in which the ADF went head-to-head with the ACLU.

About the same time ADF was being founded, Jim would become personally involved in what would become the highest profile legal battle over religious freedoms in the

'90s. Judge Roy Moore, a Circuit Court judge in Etowah County, Alabama, decided to display in his courtroom a wood carving of the Ten Commandments he had personally made. Everything was okay until some friends of the ACLU learned of the practice. So in 1995 the ACLU filed suit to force Judge Moore to remove the Ten Commandments. This launched a protracted court fight that gained national attention when Alabama Governor Fob James threatened to call out the National Guard in defense of Judge Moore. The Alabama Supreme Court threw out the ACLU's lawsuit on a technicality, enabling Moore to retain both prayer and the Ten Commandments in his courtroom, for now. Since then, unfounded ethics allegations—a form of legal harassment—have been brought against Moore. But with each new attack, Jim Kennedy and Coral Ridge Ministries stood by Judge Moore's side. The ministry contributed to Judge Moore's defense fund and helped spread the word to millions across the nation.

"Judge Roy Moore is a unique man, a true Christian statesman who I believe has been called into the kingdom 'for such a time as this,'" says Jim. "Few in America today have his depth of knowledge of America's Christian heritage. Most importantly, few have the courage to stand for his convictions against the anti-Christian tide in our society."

Of course, throughout this entire process of "reclaiming America," Kennedy has carefully preserved the integrity of the Gospel by avoiding becoming beholden to any political party. "Christians, in my opinion, should be conscript to no political party," he said. "They should be conscript to the Word of God. They should search the Scripture, ascertain what the Bible says about any issue facing our nation, and then vote their biblically informed conscience." In fact, he would say "I never talk about partisan politics." However, "when the government obtrudes itself into the moral realm, I will talk about that." Talk, indeed. But more than talk, D. James Kennedy has taken dramatic action to reclaim the land he cherishes for the glory of the Lord he loves.

It becomes clear, then, that the Cultural Mandate, like the Great Commission, calls for action—soldiers of the Cross to take their spiritual weapons into the warfare. The objective is, by living lives of holiness and proclaiming His Word through actions as well as speech, to bring all of creation under the control of Jesus Christ. Jim puts it this way:

"This nation, which is as turbulent as a storm-tossed sea, could one day be subdued by His Spirit until it lies like a calm and tranquil lake; and then, the glories of Heaven shall be revealed and reflected therein. This is the vision God holds for our nation. This is God's purpose for America. There it is, shining, dazzling in its glory. Lift up your eyes and discover what God's real purpose for your life is, and give yourself over to it—heart, mind, and soul.

"If you do this, God will bless you and make you a benediction to this country."

What has been Jim Kennedy's benediction (which literally means "blessing") on America? Perhaps his firm conviction that America can restore her greatness as men and women turn their hearts to Christ and heed his clear call for Christians to reclaim that greatness. As Sen. John Ashcroft once remarked, "Dr. Kennedy calls America to greatness; he calls individuals to godliness. And if we have individuals who are godly, we will have an America that is great."

PART SIX

THE MAN AND HIS LEGACY

PURGING THE CHURCH

*Who gave himself for us, that
he might redeem us from all
iniquity, and purify unto
himself a peculiar people.*
—TITUS 2:14

The last will and testament of Jim Kennedy has not been probated, for—as the writer of Hebrews observed— where there is a testament, there must of necessity be the death of the testator. However, wills are drawn up and bequests are made, not by the dead, but by the living. The spiritual inheritance due the heirs of the Kennedy estate has been spelled out in some detail in this account of his life and ministry, and many more benefits will be added as codicils in the productive years remaining to this servant of the Lord. In the alphabetical nomenclature familiar to hundreds of thousands of his fellow laborers, he will leave behind him:

E.E.—Without exception, Evangelism Explosion and its spectacular march from the tiny McNab schoolhouse church into every nation on earth constitute Jim Kennedy's unique and inimitable legacy to the Christian world. No other set of initials could make a more appropriate monogram to distinguish his life work and ministry.

CRPC—Certainly South Florida will be forever changed by Coral Ridge Presbyterian Church. As its founder, its builder, its guiding genius, and its only pastor, Jim has left forever the stamp of his personality on this great lighthouse of the Gospel of Jesus Christ.

CRM—Most churches have developed outreach programs, but few, if any, compare with Coral Ridge Ministries in scope, diversity, and professional standards. This mammoth communication operation broadcasts, records, programs, prints, films, advertises, publishes, and promotes the Word of God to audiences of millions in competition with the secular media.

WA—Westminster Academy has demonstrated, throughout one of the most degraded periods in the history of American schools, that a godly, healthy, and scholarly education is possible when its foundations rest upon unashamed Christian and patriotic witness and teaching.

KTS—Entering its second decade, Knox Seminary combines quality academics with the passion of its Chancellor, Dr. Kennedy: commitment to the sovereignty of God, the inerrancy of His Word, the Great Commission, and the Cultural Mandate It is meeting a desperate need in the earthly kingdom of Christ for Reformed, biblical, evangelical ministerial training in a predominantly secular environment.

WAFG—As a permanent memorial to his miraculous conversion by the preached Gospel via radio transmission, this outstanding nonprofit station is reaching South Florida listeners with good programming and Good News.

PCA—Perhaps you haven't been aware of the spiritual kinship that developed between the Presbyterian Church in America and the Coral Ridge institution. Once again, it was an unswerving devotion to Christ and an unshakable reliance on the Word of God that made Jim the catalyst in that relationship and that led eventually to his acceptance of yet one more position of national responsibility and service.

As far back as 1971, Jim identified himself with a group of Presbyterian leaders known simply as Concerned Presbyterians. What was it they were especially concerned about? A disturbing drift toward liberalism in the denomination—that is, in the Presbyterian Church of the United States, better known as Southern Presbyterians. They were concerned about increasingly liberal pronouncements regarding abortion, ordination of women as elders and as ministers, the rights of homosexuals, the inerrancy of Scripture, even the Westminster Confession of Faith, and reunion with the even more liberal northern branch of Presbyterianism (PCUSA). Such trends represented a total departure from the historic positions held by the Church.

> **J**im identified himself with a group of leaders known as Concerned Presbyterians.

In 1973 more than two hundred churches withdrew from the Southern camp as other groups joined with the Concerned Presbyterians to form the new, conservative PCA. Jim grieved over the permissiveness toward social issues, but remained with the larger body in hopes that PCUSA would turn back toward its historic positions. "We sort of drew a line," he recalls. "The line consisted of (1) if you actually change the Westminster Confession (our statement of doctrine); (2) if you go into the Northern branch; or (3) if you merge with Consultation on Church Union, a proposal to collect all mainline denominations into one—if you cross this line, we will leave. Otherwise we will not divide ourselves. They had not done any of that, so we stayed in the body.

"Well, about six years later, there was an attempt to

reword the *Westminster Confession of Faith*. That required the approval of three-fourths of the presbyteries, and it fell short. But they did manage to change the *Book of Church Order* (which required only a majority vote). In the *Book of Church Order*, which is our rule of government, are the vows the elders and the ministers take; and, of course, among those vows is subscription to the doctrines taught in the *Westminster Confession of Faith*—which we believe to be the doctrines taught in the Bible.

"In other words, by devious and unexpected means, the rope had been cut and the ship allowed to float out to sea. Now there was really no doctrinal basis at all for becoming a minister in that church because the leadership was no longer bound to anything solid. That fact was demonstrated when one minister who explicitly denied the deity of Jesus Christ was ordained anyway. When I realized that the *Westminster Confession* had been disposed of in a way that nobody had really expected, I decided it was time to leave in order to protect the purity and the integrity of the Church."

While many of the church groups which had left PCUSA earlier had done so in defiance of the Presbytery —just leaving without asking to be dismissed, throwing off authority and declaring their own independence—Jim opted not to go that route. Instead, he discussed the situation with the elders at Coral Ridge, then with all of the various organizations and ministries within the church, and finally with the full congregation. After the Session had given its unanimous vote, the entire membership of forty-four hundred voted, with one negative ballot, to transfer to the Presbyterian Church in America. Now it was Jim's assignment to go before the Presbytery of the Everglades to make the announcement.

The big problem faced by many individual churches seeking official dismissal had been the forfeiture of all their property. Coral Ridge, of course, was by far the largest church within the Presbytery of the Everglades, and its departure would reduce the size of the Presbytery by approximately one-fourth. Jim went before that august body to face the issue squarely.

"Gentlemen," he said, "you may wish to attempt to take our property as you approve our transfer to the PCA. You may want to take us to court in order to acquire legal title. However, I really would not want you to have to go to all that trouble. So if you would like to take over our property, here is the deed which I have brought along with me. All we have to do is sign, and the property is yours. I should tell you that it is going to cost you $4,000 a day to hold on to it. But if you want it, I don't want you to have to go to all the trouble of a court case."

In consideration of the fact that the church carried an enormous mortgage at that time—enough to sink the entire Presbytery financially—the members responded quickly in unison: "Oh, by no means—we wouldn't want to do that—of course not!" They then promptly voted overwhelmingly to allow Coral Ridge Presbyterian Church to go in peace from the Presbytery, they warmly praised the accomplishments of the church, they brought all of Jim's assistant ministers and elders to the front of the assembly, expressed their gratitude, sang "Blessed Be the Tie That Binds," took pictures, shook hands all around, and let the pastor and the delegation go. "It was a most amicable separation," Jim recalls.

The significance of the pastor's decision to move his church from one ruling body to another is to be found in the absolute consistency of his conviction from earliest seminary days when he first learned of a rising tide of liberalism that threatened to drown the pure scriptural doctrine he had accepted. His decision was not only studied and conscientious, but actually delayed until he felt that the fundamental purity and integrity of the faith itself was becoming imperiled. At that point, compelled by the same sort of instinct that had sent him into deep water many times before as a young lifeguard, Jim jumped in to perform a rescue operation. His goal was what it had always been—excellence in all things

The new affiliation was instantly acclaimed by his fellow PCA ministers.

for God's glory—and he was no more inclined toward compromise midway through his ministry than he had been in the beginning. The new affiliation was instantly acclaimed by his fellow PCA ministers. A typical comment came from an elderly preacher in Panama City, Florida:

> Mine is inexpressible joy over what has happened and my heart is overwhelmed with joy and gratitude, first to our loving Father who does all things well and, then, to you for your own strong decision against every inducement to keep the status quo. . . . My gladness in your coming is . . . that you love the Reformed Faith with evangelistic emphasis, that the doctrines of sovereign grace are precious to your heart. You will strengthen all who in PCA try to do more than wave the Confession as though we had a passing parade. I am profoundly grateful that you come as the man God has made you.

And, while everybody knew that the Coral Ridge pastor already had enough to do—perhaps more than three times enough—without taking on another heavy responsibility, it was not long before Jim began to receive letters from men holding the higher ranks in PCA with suggestions like this one in the mid-1980s:

> You have a much-needed contribution to make, and we are less—much less—as a denomination without your presence amongst us. . . . I realize that the demands upon your time are great and that there are many exciting opportunities for min-

istry which you must carefully weigh before the Lord as a steward of your time. However, I feel that Presbyterianism, even evangelicalism, is at a crucial juncture, and that we as the PCA can have a critical role to play in determining the course of Presbyterianism and Protestantism in America and around the globe. Your participation or lack of it has an impact on the outcome. . . . You and men like you must assume the leadership of our denomination in your Presbytery and the General Assembly. You will determine the direction of the PCA in the next few years.

Such appeals, obviously, were aimed at one objective— and that was accomplished in the summer of 1988 when Jim accepted the position of moderator of the Presbyterian Church in America. Somehow it seemed peculiarly fitting that the man who had been astonished, thirty-three years before, to be called to preach a Gospel of pure, unadulterated grace, should be at the head of the largest group of Presbyterians committed to the very same Bible-rooted doctrine of salvation by grace. The PCA has grown from 240 congregations with 40,000 members in 1973 to more than 1,404 congregations with about 290,000 members. It is one of the country's fastest-growing denominations.

A unique aspect of the legacy of Jim Kennedy is the considerable bulk of his spiritual estate bequeathed to ministers. The extent of his exposure, over the years, to fellow preachers of the Gospel is really quite staggering to contemplate. His participation on the teaching faculty of the Billy Graham School of Evangelism since 1967, for example, has brought him, as teacher, before more than forty thousand ministers. His role as founder and president of Evangelism Explosion International since 1972—plus continuing E.E. clinics for pastors started almost a decade before—put him in personal contact with at least that many more. And as moderator of PCA he has been drawn into close relationships with hundreds of church leaders, including pastors from 42 states and Canada and 403 career missionaries. Without even considering sermons, broadcasts, and printed messages, it would be safe to assume that Jim has influenced the ministries of more than 100,000 evangelicals already.

What has been the message to these shepherds who, in turn, influence the lives of their flocks? It has been twofold: (1) that ministers must be doctrinally sound on the essential elements of Christian teachings, as they preach the Gospel of Christ; and (2) that they must be and must live as Christ would want His disciples to live.

These two characteristics are itemized in fifteen affirmations,[10] which the Coral Ridge pastor has set before his church and which he endorses for all ministers and the ministries they lead:

Affirmation I
We confess Jesus Christ as God, our Lord and Savior, who is revealed in the Bible, which is the infallible Word of God.

Affirmation II
We affirm our commitment to the Great Commission of our Lord, and we declare our willingness to go anywhere, do anything, and sacrifice anything God requires of us in the fulfillment of that Commission.

Affirmation III
We respond to God's call to the biblical ministry of the evangelist and accept our solemn responsibility to preach the Word to all peoples as God gives opportunity.

Affirmation IV
God loves every human being, who, apart from faith in Christ, is under God's judgment and destined for Hell.

Affirmation V
The heart of the biblical message is the Good News of

God's salvation, which comes by grace alone through faith in the risen Lord Jesus Christ and His atoning death on the cross for our sins.

Affirmation VI

In our proclamation of the Gospel we recognize the urgency of calling all to a decision to follow Jesus Christ as Lord and Savior, and to do so lovingly and without coercion or manipulation.

Affirmation VII

We need and desire to be filled and controlled by the Holy Spirit as we bear witness to the Gospel of Jesus Christ, because God alone can turn sinners from their sin and bring them to everlasting life.

Affirmation VIII

We acknowledge our obligation, as servants of God, to lead lives of holiness and moral purity, knowing that we exemplify Christ to the Church and to the world.

Affirmation IX

A life of regular and faithful prayer and Bible study is essential to our personal spiritual growth, and to our power for ministry.

Affirmation X

We will be faithful stewards of all that God gives us, and will be accountable to others in the finances of our ministry, and honest in reporting our statistics.

Affirmation XI

Our families are a responsibility given to us by God, and are a sacred trust to be kept as faithfully as our call to minister to others.

Affirmation XII

We are responsible to the Church, and will endeavor always to conduct our ministries so as to build up the local body of believers and serve the Church at large.

Affirmation XIII

We are responsible to arrange for the spiritual care of those who come to faith under our ministry, to encourage them to identify with the local body of believers, and seek to provide for the instruction of believers in witnessing to the Gospel.

Affirmation XIV

We share Christ's deep concern for the personal and social sufferings of humanity, and we accept our responsibility as Christians and as evangelists to do our utmost to alleviate human need.

Affirmation XV

We beseech the body of Christ to join us in prayer and work for peace in our world, for revival and a renewed dedication to the biblical priority of evangelism in the Church, and for the oneness of believers in Christ for the fulfillment of the Great Commission, until Christ returns.

"It is our hope," Jim concludes, "to truly strive for excellence with our efforts in all we do, so that God may be glorified. In affirming our belief in these principles, we are not claiming to be perfect. We do state that we are attempting, as sincere Christians, to honestly conduct ourselves in such a way as to please God in our doctrinal teaching, our personal lives, and our financial affairs. It is our intention to be good stewards and faithful witnesses for God. We hope you share our vision for a godly ministry as set forth here. If you do, then please join with us in prayer that God may bless our efforts to reach the nations for Christ so that our Heavenly Father's name might be honored and His will done in all the earth. Amen!"

SONGS IN THE NIGHT

I waited patiently for the LORD; and
he inclined unto me, and heard
my cry . . . And he hath put a
new song in my mouth.
—PSALM 40:1, 3

When a man arrives at the peak of his career with a record of excellence in all things—with phenomenal achievements and successes and recognitions—then the deep, dark valleys through which he has had to pass tend to be concealed from view. Like most of us, Jim Kennedy has had to grapple with some harsh realities along the way; he has learned to endure hardness as a good soldier of Jesus Christ. While he has not advertised the times of testing, they have nevertheless been a very real part of the record. And, after all, this is the record of a life.

The opening chapters of this work called attention to a devastating, traumatic childhood, which he miraculously overcame without lasting damage to mind and body. The emphasis here, however, is on the Christian struggle, after the experience of regeneration in early adulthood. With all of his demonstrated courage, contagious optimism, remarkable logic, and unshakable faith, Jim acknowledges, "There is the dark night of the soul that all of us must pass through. There is the deep valley, the great darkness; no life can be spared it."

Quoting his favorite preacher, Charles Spurgeon, he explains, "It is easy to sing in the day time. Most birds do it. And many men do it, too. It's easy to sing when our cup is brimming full; when wealth rolls in abundance and health is ours; when all things are going well; when success crowns our every effort. It's easy to sing in the daytime.

"But what about when life crumbles in and the night time comes? Then the songs choke in the throat. It's easy for the aeolian harp to give its sweet music when the soft winds blow, but what about the time when that dead stillness of soul comes and hope has flown? Now from whence shall come the fullness of music? It is easy to make a crown when jewels are scattered at our feet. But when there is nothing but hard stones, of what shall we make our diadem?"

No doubt the first "deep valley" encountered as a servant of God was the utter despair of a new young pastor discussed in earlier chapters, when his church attendance plunged month after month almost to the point of extinction. But the words quoted above stemmed from an even more heart-wrenching set of personal circumstances. They are from a sermon he brought to his congregation in September of 1967, about six weeks after tragedy struck his family. Jim had just undertaken study for an advanced degree at the Chicago Graduate School of Theology when the malignant claw of cancer reached out to threaten the life of his beautiful wife while they were living at Winona Lake, Indiana.

"I was sitting in the lobby of the hospital where Anne had been taken for a biopsy," Jim recalls. "After the report came back from the laboratory, the doctor came out to see me. I will never forget the impact his words had on me. He had previously told us that in 99 percent of such cases, the tumor proved to be benign. But he walked right up to me and said, 'Your wife has cancer.'

"If this doctor, who was a huge man weighing about 250 pounds, had walked up and hit me in the stomach with his fist, the impact would have been no different. As I stood there, the room seemed to spin around and around. He must have talked for about two minutes, as he asked for my permission to proceed immediately with the surgery. My head was swimming all that time and I was losing touch with my environment. As soon as the doctor left, I literally dove for a couch nearby and passed out like a light. I never realized before that mere words could carry such a physical impact."

When Jim returned weeks later to the church, there was scarcely a dry eye in the congregation as he unburdened his heart to them. "I think perhaps the most difficult task that has ever fallen to me," he said from the pulpit, "was that of breaking the unexpected news of what she had to my wife. I looked at her on that bed, realizing that she was ignorant of her condition, and that she was hoping to rise up and go home in a few moments.

I looked down at her and she said to me, 'It is benign, isn't it?'

"And I said, 'No, dear, I'm afraid it's cancer.' Never have I felt words shaped so sharply into a knife; I felt like Abraham—as if I had driven that knife into her heart. But I want you to know that that knife was driven into my heart as well. It plunged deep into my soul. As I walked those halls that day, with no one to talk to, there was one thought that kept coming back to my mind. It was the words of Lincoln in the depths of the war, after the

"It is benign isn't it?"

"No, dear, I'm afraid it's cancer."

death of his son, when he said, 'I think that I shall never be glad again.' And on that day, I did not see how I could ever be glad again. It did not seem to me that I could ever stand in the pulpit and lead in songs of praise. I was plunged into the dark night of the soul."

But at the same time he shared his grief, Jim shared also the inspiration that came to him in those dark hours: "But God giveth songs in the night. It was very shortly thereafter, while riding in my car, the words of the Doxology burst spontaneously from my lips: 'Praise God from Whom all blessings flow; praise Him all creatures here below.' And the words of the Gloria Patri: 'Glory be to the Father, and to the Son, and to the Holy Ghost.'

"That is a song that only God can give. But His Word stands sure that God indeed gives songs in the night. I shall not forget hearing my wife pray: 'I thank Thee, Lord, for what has happened to me this summer.' These are wonderful songs. They are divinely given songs. For I am not strong, and neither is she.

"But the world listens with an attentive ear to those songs. May I say, I rejoice that a woman across the hall with a broken shoulder, bemoaning her fate and having no hope, was so astounded by the testimony of Anne that she asked Christ to come into her life. And Anne's joyous response to the telephone calls that came in was such that the telephone operator of the hospital asked to come and see her in her room. She came again and again, and the night before we left she asked Christ into her life. These are songs the world desperately needs to hear.

"Do you know why and how we can have that song in the night? It is only when we know that God is in it, as did Paul and Silas when they sang hymns at midnight while bound in stocks inside a filthy dungeon. There is the secret that can turn gloom into joy and that can illumine the heart!

"What is the night of your soul? Is it a financial reversal? 'This thing is from Me'—that you may draw upon His riches. Is it sickness? 'This thing is from Me'—that in your weakness His strength may be made perfect. Do others turn their backs on you? 'This thing is from Me'—that you may be drawn closer to Him."

Yes, here is a man who is acquainted with grief. He knows what it is to be in repeated discomfort from attacks of asthma, and to be in almost constant pain through his adult years because of compressed vertebrae—both ailments requiring medication on a daily basis. He remembers the keen disappointment of rejection by the Foreign Mission Board because of his physical problems.

He is no stranger to the threats of desperate men who have resented his testimony for Christ and his call for righteous living. On three occasions Jim has been the target of what the Bible calls "liers in wait"—in plain language, people who meant to kill him. In one instance, the death threat was not particularly dramatic, but it was disturbing nonetheless. It began with a rage-filled letter, criticizing the pastor, which was followed by a series of notes

He is no stranger to the threats of desperate men.

that became increasingly more belligerent and menacing in tone. Finally, the writer said that he was going to kill the preacher. Certain peculiar expressions in the letters led some of the assistant ministers to suspect a man who had been coming to them for counseling and who obviously had mental problems. The ministers got in touch with the suspect and persuaded him to come to the pastor's office in their presence, aware that it could be a dangerous situation.

"I didn't sit in my usual chair across the desk from him,"

Jim said, "but I took a chair which I pulled up close beside his. In case he should go for a gun, I wanted to be in a position where I knew I could prevent him from ever getting it out of his belt or his coat. However, whether he was armed or not, we were successful in talking him out of his notion. The letters stopped coming, and that was that."

Another instance in the old church on Commercial Boulevard came a little closer to erupting in an act of violence. Jim had led a woman and her two teenage sons to Christ. The husband and father was an alcoholic who was the absolute terror of his neighborhood. The people who lived around him would run into their homes as they saw him coming down the street yelling and cursing. Sometimes he would even bang on their doors, daring them to come out. The pastor had never laid eyes on the man, but word came to the church that he has spreading the news that he was going to "kill the preacher who loused up my family."

Sure enough, he showed up at the church on Sunday, intoxicated and carrying a concealed pistol. His plan was uncomplicated: he was going to step into the sanctuary and unload his gun at the preacher. Fortunately, an alert usher standing in the narthex saw the man enter, pull the pistol out of his belt, and proceed unsteadily toward the door of the sanctuary, where the service was in progress. The usher, a large young man, easily took the weapon away from the intruder and muscled him right out of the building and on his way down the sidewalk. He made no effort to have the man arrested, and no one inside the church was aware of what had taken place until they saw the usher's evidence.

"Actually," Jim remembers, "I had a guest preacher that day, Dr. William Childs Robinson, who was the greatest theologian I ever studied under. Since the would-be assassin had never seen me, he could have shot the wrong preacher. But who knows? With both of us on a not-too-large platform, he could have gotten both of us if his aim were any good."

The third incident bordered on the sensational. It was on

a Saturday when a wild-looking individual, dressed only in a pair of cut-off, blue-jean shorts and carrying a club, rode up on a bicycle. He stopped at the tennis courts behind the church (on Federal Highway) where Jim's daughter Jennifer was playing tennis. Banging on the metal fence with his club, he bellowed out, "Is the Lord of this place here?" Jennifer, startled at his bizarre appearance and question, answered, "Well, if you mean the minister, you'll have to inquire inside the church."

With those instructions, the strange visitor rode around to the office entrance and approached the receptionist's desk, banged his club on the counter, and repeated his menacing question, "Is the Lord of this place here?" When informed that the preacher was not in the church at the time, he said to the receptionist, "Well, tell him that at high noon tomorrow I'm going to come and do him in."

The terrified girl at the desk began calling leaders of the church membership, and soon the Session was apprised of the threat. The Fort Lauderdale police were notified by the elders, and at a tense worship service the next day, approximately a dozen uniformed and plainclothes officers were stationed at strategic points inside the sanctuary—including one who was seated behind the lectern. All went quietly, and after church the preacher stood at the front door to shake hands with the departing congregation.

As the last parishioner left, a car swerved off the street and into the church driveway. Oddly enough it went undetected by any of the policemen still inside the church. But by coincidence, a passing patrolman in a squad car noticed something strange about the traffic maneuver and followed the car into the drive, parking immediately behind it. The driver panicked, left his car with the door standing open, and dashed around the side of the church building and across a parking lot. Several policemen quickly took up the chase, which led into an adjacent residential area, but by hurdling a series of fences, the fugitive was able to elude his pursuers and vanished.

In their follow-up investigation, the police traced the mystery man's address from the abandoned car and made an unsettling discovery in his apartment. What they found was a television set split almost in half, with the ax still deeply embedded in it. Recalling the weird situation, Jim says with a hearty laugh, "I don't know what I preached on, but I really reached the guy. Peter Marshall once commented that, when the apostles preached, they didn't get a pat on the hand and a 'Nice sermon, preacher.' He said there were either riots or regeneration. I certainly said something that got a response from that fellow. I understand the police did catch him, but I never knew the outcome of it. We never heard any more from him."

Few laymen are ever aware of the real cost of preaching the Gospel and standing for Christian principles without compromising. One typewritten—and, of course, unsigned —note in the office files reads: "Best change the locks on the door. Definite and clear signs that the WOLF is on the prowl again. You'd better think twice." A phone call—the voice sounded like that of a young man—told the pastor's secretary, "Tell him he dies tonight." Communications like a telephoned bomb threat don't particularly brighten a minister's day, as they are sorrowful reminders of the ever-present depravity of the human soul. Fortunately, such gestures are infrequent. Whether the opposition is in the form of petty criticism or a heavy-weight lawsuit, Jim does not cave in under pressure nor does he seek commiseration. Rather, he rejoices as he recalls the promise of Jesus: "Blessed are ye, when men shall revile you, and persecute you, and say all manner of evil against you falsely, for my sake. Rejoice, and be exceeding glad: for great is your reward in Heaven." He is able to say with Paul, "I have learned that in whatsoever state I am, therewith to be content."

"This is something that is really foreign to human nature," Jim admits. "It is quite incongruous to the normal way of acting and reacting to our circumstances. It is something which must be learned, and often the school is hard and the lessons try us to our depths. Weeds grow swiftly. We do not need to cultivate thorns and thistles and brambles, for these grow profusely in the fallen nature of man. But if we would have precious flowers, the luxurious garden, there must be the tender care of the gardener. We must learn. Therefore, let us be patient students in the college of contentment. For this indeed is a great lesson to be learned."

It is a lesson which Jim has learned straight out of the Bible, as taught by the Holy Spirit. Like Job, he has looked to "God my Maker, Who giveth songs in the night." Because he was prepared for God to put a new song in his mouth, he could put a new song in the hearts of his church family and others with whom he has come into contact. What many would regard as calamities, he has been enabled by the grace of God to pass along as blessings to those around him.

That is a legacy worth more to the recipient than all of the world's sweepstakes awards added together.

MEASURE OF A MINISTRY

Behold, now, here is in this city
a man of God, and he is an honourable man.
—I SAMUEL 9:6

Perhaps no one can more reliably evaluate the life and work of Jim Kennedy than the thousands of his peers in the Christian ministry and in public life who have known him through the years. A few of these were asked to add personal comments to this biography and their responses are presented in random order:

Dr. Adrian Rogers
Pastor, Bellevue Baptist Church
Memphis, Tennessee
(Former President, Southern Baptist Convention)

James Kennedy is a most remarkable man. I see in him a combination of scholarship, piety, and ironclad courage. These things are not often brought together in one human being. He is a preacher's preacher. When I hear him on the radio or in person or watch him on television, I am enriched and informed. He is not saying the same tired things that so many say, but is remarkably fresh and always powerfully prepared.

When the history of the twentieth-century Church is written, the name James Kennedy will be a significant factor in that history.

Dr. Billy Graham
Billy Graham Evangelistic Association
Minneapolis, Minnesota

It has been my privilege to know Dr. D. James Kennedy for many years. We have watched his church grow from a small congregation to one of the great mega-churches in America. We have appreciated his willingness over the years to take time out of his own busy schedule to come and speak at many of our schools of evangelism across America, sharing with thousands of pastors. He has been a great friend to me, my family, and my team. We thank God for Jim Kennedy.

Charles W. "Chuck" Colson,
Founder, Prison Fellowship Ministries
Washington, D.C.

I have a deep respect and affection for Jim who is clearly one of our nation's great preachers. His ministry has challenged me personally and I have treasured our times of fellowship together. He has a great mind, which he uses for God's glory. I am proud to serve with him in the cause of Christ.

Paul Weyrich
President, Free Congress Foundation
Washington, D.C.

The remarkable thing about Dr. Kennedy is the credibility he has in the political community in Washington. That is

undoubtedly because, in an era when scandals and misman-
agement have rocked many television evangelists, Jim
Kennedy has neither problem. Hence, he stands out as someone who has maintained a steady course during rocky times.
I have heard high government officials and important
conservatives from think tanks and other outside groups
discussing Dr. Kennedy's sermons and even his observations
about the creed. I know of no one else who has this sort of
following here, and I believe it is mainly because his teaching
is so firmly rooted and so intellectually sound.

Dr. Robert P. Dugan, Jr.,
Former Vice President, National Association of Evangelicals
Washington, D.C.

My friend Jim Kennedy has honored God with the quality of
all his work—whether with his intellectually credible, biblical
preaching, construction of a magnificent twentieth-century
cathedral, or design of a magnificent evangelistic tool. Several
years back, a professor from [what was then] West Germany
spent time in my office inquiring at length about the vitality
and impact of evangelical Christianity in the United States.
As he left, he asked if I would procure for him video tapes of
two evangelical television ministries. Because I wanted him
to see the best evangelicals were producing, one of those was
a tape of a service at Coral Ridge. The professor wrote back
from Germany, expressing his pleasure, and hint of surprise,
at the quality of such an evangelical television outreach. That
anecdote exemplifies Dr. Kennedy's ministry.

Mr. Jack Eckerd
Clearwater, Florida
(Founder, Eckerd Drug Stores)

Once in a great while—when it is needed most—God provides a special spokesperson. One who possesses a rare blend

of insight into people, a commitment to God, a voice that can be heard above the roar of worldly concerns, and the heart of a servant. Jim Kennedy is this kind of person. From his pulpit, he looks at our nation, sees its pestilence, and feels its hurt. Searching the heart of God for answers, he boldly sets the record straight with eloquence and enthusiasm.

Dr. Henry M. Morris, President Emeritus
Institute for Creation Research
Santee, California

Dr. James Kennedy is both a distinguished colleague and an honored friend. His ministry has been unique in modern history as a prime example of both warm spiritual devotion to the Lord Jesus Christ and knowledgeable intellectual commitment to the integrity and authority of the Holy Scriptures, the Word of God. In addition to his evangelistic ministry as multiplied many times throughout the nation by the Evangelism Explosion program, his strong and courageous stand on the truth of special creation, which is so needed in our day, but which is often ignored by other theologians and pastors, has been especially significant and valuable. He has had a great and beneficial influence on multitudes of people and deserves thanks and congratulations for his unique contribution.

Dr. John W. Whitehead, President
The Rutherford Institute
Charlottesville, Virginia

James Kennedy's willingness to speak out on key issues and to stand for truth have always impressed me. Even more impressive is his commitment not to only speak truth but to act on it as well. Jim, thus, does not just talk about Christ. Instead, he works to act like Christ.

Wendell R. Bird
Attorney At Law
Atlanta, Georgia

Dr. D. James Kennedy is the intellectual leader among the national spokesmen for conservative evangelical Christianity. With his earned Ph.D. degree, with his immense knowledge on such a variety of subjects, and with his logical and convincing delivery, he leads in brilliantly presenting the positive arguments for biblical Christianity and a Christian world view.

Lt. Gen. Daniel O. Graham (Deceased)
Founder, High Frontier
Arlington, Virginia

Dr. D. James Kennedy was an early supporter of nonnuclear defenses in space against Soviet nuclear missiles—the program called SDI by the government, and sarcastically "Star Wars" by its opponents. It did not take Dr. Kennedy long to see that pursuing such defenses gave America the moral high ground in the strategic struggle with the USSR—it really is "better to defend lives than merely to avenge them" as President Reagan was later to say.

Dr. Kennedy made a wise comparison between the modern day debate over SDI and the biblical debate which raged about the Prophet Nehemiah over rebuilding the walls of Jerusalem. Nehemiah was faced with naysayers who said it couldn't be done, the walls would be too expensive, and that Jerusalem's enemies could easily overcome the walls—precisely what we hear from the anti-SDI naysayers of today.

Good Christians understood what Dr. Kennedy was saying, and my organization, High Frontier, presented Dr. Kennedy an award for his labors on behalf of sensible and ethical defenses.

Howard Phillips, Chairman
The Conservative Caucus, Inc.
Vienna, Virginia

I am grateful for the opportunity to express my profound admiration for Dr. D. James Kennedy, one of the most remarkable men of the twentieth century.

Dr. Kennedy has marshalled his exemplary character and gifted intellect to make the relevance of God's Word to today's events clearly evident to all who hear his message.

Dr. Tim LaHaye,
President, Family Life Seminars
Washington, D.C.

Dr. D. James Kennedy is one of the most respected voices on Christian television and radio today. His programs are first-rate productions, and his message of the Gospel is always presented with intelligence and compassion, leading many souls to make a clear-cut decision for our Lord.

He does not skirt the difficult issues of our day, which many TV evangelists seem afraid to mention, but deals with them forthrightly. In a day when Christians are unable to trust some media evangelists, he stands tall as a man of utmost integrity. He is unsurpassed as a Presbyterian pastor, is exemplary in his moral conduct, and has provided thousands of churches with soul winning training tools that have contributed greatly to the enormous soul-harvest our nation has been experiencing during this past decade.

I pray God will protect him and give him another two decades of faithful ministry.

Mrs. Phyllis Schlafly, President
The Eagle Forum
Washington D.C.

Dr. Kennedy has been an inspiration and encouragement to me, as to millions of others. In these uncertain times, he consistently sounds a certain trumpet. His is a voice of clarity and truth, and I know he is responsible for bringing many, many people to know Jesus Christ. I am personally grateful for his ministry.

John Ankerberg, Host
The John Ankerberg Show
Chattanooga, Tennessee

The breadth of Dr. Kennedy's interests, his knowledge of Scripture and his discernment of God's will in current events has always amazed me. I thank God for the ministry He has given to him and for the different occasions Dr. Kennedy has been able to appear on our television program to either debate an opponent or explain the faith once given to the saints.

Dr. R. J. Rushdoony, President
Chalcedon Foundation
Vallecito, California

Since about 1840, at least, Christianity in the United States has been, with some ups and downs, in a growing recession. While church membership in ratio to the population has increased, personal commitment has declined, together with family life, private worship, and the relevance of the faith to society. At the same time, as America has moved from a rural to an urban culture, the urban super-church, with a vast membership, has become commonplace, and a part of the problem usually, because it has been institution-centered. It has stressed its own growth, not the kingdom of God.

Coral Ridge Presbyterian Church and Coral Ridge Ministries, under the leadership of Dr. D. James Kennedy, represents a major countertrend in which a major ministry ministers to the Church at large. This is evidenced not only in the local ministries begun under Dr. Kennedy, but also in his television ministry. His Evangelism Explosion program is used worldwide and by very diverse churches theologically so that Dr. Kennedy's ministry has touched church circles normally without contact with any Presbyterian pastor. Our Lord says, "whosoever will be great among you, let him be your minister" (Matt. 20:16), and Dr. Kennedy has been a serving minister.

Every pastor in this humanistic age faces a problem. The church members say, "Meet our needs," whereas Christ requires His servants to do His will, not man's. No church is without this problem, and it is a burden for faithful pastors. It requires patience, tact, and ability to cope with our era's besetting sin.

I have noticed that the problem can be especially severe in areas where retired people make up a disproportionate amount of the congregation. It has been no small accomplishment on the part of Dr. Kennedy to work in such a community and channel its interests into a world ministry.

Dr. Ben Armstrong,
Former Executive Director, National Religious Broadcasters
Manassas, Virginia

When visiting Coral Ridge Presbyterian Church, I was asked to participate in the service. I could not help but admire the beautiful organ, the marvelous choir, the crowded sanctuary of avid churchgoers, the striking stained glass windows, and the fabulous Gothic architecture, including the tallest spire on the east coast of Florida.

I had played competitive tennis with Jim the day before and had felt the impact of his blazing serve. Jim was now preaching to his congregation with the same "blazing serve." Following the service, I talked earnestly with Jim about the need for him to get into television. He asked what kind of a program I would suggest. Immediately I said there was no doubt about it. "You need to do just what you do best—put your Sunday morning service on television. All of the ingredients for great television are here."

Jim asked, "But what kind of interference will I suffer from the intrusion of cameras and so forth?" "Forget about that," I said. "It is nothing compared to the outreach to the millions you would have outside the church." I recommended Shorty Yeaworth from Good News Productions, Chester Springs, Pennsylvania, to help him produce the program. Also, I told Jim that the evangelical outreach needed not only "visceral impact," but also cerebral leadership and that his kind of a program would provide both aspects.

The rest of the story is history.*

*Dr. Armstrong's urging was a significant factor in Jim's decision to go into television.

Dr. Bill Gothard, President
Institute in Basic Youth Conflicts
Oak Brook, Illinois

Courage, consistency, and vision are but three of the many outstanding qualities which characterize for me the life and ministry of Dr. James Kennedy. I have been grateful for Dr. Kennedy's willingness to speak out on issues which affect the cause of Christ. It is thrilling to know that hundreds of thousands will be in heaven because of the anointed ministry of Evangelism Explosion which Dr. Kennedy pioneered and has maintained over these many years. What a glorious entrance Dr. Kennedy will have in heaven as a result of his wise and diligent labors for the Lord.

Richard G. Capen, Jr., Former Chairman and Publisher
The Miami Herald
Miami, Florida

Few religious leaders in South Florida have had a more inspiring impact on our region than Dr. Jim Kennedy. The growth of his South Florida church, coupled with the impact of his television ministry have been impressive indeed. I'm a better person for having been touched by his example, for he has been a valued friend, a dedicated religious leader, and a wise counselor.

Dr. Duane Gish, Senior Vice President
Institute for Creation Research
Santee, California

To me, Dr. D. James Kennedy is one of the great heroes of the faith of the twentieth century. His life and ministry have been a great inspiration to me as I have had the privilege of being associated with Dr. Kennedy personally in seminars and debates in his church and have had the privilege of personally hearing some of his lectures and have enjoyed his television ministry. He has stood unflinchingly for the truth of the Word of God and has preached fearlessly those doctrines based upon the Word of God which are not popular in many circles today, such as the doctrine of special creation that we find in the early chapters of Genesis. I love, honor, and respect this great man of God, this minister of Jesus Christ.

Dr. Bill Bright, President
Campus Crusade for Christ International
Orlando, Florida

Dr. D. James Kennedy is, in my opinion, one of the great Christian statesmen and leaders of our time. Many things impress me about Jim. He has a warm heart for God and a brilliant mind. The content of his sermons is always superb and stimulating, first class. He has built a great church and a powerful nationwide television ministry. But the thing that impresses me above all of his other achievements is his emphasis on evangelism and helping to fulfill the Great Commission, which has resulted in his developing and leading Evangelism Explosion, which has touched the lives of many millions of people around the world.

I first met Jim at a Presbyterian pastors and lay leaders seminar in Florida, more than twenty-five years ago. Approximately twenty churches were represented, and each pastor had brought a number of his laymen. I was most impressed with Jim because he, more than any of the other pastors, seemed to have a heart for evangelism and was not only teaching it but demonstrating it by leading his laymen as a model. A year later Jim called to ask me to come back to Florida for another weekend of training, stating, "We have seen 300 people come to Christ in our church since you were here last year, and we want you to teach them what you taught us." I returned with the promise that other churches would get involved as well. And, again, God met with us in a special way. At that time Jim had a modest church with folding chairs beside a fire station in Coral Ridge, but had a heart and vision for the world. I remember going with him to a very choice location of the city, an open field, which we claimed together in prayer as the site for his new church. Some years later, God provided the property, which is now the site for the Coral Ridge Presbyterian Church.

My interest and prayer is to follow Jim through the years. He is truly an inspiration to me and to all who really know and understand his brilliant mind and great heart for God. Few people have contributed more to evangelism than he.

Dr. Ben Haden, Founder
Changed Lives
Chattanooga, Tennessee

My friendship with Jim Kennedy dates back to 1963 when I entered my first pastorate at Key Biscayne Presbyterian Church in Miami. Those were the early days when Coral Ridge was still under 1,000 membership.

The strong evangelistic effort by Jim Kennedy and his church members was well under way. My wife and I asked whether we could "observe." Jim Kennedy invited us to accompany him one night. We jumped at the chance.

We went to a duplex of a young couple from Illinois. They had several Bibles—even a lampshade with Scripture printed on it. They had first met at a Christian retreat. Both had received two full years of Christian instruction before joining their church in Illinois. Their only intention was to join Coral Ridge Presbyterian Church by transferring their earlier church membership. Little did they expect Jim Kennedy to challenge their faith.

No matter what their intentions were, Jim Kennedy assumed *nothing*. He shocked them by asking what they could tell God in response to His question: "Why should I let you into my heaven?"

The wife said she had tried to live a *good life*. Her husband said he had always *tried to keep the Ten Commandments*. Within 45 minutes they both confessed Jesus Christ for the first time in their lives—acknowledging they were sinners and without any hope except for the mercy of God and the blood of Christ. It was an unforgettable evening. As we left, both my wife and I were silent. We had witnessed something sacred. Inwardly we realized how many millions of church people would have given the same answers as the couple originally gave—and how they would be equally confident of salvation by works or "just by trying."

In my opinion, Jim Kennedy is among the handful of men most used by the Lord to win people to Jesus Christ in a fashion where they clearly understand it is by His blood alone and not by any personal virtue.

The Lord has had His hand on Jim from the day he first learned that people already knew how to go to hell—and needed direction on how to go to heaven.

Jim is an intellectual soul winner grounded in simplicity. He has centered his life on the ultimate question rather than the side issues.

Edith (Mrs. Francis) Schaeffer
Rochester, Minnesota

Fran and I appreciated the clarity of Jim Kennedy's proclamation of truth. We always felt encouraged by his scholarly and carefully presented studies based on the inerrant truth of the unchanging Word of God. Although Fran has been in heaven almost five years, I know he would join me, if possible, in expressing constant satisfaction in Jim's courage to take a stand where he believed it was right, no matter how unpopular that might be. I do not believe that God's assessment of His servants is anything we have the weights and measurements for. Certainly the word success with a capital S is not that which God would use to describe those to whom He will say, "Well done, thou good and faithful servant." Although the "measure" is hidden from us, I do believe that in our lifetimes we have a glimpse of those whom we recognize as being solid walnut and not veneer.

Marlin Maddoux, President
International Christian Media
Dallas, Texas

Dr. Kennedy is an innovator with a creative talent. His enthusiastic work to further God's kingdom has had a profound impact on America. He was one of the first to date to speak out publicly on important issues, often addressing and tackling problems which others had wished would solve themselves. Countless people have been inspired and motivated to greater church, community, and national involvement as a result of the example set by his boldness and zeal. The benefits of his Evangelism Explosion will be seen and felt for generations to come.

Dr. John Haggai, Former President
Haggai Institute for Advanced Leadership Training
Norcross, Georgia

I feel that Dr. Kennedy is my constant traveling companion. Wherever I go in the world, I meet people who have been blessed by his Evangelism Explosion principles. I commend him for his sensitivity to cultural distinctives and for the remarkable freedom from Western ethnocentricity this program enjoys.

When reflecting on the superb and sterling life and work of this man of God, I marvel at the powerful way he moves toward well defined, Spirit-ordained objectives. Only in heaven will we fully know Dr. Kennedy's global impact for God—and therefore for good.

Dr. Leighton Ford
Evangelist

The name of D. James Kennedy is known for many things to

many people—pastor of a magnificent congregation, intelligent preacher to a national audience, man of strong convictions, founder of Evangelism Explosion.

But when I think of Jim Kennedy, I think of a young man with a vision and a handful of believers who went door to door introducing people to Jesus Christ and found an approach and a strategy which have inspired and helped people around the world to effectively share their faith.

Younger leaders, especially, look with awe at someone of the stature of a D. James Kennedy. They need to remember that it was Jim Kennedy who, like them, was a faithful follower and servant of Jesus Christ, a steward of the good news and who wasn't afraid to start at the bottom. From there God has raised him up to a mighty ministry. I think Jim Kennedy's story ought to say to each one of us, "Despise not the day of small beginnings."

Rev. Frank M. Barker, Pastor
Briarwood Presbyterian Church
Birmingham, Alabama
Former Moderator of the Presbyterian Church in America

Jim Kennedy and I were in seminary together and have been close friends ever since. Jim has never wavered from his commitment to preaching the gospel straight and true or from the goal of fulfilling the Great Commission.

God's leading in his life by showing him his own inability to effectively share the gospel and then guiding him to a development of the methodology of EE has been a tremendous blessing to the entire church. One of my great goals as a pastor is to enable my people to do the work of ministry and Jim's work has helped me immensely in doing that. Jim has not let success go to his head, but has continued to make himself available to those who seek his wisdom and help. Jim's insights between Christianity and culture, as well as the need for Christianity to effect our political involvement, has been crucial in helping Christians around the nation understand the issues and be involved.

In an age when TV evangelists are automatically suspect, Jim's demeanor has always been absolutely above reproach. I thank God for giving Jim to all of us and I pray for him regularly.

Edward E. McAteer, President
The Religious Roundtable
Memphis, Tennessee

Some historians when recording Christian American history maintain that it was not the politicians, the businessmen, nor even the military establishment which turned the tide during the American Revolution. They maintain that those who were mainly responsible for the "turning of the tide" were an elite group of clergymen called the "Black Regiment of the Continental Army."

These men spoke out against the Crown and the Parliament. They spoke for that which was right and against that which was wrong.

Their preaching inspired the Potato Farmers of the new republic to rise up behind General George Washington and help him win the victories that have resulted in our cherished freedoms for the past two hundred years.

In my knowledge of Dr. James Kennedy, I rate him as a modern day General of the "Black Regiment" of the American army.

Dr. James C. Dobson, President
Focus on the Family
Colorado Springs, Colorado

There are many things I might say about Dr. Jim Kennedy given the space and time. Naturally, personal experience always creates the strongest impressions. I particularly recall how Jim made himself a spokesman and advocate for Joan Andrews, the courageous young woman who went to prison in Florida for attempting to save the lives of unborn children. As a guest on our Focus on the Family radio broadcast, he asked listeners to write letters of recommendation that Joan be set free. It's risky for a man in such a prominent position to take a strong stand on such a controversial matter, but that didn't stop James Kennedy. Neither was he afraid to stand with us against that blatantly anti-Christian film *The Last Temptation of Christ* and the so-called "Civil Rights Restoration Act." But that's characteristic of the man. He doesn't hesitate to apply biblical principles to current issues or to act according to his convictions. He's been a valuable ally in the battle for Christian values, and we need more like him!

Like so many others, I've also been affected by Dr. Kennedy's Evangelism Explosion program. Evangelism Explosion is an expression of the one ruling passion of Jim's life—his desire to see the Gospel spread to every man, woman, and child on earth. And it's taken us a long way toward achieving that goal, too. Evangelism Explosion is now present and operating in every city in the United States and in 95 other countries [now in every nation on earth]. It's had a tremendous effect in motivating and mobilizing our churches for the work of the kingdom here in Southern California. Jim's zeal for leading people to the Savior is also reflected in the tremendous growth his own congregation has experienced under his leadership—not only in numbers, but in the quality and extent of outreach. It's worth mentioning here that Coral Ridge's television ministry was the only such program that actually grew during 1988.

God has clearly blessed James Kennedy. I thank the Lord for all the marvelous work He's enabled Jim to accomplish and for the privilege of being his brother in Christ.

Her Excellency Faith R. Whittlesey, President
American Swiss Foundation
New York, New York

I got to know Dr. Kennedy and his work as a result of my service in the White House as a member of the senior staff from 1983 to 1985. From that perspective, I learned that Dr. Kennedy was viewed as one of the natural and most effective leaders of the evangelical Christian movement in the United States. The more I heard of Dr. Kennedy, the more I came to admire his ministry and the example of Christian commitment he represents.

Dr. Jay Grimstead, Director
Coalition on Revival
Sunnyvale, California

Jim Kennedy is one of my own modern-day heroes of the faith. He is a model of dignified, orthodox statesmanship. I consider him to be a leader whose worldview incorporates the historic theologies of Augustine, Calvin, Luther, Whitefield, Spurgeon, Warfield, and the late Francis Schaeffer. If Jim's worldview and his commitment to extending the kingdom of God on earth were incorporated into the minds and lives of the Bible-believing pastors of America today, it would only be a few short years until this country could be turned around and once again be established on the Pilgrim/Puritan biblical foundations which made it a great Christian nation.

The Honorable Jack Kemp, Co-Director
Empower America
Washington, D.C.

The life, struggle, and witness of Dr. James Kennedy has been an inspiration to millions of people around the world, including the Kemp family via his television ministry and writings.

Throughout his life, Jim has been a tireless champion in the fight to restore traditional Judeo-Christian values throughout America and a leader in alerting the nation to the "American Tragedy" of pornography, and the battle to help end this scourge in our country. We are proud to be able to call ourselves both friends and fans of Dr. James Kennedy.

The Honorable William L. Armstrong
Former United States Senator from Colorado

Jim Kennedy has made an extraordinary contribution to the thought life of America. His sermons set a high standard of faith and intellect. He manages to address the most important issues of life in an appealing and thoughtful manner, without sophistry and pretension, but with great power. His faithful testimony and service are an inspiration to me as they are to countless others.

Zig Ziglar
The Zig Ziglar Corporation
Carrollton, Texas

Recently, when I finished a prayer breakfast in Nashville, Tennessee, a lady approached me and, with considerable enthusiasm, simply said two letters, "E-E." What a delight it was to meet her, as she expressed her familiarity with Evangelism Explosion, which was the second book I read after I became a Christian in 1972. From that date until this, it has been my privilege to use what Dr. Kennedy taught me to win many people to Christ. However, that work of Dr. Kennedy's only touches the surface of his incredible ministry. His intellectual capacity is exceeded only by his deep conviction and love for Christ. His concern for our country, as well as his compassion for the lost and downtrodden, is certainly an inspiration to millions of Americans. In my personal life, I have found very few people I could admire and respect in every area of their lives. Certainly Dr. Kennedy fits in that category. He truly "walks the walk" and teaches by example. That is so extremely important because sometimes sermons and lectures are a little confusing, but the example we set is crystal clear. The example Dr. Kennedy is setting for millions of Americans is certainly an encouragement to all. I know his love and integrity have inspired me to renew my commitment and serve my Lord more effectively.

Jay Van Andel, Co-founder
Amway Corporation
Ada, Michigan

It's a rare privilege to have an ongoing relationship with a man of God who has touched so many lives in such a positive manner. Jim Kennedy has inspired me with his deep-seated faith. Jim does not just preach Christianity; he lives it to the fullest each day. This is what has enabled him to positively affect so many people, including me.

Richard P. Bott, President
Bott Broadcasting Company
Overland Park, Kansas

First of all, he is truly one of a kind. He has the grace and style that make him every inch a gentleman and a man's man. He presents himself and the overall Coral Ridge ministry to a world of people who hunger to know truth, in an unvarnished, yet gracious manner.

Further, Jim's radio/television ministry is one which seems to be able to take the high road on so many of the sensational issues, including recent scandals. At the same time, he never avoids addressing the substantive, truly important issues which Christians face everywhere—the issues about which we all really need leadership from a biblical worldview.

Jim also gives the Christian community across America the type of leadership that leads to informed understanding. And he does all this without any sign of worry about so-called popular opinion. To take a stand requires both ability and courage, and Jim Kennedy has both. I would say he "has it all together."

Richard A. Viguerie
Conservative Activist

As a Catholic, I feel that James Kennedy reaches across Christian denominational lines as effectively—bringing the truth about the spiritual, physical, and mental aspects of our lives—as any minister of the gospel in America today. Perhaps his title should be: God's Great Communicator.

Sam Moore, Chairman
Thomas Nelson Publishers
Nashville, Tennessee

Dr. James Kennedy is one of God's champions of our time. He has through Evangelism Explosion and *Truths That Transform* presented God's message to millions of people. I am pleased to tell you he is making an impact on this world by preaching a faithful and true message of the gospel of Jesus Christ. It is with great honor that I count Dr. Kennedy my friend.

Dr. Jerry Falwell, Pastor
Thomas Road Baptist Church
Lynchburg, Virginia

It is a great privilege to say a few words about Jim Kennedy and his ministry.

Jim Kennedy is to be considered among God's most faithful servants, and I am proud to call him my friend. God has gifted him with a brilliant mind, and he has used that mind to clearly articulate the gospel of Christ to a lost nation and world. Because of his unswerving faith, I consider Jim Kennedy to be a Presbyterian pillar in our nation.

Richard M. DeVos, Co-founder
Amway Corporation
Ada, Michigan

D. James Kennedy is a preacher, pastor, patriot . . . and a pretty fair tennis player, too!

He's a theologian who relates to the real world; an evangelist who knows how to share the gospel in a most direct way; a man who is humble, unselfish, and doesn't know the words, "What's in it for me?"

Rev. Kennedy Smartt
Former Moderator
Presbyterian Church in America

Jim Kennedy is one of the most unique and interesting persons I have ever known. He is at once retiring and self-effacing as well as bold and ambitious. He is timid as well as assertive and blunt as well as diplomatic. He is often misunderstood because of this, but few men in the twentieth century have been used in such a significant way as he.

He would be great if he were only the founder and pastor for the Coral Ridge Presbyterian Church, or as the founder and speaker of the Coral Ridge Ministries radio and television programs, or as the founder, author, and president of Evangelism Explosion. But to realize that this one man is all three of the above is mind-boggling to say the least. But history will probably come to the decision that considering all of the above, his most significant achievement will have been the latter. History may very well show that there has been no missionary or evangelistic organization throughout all the centuries that has contributed as much to the growth of the church of Jesus Christ worldwide as has the evangelism/discipleship ministry of Evangelism Explosion.

Dr. John Wesley White
Associate Evangelist
Billy Graham Evangelistic Association

It is my privilege to hold area-wide crusades in the smaller cities of the United States, Canada, and the British Isles, something I've been doing as an associate evangelist to Billy Graham for a full generation. Throughout these three countries, I have never yet been in a community where Dr. Kennedy's deep impact in evangelism has not been felt strongly through the E.E. movement which he brought into being and spearheaded. Add to this the week-by-week influence he is having via his nationwide television ministry in confirming evangelical believers in the fundamental basics of their faith, and one can realize just how twofold the ministry of this distinctive preacher of the Word of God has been in our generation. Add to this the joy of personal fellowship I have experienced in the many Billy Graham Schools of Evangelism in which Dr. Kennedy and I have jointly proclaimed the Word of God, and it can be realized how great my appreciation of his service in the kingdom of God has been.

Dr. John Gerstner (deceased)
Professor-at-Large
Ligonier Ministries
Ligonier, Pennsylvania

It was my privilege to preach a week for Dr. Kennedy and Coral Ridge before he and they became world famous for the proclamation and propagation of the gospel. After one evening address, a young man about eighteen came forward to talk about the invitation to accept Christ. Dr. Kennedy's answers to the teenager's questions gave the finest half-hour summary of the Christian message that I have ever heard or read. That God saw fit to explode that statement of the evangel around the world, though it makes me profoundly grateful, has never surprised me.

Rev. Donald E. Wildmon, Founder & Executive Director
American Family Association
Tupelo, Mississippi

Praise God for Jim Kennedy! I believe in everything he stands for and pray that God will enable him to keep on keeping on in the wonderful work he is doing for the Gospel of Jesus Christ and the betterment of our nation and our world.

Dr. Robert Schuller, Pastor
Crystal Cathedral
Garden Grove, California

*Divine
—Truly of God—"You have not chosen me—I have chosen you."

*Daring
—He knows the right questions and has the courage to put it to the strongest test—"If you died tonight . . ."

*Dedicated
—To the "Faith of the Fathers," once and for all delivered to the household of faith!

I am proud to know him as a colleague in Christ's work!

**Dr. Joel Nederhood, Director (retired)
The Back to God Hour
Palos Heights, Illinois**

Surely within the Reformed community, all of us are in debt to D. James Kennedy for his unquestioned enthusiasm for Reformed Christianity. I remember that when my predecessor, Dr. Peter Eldersveld, would tell me about visiting Coral Ridge Presbyterian Church, he would dwell on Kennedy's steadfast proclamation of sovereign grace. In a time when the robust message of Calvinism is largely ignored, his emphasis is increasingly valuable.

I admire him greatly for his vision; he has been gifted with a boldness and single-mindedness that has enabled him to carry significant ideas from conception to actualization. The leadership he has given in Evangelism Explosion is unique, and its impact will be abiding. The church he serves, his growing television outreach, his emphasis on Christian day school education, and the radio station that serves South Florida testify to his unusual ability.

We who are his colleagues in broadcasting the Gospel are thankful for his unwavering dedication to principles of honesty and candor. His integrity is an inspiration. His commitment to the growth of outreach while remaining true to high ethical standards provides us with a stirring example.

Dr. Kennedy, who never ceases to be amazed by God's amazing grace in his own life, speaks with a conviction that comes from an assurance that the God who saved him so marvelously is able to do the same in the lives of those who hear him. There is an excitement about him that we recognize arises out of his own rescue from a life that could have easily been spent in the pursuit of conventional success. He knows the futility of such pursuits and helps us all seek more worthy goals.

Today, he stimulates us all to assess the neo-paganism that has captured our society and to formulate a message of response that can be translated into appropriate action.

The Honorable Paul Pressler
Retired Justice, Texas Court of Appeals
Houston, Texas

Dr. D. James Kennedy is one of God's greatest. He has had the courage to stand where others would not. He has applied Christian principles to our everyday life in such an effective way that it has brought to people's realization the need for being consistent in their theology as it affects our government and through the application of biblical principles. While he has alerted us to this responsibility he has never forgotten the fact of the simplicity of the gospel, and that a person must come to know the Lord Jesus Christ as personal Savior. Jim Kennedy is God's man for this hour and has been greatly used of Him.

THE GREATEST SERMON OF ALL

So teach us to number our days,
that we may apply our hearts
unto wisdom.
—PSALM 90:12

The first biographer, Moses, gave the world its most unforgettable life stories. What classics can compare with those immortal portrayals in the Pentateuch of personalities like Noah, Abraham, Isaac, Jacob, Esau, Joseph, and of the wives, relatives, friends, and enemies with whose experiences their own were so poignantly intertwined? It was Moses himself who reminded us that each individual weaves a story out of the materials which the process of living presents—that "we spend our years as a tale that is told."

One divine technique or strategy employed throughout the Word of God should not be overlooked. The whole Bible, after all, is a gracious condescension on the part of a loving Author (your dictionary tells you that the root meaning of the word author is Creator). Because God the Father wanted His creatures to know Him and to love Him and to give Him glory, He has accommodated Himself to us in a most amazing way. He has chosen to reveal Himself, not only in the wonders of the universe and in the providential turns of human history and in the promptings of the inner consciousness—but primarily in the ordinary format of a book. Imagine the almighty Creator deciding to package His eternal, unchanging message to man in the fragile, vulnerable dimensions of a book that can be made to look like other books on the shelf!

There is a divine strategy employed throughout the written Word of God.

That's what He did, and He filled that book with the simple but matchless stories of the lives of many, many people, beginning with a brief biography of the first Adam and ending with that of the Second Adam. The life of Jesus was of such magnificence and of such magnitude that the Holy Spirit assigned four biographers and more inspired New Testament commentators than that to report and to assess that one life from different points of view.

Why is so much biography in the Bible? Scripture is clear on the purpose—these "happenings" in the lives of individuals, as Paul expressed it, were "examples . . . written for our admonition, on whom the ends of the ages have come." Even as we reverently set apart from all others the account of the Savior's life, which is beyond comparison with others, we can readily see that human biography is a powerful instrument of instruction. There is simply no better way to learn about life than to learn about lives; this has been the motivating conviction of biographers from Plutarch to Boswell to Manchester. Unlike experience, which is universally recognized as a hard and often a cruel and destructive teacher, the study of the lives of those preceding us or around us provides a safe and rewarding route to wisdom. Entire educational systems are built on the salutary advantage of learning by precept and by example. America's beloved bard, Longfellow, has been reminding us for more than a century:

> Lives of great men all remind us
> We can make our lives sublime,
> And, departing, leave behind us
> Footprints on the sands of time.

If these rather lofty lines may be brought down to humble application to the present work, it is to be hoped that the relating of the story of Jim Kennedy's life adds up to more than possible diversion or entertainment for the reader. It is a story with a powerful didactic thrust. The lesson of grace is taught in diverse ways, but none are so convincing as those that show and tell the transformed life. How easy, how "natural," how credible it would have been for that young Tampa dance instructor to continue along the broad road that leads to popularity, to worldly success, and to destruction! How unlikely, how improbable, how unbelievable that he could be turned 180 degrees by a portion of an unwelcome radio message, to become irrevocably committed to a wholly different kind of life! That pivot point, the events that led up to it, and the miracles that have ensued from it have been the subject of this book.

The exciting good news—or the "teaching moment," as the educators call it—flowing out of the biography of Jim Kennedy is precisely this: the same miraculous grace that transformed his life is available to anyone who will hear the Gospel. Because it is not the power that generates from any human source, but the power available of God unto salvation to everyone who believes, the Gospel of Jesus Christ can make the difference in your life story that you can never weave into the narrative by your own ingenuity.

Jim Kennedy has been able to accomplish so much in the past three decades because he made the discovery at one time (1) of the certainty of an eternal paradise and (2) of the power for doing good that can revolutionize a life totally yielded to the service of Christ in this world. The letters of commendation in the preceding chapter simply bear witness to the scriptural truth that the greatest sermon of all is not delivered by one's lips, but by one's life. As the earliest Christians were told: "You are our epistle written in our hearts, known and read by all men; you are manifestly an epistle of Christ, ministered by us, written not with ink, but by the Spirit of the living God, not on tablets of stone, but on tablets of flesh, that is, of the heart." Jim has furnished living testimony that he can do all things through Christ who strengthens him.

And you? The lesson is a simple one. Without Christ you can do nothing—nothing at all that matters. With Him, you can do all things. You can make a difference. In the familiar words of Jim Kennedy, "You can change the world!"

APPENDIX

The text of the radio sermon by Dr. Donald Gray Barnhouse that led to the conversion of D. James Kennedy in 1954 is reprinted here in full.[11] However, Jim, who was not quite twenty-four at the time, slept through the first nine paragraphs. When his clock radio came on at the tenth paragraph, he heard Barnhouse's electrifying words—words that changed his life.

Entitled simply, "Your Right to Heaven," this sermon is also the source for one of the two diagnostic questions (in somewhat altered form) essential to the effectiveness and the success of Evangelism Explosion.

Among the various rights of men and nations there is one which every man, woman and child must consider—the right to enter Heaven. Have men a right to enter Heaven? This question was anticipated many years ago by the apostle Paul. In language clear, concise, and unequivocal, the great apostle in his letter to the Romans states that no man has any right whatsoever to enter Heaven. In the third chapter of his epistle to the Romans, verses 19 and 20, Paul says, "Now we know that what things soever the law saith, it saith to them who are under the law: that every mouth may be stopped, and all the world may become guilty before God. Therefore by the deeds of the law there shall no flesh be justified in His sight; for by the law is the knowledge of sin." In this passage Paul states that, in the light of man's record and God's perfect standard, no man has a right to enter Heaven.

When you first read this you may be shocked and insulted. But look for a moment at the words of the apostle and you will see immediately that there can be no other answer. Let me approach this problem as if you are a patient who has just come to me, a doctor, to find out the state of your health. For just as a doctor has certain diagnostic questions that become almost routine for use with practically every patient, so there are spiritual diagnostic techniques. When a person comes to me with a problem, I follow a definite procedure. First of all, I must find out whether I am dealing with the needs of a believer in Christ or an unbeliever. I ask, "Have you been born again?" If there is an immediate, clear-cut testimony that shows knowledge of redemption and a faith that is committed to Christ as Savior and Lord, the problem itself can be dealt with. But if there is any hesitancy, any wavering, any doubt as to the person's personal salvation, that has to be dealt with first. I say, "Perhaps I can clarify your thinking with a question. You know that there are a great many accidents today. Suppose that you and I should go out of this building and a swerving automobile should come up on the sidewalk and kill the two of us. It is God Himself you must face. And if in this next minute He should say to you, 'What right do you have'—not, 'Why would you like to come,' but— 'What right do you have to come into My Heaven?' what would be your answer?"

Literally hundreds of people have had their thinking brought to clarity by following this line of thought. There are three possible answers to this question.

The first answer will be variations on the theme of presenting one's life and works to the scrutiny of God and claiming that he has done the best that he could. Surely, he reasons, God would not be too hard on a sincere man who has plugged along without harming his neighbors too much. The variations are many; a person may boast to have lived always by the Golden Rule, or assert that he has lived up to a certain code. Or he may insist that he has never been guilty of murder, adultery, and other gross sins.

Two particular conversations will illustrate this tactic to present works to God as the price of entry into Heaven. Early in my ministry I knew a man casually who happened to live a few doors from the church. When I spoke to him about his soul, he laughed me off patronizingly, telling me that he was not the kind of man that needed the church or anything else. He was an active member of a lodge, he said, and if any man lived up to the high principles of that particular lodge, he would be all right.

I saw him from time to time and whenever I attempted to speak to him about his soul he would tell me, once more, that he was living up to his lodge obligations. I am not speaking against lodges here. If you want to drill and exchange passwords and handgrips, and if you want to have an insurance and benevolence scheme with some other men and women, go right ahead. But if you say you can go to Heaven by living up to a society's obligations and principles, you are desperately mistaken.

The sequel of the story will reveal the poverty of any such idea. The day came when this man was stricken with a serious illness and was not expected to live out the day. I went to see him. A member of his lodge was already there on what they called the deathwatch, so that no member of their group would have to die alone. This man was seated across the room from the bed, reading a magazine. I had scarcely entered the room when his successor came, and the "watch" changed, one man leaving and the other man taking his place. The sick man's case was desperate, and a desperate remedy was necessary.

Sitting down by the man's bedside, I said to him, "You do not mind my staying a few minutes and watching you, do you? I have wondered what it would be like to die without Christ. I have known you for several years now as a man who said he did not need Christ but that his lodge obligations were enough. I would like to see a man come to the end that way, to see what it is like."

He looked at me like a wounded animal and slowly said, "You . . . wouldn't . . . mock a . . . dying man . . . would you?" I then asked him what he would answer when God asked him what right he would have to enter the Lord's holy Heaven. Great tears ran down the man's pale and wrinkled cheeks, and he looked at me in agonized silence. Then, swiftly, I told him how he might approach God through the merits of the Lord Jesus Christ. He then began to say that his mother had taught him these things as a child, but that he had abandoned them. But in those moments he came back to God through Jesus Christ, and in a little while he had the members of his family called that they might hear his testimony of faith. They even heard him say that he wished that his story might be told at his funeral, which it was a few days later. A second story illustrates the same point from . . .

At this precise juncture in the message Jim was startled awake and heard these life-changing words:

. . . another angle. A young officer of the United States Marines came to visit our church during the war. His brother had become a believer, and the marine was intrigued with the change that had come over his brother. When he was asked if he were saved, he wavered in his reply. Next came the diagnostic question: "What answer would you give if death had just claimed you and God should say to you, 'What right do you have to come into My Heaven?'" He replied that he would say something like, "Well, God, I have never committed any great sins."

"Lieutenant, permit me to be very frank. If you dared attempt any such answer, you could never enter Heaven." He broke in to say, "I have been giving much thought to these things recently, for we have been practicing crawling across a field under live ammunition bursts, and I have wondered what would happen to me if I humped too high." I replied, "Lieutenant, suppose you drive a car up the main street of your city at eighty miles an hour, through all the traffic lights, without any regard to the police whistles. Finally, you are overtaken, and you reach out and slap the policeman. When they finally get you to the court, they throw the book at you. The total of your fine is three hundred dollars. You have no money, but your brother pays your fine for you; and while he is doing it, you start for the door. A policeman says to you, 'What right do you have to leave the court room?' Note the phrase—what right? Would you say to him, 'Why, there's my record. I am the man who drove the car up the street at eighty miles an hour and slapped the policeman; so now let me go'?" He answered, "Of course not; I would say that my fine had been paid."

"Exactly! It is not your record that lets you go free; it is your record that brought you there in the first place. And if any man thinks he can arrive in Heaven because of his record, he is not really thinking. It is his record that raises the question. If he had no record with sin in it, he could say, 'Move over, God, and let me sit down on the throne with you. I've arrived at last, and my record brought me in.'

"The lieutenant shook his head and said, "Of course, I see it plainly now. It is not my record, but the fact that the Lord Jesus Christ paid my fine by dying on the cross." And thus another man passed out of death and into life.

On another occasion, several years before World War II, we were crossing the Atlantic. It was summer, and I was asked to preach at the Sunday service the second or third day out. After that I had several conversations about spiritual matters with people who came up to ask questions. One conversation was with a young woman who was a professor of languages in one of the Eastern U.S. colleges. I asked the diagnostic question: "If this ship should go to the bottom of the sea, and we were what men called dead, and God asked you: 'What right do you have to come into My Heaven?' what would you say?"

She answered, "I wouldn't have a thing to say."

I replied, "You are quoting Paul in Romans 3:19." She was puzzled. I then opened the New Testament to the text (Rom. 3:19) and asked her to read it: "Now we know that what things soever the law saith, it saith to them that are under the law: that every mouth may be stopped, and all the world may become guilty before God." When she had finished, I said, "What does it say? That every mouth may be . . ." And she read it slowly ". . . stopped. That every mouth may be stopped." "That's right. You said it in modern English—'I wouldn't have a thing to say.' God says that your mouth would be stopped. It is the same thing." And then I led her to see that there is another answer, a great and wonderful answer to the question.

Yes, there are only three possible answers. One: "I'm relying on my record." This is an answer that exists only in present imagination but will never even be uttered when men stand in the clear light of truth "without excuse" (Rom. 1:20). Two: "I wouldn't have a thing to say." That is the horrible truth. You would be speechless as you confronted the Savior who now had become your outraged Judge. The men who pause briefly at the judgment bar of God before going to their eternal doom will never open their lips in their own defense. They will know then that they have no defense, and that they are, indeed, without excuse.

If there is a word spoken at the judgment bar of God by human beings who are being sent to their place in outer darkness, it will be that which is forced from their reluctant lips by an all-powerful God. They will cry, "It was all true, O God. I was wrong. I knew I was wrong when I made my excuses.

But I hated and I still hate righteousness by the blood of Christ. I must admit that those despised Christians were right who bowed before Thee and acknowledged their dependence upon Thee. I hated their songs of faith then, and I hate them now. They were right, and I hated them because they were right and because they belonged to Thee, and I hate them now because they belong to Thee. I wanted my own way. And I still want my own way. I want Heaven, but I want Heaven without Thee. I want Heaven with myself on the throne. That's what I want and I do not want anything else and never, never will I want anything other than Heaven with myself on the throne. I want my way. And now I am going to the place of desire without fulfillment, of lust without satisfaction, of wanting without having, of wishing but never getting, of looking but never seeing, and I hate, I hate, I hate because I want my own way. I hate Thee, O God, for not letting me have my way. I hate, I hate. . . ." And their voices will drift off to utter nothingness moaning, "I hate. . . ."

And though there may be such a chorus of the damned, there will never be a word allowed in self-defense. They will see truth by the light of truth and will attempt subterfuge no more. Every mouth will be stopped along that line.

Will you sing this chorus of hate? Will you be a member of the chorale of the damned? You need not be. It is true that you can in nowise say that your record gives you the right to enter Heaven. And perhaps you, too, are in the position of the woman who said, "I haven't a thing to say," for your mouth is stopped and will be stopped on that great day of judgment. But there is a wonderful third answer to the question, "What right do you have to enter Heaven?" The same apostle that wrote the terrible words which point out to us that our record is not satisfactory to God, also has set forth God's wonderful provision. We read a few verses further on, "Being justified freely by his grace through the redemption that is in Christ Jesus: whom God hath set forth to be a propitiation through faith in his blood, to declare his righteousness for the remission of sins that are past, through the forebearance of God; to declare, I say, at this time his righteousness: that he might be just, and the justifier of him which believeth in Jesus" (Rom. 3:24-26 KJV). This is the answer. This gives us the right to enter Heaven.

> In my hands no price I bring,
> Simply to Thy cross I cling. . . .
> These for sin could not atone;
> Thou must save, and Thou alone.

> Rock of Ages cleft for me,
> Let me hide myself in Thee.

This is your only plea. This is your only right to enter Heaven. Accept the Lord Jesus Christ as your own personal Savior, and come to know the assurance and peace which He gives.

> The holy, meek, unspotted Lamb,
> Who from the Father's bosom came,
> Who died for me, even me, to atone,
> Now for my Lord, and God, I own.

> When from the dust of death I rise
> To claim my mansion in the skies,
> Even then this shall be all my plea—
> Jesus hath lived, hath died for me!

> Ah! give to all Thy servants, Lord,
> With power to speak Thy gracious Word,
> That all who to Thy wounds will flee,
> May find eternal life in Thee.

NOTES

1. D. James Kennedy, *Why I Believe* (Waco, TX: Word, 1981), 136-7.

2. D. James Kennedy, Preface to *The Greatest Story Ever Told* by Fulton Oursler, special ed. (Ft. Lauderdale, FL: Coral Ridge Ministries, 1981).

3. Darrel Eiland, "Key to Church Growth," *Christian Herald*, Feb. 1984, 21.

4. D. James Kennedy, *Evangelism Explosion*, 3rd ed. (Wheaton, IL: Tyndale House, 1983), 24-44. Used by permission.

5. Paul M. Weyrich, "Emerging Leader of the Religious Right," *Conservative Digest*, Mar. 1988, 48.

6. Margaret N. Barnhouse, *That Man Barnhouse* (Wheaton, IL: Tyndale House, 1987), 32.

7. Weyrich, "Emerging Leader," 48-49.

8. Sir Arthur Keith, *Evolution and Ethics*. Quoted from D. James Kennedy, "The Descent of Man," Issues 1985 (Ft. Lauderdale, FL: Coral Ridge Ministries, 1985), 18.

9. Weyrich, "Emerging Leader," 49.

10. Adapted from Billy Graham, *A Biblical Standard for Evangelists* (Minneapolis, MN: Billy Graham Evangelistic Associates, 1984).

11. *Your Right to Heaven* by Donald G. Barnhouse (Grand Rapids, Mich.: Baker Book House, 1977), pp. 43-52. Used by permission.

About the Author

Dr. Herbert Lee Williams was a practicing journalist on five newspapers, and a journalism educator for forty years, teaching at the University of Mississippi, Boston University, Stephens College, Michigan State University, and Memphis State University, where he served as chairman, obtaining national ACEJ accreditation, a graduate program, and a million-dollar journalism building for that institution. He was employed by former President Harry S. Truman during most of 1954 as a researcher and writer for his memoirs. Since 1989, he has worked at Coral Ridge Presbyterian Church in research and writing for the Senior Minister, Dr. D. James Kennedy.